Epistemology and the Psychology
of Human Judgment

Epistemology and the Psychology of Human Judgment

Michael A Bishop

J. D. Trout

UNIVERSITY PRESS

2005

OXFORD
UNIVERSITY PRESS

Oxford   New York
Auckland   Bangkok   Buenos Aires   Cape Town   Chennai
Dar es Salaam   Delhi   Hong Kong   Istanbul   Karachi   Kolkata
Kuala Lumpur   Madrid   Melbourne   Mexico City   Mumbai
Nairobi   São Paulo   Shanghai   Singapore   Taipei   Tokyo   Toronto

Copyright © 2005 by Oxford University Press, Inc.

Published by Oxford University Press, Inc.
198 Madison Avenue, New York, New York 10016

www.oup.com

Oxford is a registered trademark of Oxford University Press

Library of Congress Cataloging-in-Publication Data

Bishop, Michael A
Epistemology and the psychology of human judgment / Michael A Bishop, J. D. Trout.
   p. cm.
Includes bibliographical references and index.
ISBN 0-19-516229-3; 0-19-516230-7 (pbk.)
   1. Judgment.   I. Trout, J. D.   II. Title.
BF441 .B616 2004
121—dc22   2004043889

9 8 7 6 5 4 3 2 1

Printed in the United States of America
on acid-free paper

To our wives, Loretta Torrago and Janice Nadler,
and to the veritable basketball team we produced while writing this book:

Miguel Bishop Torrago 7/5/2000
Daniel Bishop Torrago 9/26/2001
Nicolas Bishop Torrago 3/19/2003

Jack Nadler 7/5/2000
Jessie Nadler 4/14/2004

Miguel and Jack, our first children, were born on the same day. Our actuarial outlook counsels that this is an unimpressive coincidence. But really, what are the chances?

Preface

This book began in our classrooms. At some point, we discovered that we both teach critical thinking courses that are idiosyncratic in the same ways—in short, as though they are courses in the psychology of judgment. For example, we both had our students read Robyn Dawes's *House of Cards* (1994) and Thomas Gilovich's *How We Know What Isn't So* (1991). We independently arrived at the idea that there were epistemological lessons to be drawn not just from the heuristics and biases tradition (which has received attention from philosophers) but also from the fascinating research on linear predictive modeling. But we also recognized that psychologists for too long had been wrestling with normative, epistemic issues with much too little useful input from philosophers. In their classic book *Human Inference: Strategies and Shortcomings of Social Judgment* (1980), Richard Nisbett and Lee Ross call for greater participation from philosophers in tackling the normative issues that arise in psychology.

> [W]e have become increasingly aware of the difficulty of defining what is "normative" when one moves beyond the relatively simple question of how to solve correctly some particular problem. "Normatively appropriate" strategies for the solution of some problems are extremely time consuming and expensive. It may be clear what must be done if one wishes a correct answer to such problems, but sometimes it may be even clearer that the correct solution is not worth the effort. This gives rise to more important questions of normativeness which are not fundamentally empirical in nature: How much effort, for what kinds of problems, should be expended to obtain a correct solution?

We have become excited by such normative questions and are pleased that our book highlights them. We have not been able to make much progress toward their solution, however.... It is our hope that others, particularly philosophers who are more comfortable with such questions, will be motivated to pursue them. (Nisbett and Ross 1980, 13–14)

It is rare for scientists to call on philosophers to contribute in substantive ways to their scientific projects. Rarer still for scientists who are at the top of their field.

Armed with the suspicion that there was something useful for philosophers to do in this area, we organized a symposium at the 2000 Philosophy of Science Association meeting in Vancouver. The purpose of the symposium was to explore the connections between research on predictive modeling and philosophy (see Dawes 2002, Faust and Meehl 2002, Bishop and Trout 2002). We have also presented these ideas to a number of audiences at Bryn Mawr College, California State University at Long Beach, Howard University, Northwestern University, University of Illinois, University of Innsbruck, University of Utah, and Washington University in St. Louis. In almost every venue, there were philosophers whose reaction to these issues was similar to our own: the normative issues raised by the psychological literature are interesting and important, but analytic epistemology does not have the resources to adequately address them. So we sat down to write this book.

Our goal in this book is to bring whatever philosophical expertise we can to bear on the sorts of normative issues that bedevil psychologists (like Nisbett and Ross). With a few notable exceptions, the normative concerns of epistemologists and psychologists have inhabited different intellectual worlds. When philosophers do discuss psychological findings, it is usually to dismiss them as irrelevant to epistemology. This book will have achieved its goals if it leads at least some philosophers and psychologists to admit (even if ever so grudgingly) that their field of study would benefit from closer cooperation with their sister discipline.

This book is the product of somewhat unusual philosophical training. But then again, our philosophy teachers were an unusual collection of curiosity, talent, and trust. We are grateful to Richard Boyd, Philip Kitcher, Robert Stalnaker, and Stephen Stich, each of whom taught us in his own way the value of pursuing interesting but risky projects. They also encouraged us to explore issues that lie outside the disciplinary confines of philosophy. In so doing, we were lucky to learn psychology, in graduate school and after, from Frank Keil, Richard Nisbett, David Pisoni,

V. S. Ramachandran, Robert Remez, Roger Shepard, and Gary Wells. These psychologists instilled in us an appreciation for a science of the mind and (probably unwittingly) a recognition of its relevance to philosophical questions.

Given our general outlook, we doubt that we can very reliably identify the most important intellectual influences on our epistemological views. But we are confident that they include Richard Boyd's "Scientific Realism and Naturalistic Epistemology" (1980), Alvin Goldman's "Epistemics: The Regulative Theory of Cognition" (1978) as well as *Epistemology and Cognition* (1986), Philip Kitcher's "The Naturalist's Return" (1992) as well as chapter 8 of *The Advancement of Science* (1993), Hilary Kornblith's *Inductive Inference and Its Natural Ground* (1993), and Stephen Stich's *The Fragmentation of Reason* (1990).

For useful conversations about the material in this book, we would like to thank our colleagues and friends: Paul Abela, Robert Baum, Travis Butler, Douglas Epperson, Joe Kupfer, Dominic Murphy, Gary Pavela, Bill Robinson, Abe Schwab, Peter Vranas, Daniel Weiskopf, and Gary Wells. We would like especially to thank Joe Mendola, Michael Strevens, and Mark Wunderlich, who gave us detailed comments on earlier drafts of this book, and James Twine, who supplied excellent research assistance. We are also grateful to the National Science Foundation for grants SES#0354536 (to MB) and SES#0327104 (to JDT) in support of the research culminating in this book. The findings in Arkes (2003) should keep us modest.

Contents

Epistemology and the Psychology of Human Judgment

Introduction

The first three chapters of the book introduce the basic building blocks of our epistemological approach and of our epistemological theory. Chapter 1 introduces the basic motives and methods of our epistemology. The goal is to give the reader a clear conception of our overall project. As a result, the opening chapter is not weighed down with arguments and qualifications—that comes later. Chapter 2 introduces Statistical Prediction Rules (SPRs) and offers an explanation for their success. SPRs are simple, formal rules that have been shown to be at least as reliable, and typically more reliable, than the predictions of human experts on a wide variety of problems. On the basis of testable results, psychology can make *normative recommendations* about how we ought to reason. We dub the branches of psychology that provide normative recommendations "Ameliorative Psychology." Ameliorative Psychology recommends SPRs on the basis of testable results: SPRs are reliable, they tend to be easy to use, and they typically address significant issues. In addition, taking seriously the success of SPRs requires us to impose discipline on a human mind that is much too easily tempted by appealing distractions. Certain lines of evidence, no matter how subjectively attractive or how consecrated by the concepts central to our epistemological tradition, are to be ignored except in extreme cases. In chapter 3, we identify some of the basic building blocks of the epistemological framework that supports the recommendations of Ameliorative Psychology. The framework assesses the epistemic merit of reasoning strategies in terms of their robust reliability, their feasibility and the significance of the problems they tackle. We then argue that this framework offers a new way to think about applied epistemology. In particular, it suggests that there are four and only four ways for people to improve their reasoning.

The middle three chapters of the book (4, 5, and 6) articulate the central features of our theory of epistemic excellence, Strategic Reliabilism. Strategic Reliabilism holds that epistemic excellence involves the efficient allocation of cognitive resources to robustly reliable reasoning strategies applied to significant problems. Chapter 4 takes up what is the central notion of Strategic Reliabilism: what it is for a reasoning strategy to be robustly reliable. Chapter 5 defends a cost-benefit approach to epistemology and offers an account of what it is for cognitive resources to be allocated efficiently. Chapter 6 argues that a genuinely normative epistemological theory must include some notion of significance, and it addresses the issue of what it is for a problem to be significant.

The final three substantive chapters of the book (7, 8, and 9) put our views about epistemology to work. In chapter 7, we criticize the approach that has dominated English-speaking philosophy over the past half-century or so—what we call Standard Analytic Epistemology (SAE). SAE names a contingently clustered set of methods and motives. By comparing our approach to that of SAE, chapter 7 identifies some of the troubles with SAE and argues that they are serious enough to motivate a radically different approach to epistemology. Chapter 8 takes Strategic Reliabilism, which has been extracted from psychology, and turns it back on psychology. We use Strategic Reliabilism to resolve two debates about whether certain experimental findings demonstrate deep and systematic failures of human reasoning. This chapter illustrates one of the main benefits of our approach to epistemology: it can be used to adjudicate disputes that arise in psychology that are, at bottom, normative epistemological disputes about the nature of good reasoning. Chapter 9 attempts to consolidate some of the lessons of Ameliorative Psychology with some handy heuristics and illustrative injunctions. We explore the empirical research that shows how we can enhance the accuracy of diagnostic reasoning, reduce overconfidence, avoid the regression fallacy, improve our policy assessments, and restrain the unbridled story-telling surrounding rare or unusual events. We have no doubt that many significant problems we face are best addressed with institutional measures, and on this issue much research remains to be done. But for those problems tractable to voluntary reasoning strategies, the simple strategies recommended in this chapter can improve reasoning at low cost and high fidelity.

Chapter 10 briefly sums up our view and points to some of the challenges that remain in the construction of a naturalistic epistemology.

The Appendix considers 11 objections that we expect philosophers to level against our views. Some will undoubtedly complain that we have missed some serious objections, or that our replies to the objections we do consider are by no means conclusive. Granted. But our goal in the Appendix is not the wildly ambitious one of overcoming all serious objections. Instead, our aim is to offer some sense of the resources available to the naturalist for overcoming what many proponents of SAE are likely to consider devastating objections.

1

Laying Our Cards on the Table

It is time for epistemology to take its rightful place alongside ethics as a discipline that offers practical, real-world recommendations for living. In our society, the powerful are at least sometimes asked to provide a moral justification for their actions. And there is at least sometimes a heavy price to be paid when a person, particularly an elected official, is caught engaging in immoral actions or defending clearly immoral policies. But our society hands out few sanctions to those who promote and defend policies supported by appallingly weak reasoning. Too often, condemnation is meted out only after the policies have been implemented and have led to horrible results: irresponsible war and spilt blood or the needless ruin of people's prospects and opportunities.

Epistemology is a serious business for at least two reasons. First, epistemology guides reasoning, and we reason about everything. If one embraces a defective morality, one's ability to act ethically is compromised. But if one embraces a defective epistemology, one's ability to act effectively in all areas of life is compromised. Second, people don't fully appreciate the risks and dangers of poor reasoning. Everyone knows the danger of intentional evil; but few fully appreciate the real risks and untold damage wrought by apparently upstanding folk who embrace and act on bad epistemological principles. Such people don't look dangerous. But they are. An example of the costs of upstanding people reasoning poorly is the surprisingly strong opposition in the United States to policies that would provide opportunities and services to the disadvantaged (e.g., in terms of education and basic needs such as health care). Much of this opposition is not based on the rejection of a moral principle of equal opportunity, but instead on poorly-arrived-at empirical views. Some people reject redistributive social policies on the grounds that they are *inevitably* ineffective; others rely on clearly mistaken views about what percentage of the federal budget actually goes to pay for such programs. That's not to say that there aren't good arguments against some redistributive policies. Some can backfire, and others (particularly those that benefit the non-poor) can be very expensive. But sound comparative policy analysis provides no support to a *principled* opposition to redistributive social policies. People who defend appalling social policies often do so on the basis of weak reasoning about factual matters rather than on the basis of backward moral precepts.

One might think that our call for a more prescriptive, reason-guiding epistemology is more appropriate for the areas of "critical thinking" or "informal logic" (Feldman 1999, 184–85, n10). The problem with this suggestion is that these areas, as exemplified in textbooks, are completely divorced from contemporary epistemology. This bespeaks deep problems both for critical thinking courses and for contemporary epistemology. Epistemology, if it is to achieve its normative potential, must make firm contact with the sorts of reasoning errors that lead to horrendous and avoidable outcomes. And critical thinking courses must be informed by a theory about what makes reasoning good or bad. We do not have in mind a thin epistemological "theory" (e.g., "premises should be true and support the conclusion") that yields a long list of informal fallacies. Rather, an effective critical thinking course should be informed by a theory that (among other things) helps us to recognize, anticipate, and compensate for our cognitive frailties. In other words, such courses should be informed by a deeply naturalistic epistemological theory.

We have written this book driven by a vision of what epistemology could be—normatively reason guiding and genuinely capable of benefiting the world. If our tone is not always dispassionate, it is because our profession has so clearly failed to bring the potential benefits of epistemology to ordinary people's lives. We are under no illusions, however. This book is, at best, a modest first step toward the construction of an epistemological theory with concrete, prescriptive bite. And even if our theory should be somewhere close to the truth, we are not sanguine about the potential of philosophy to influence the world. Sometimes, though, life rewards wild-eyed optimists. If in our case it doesn't, we fall squarely within what is best in our philosophical tradition if our reach should exceed our grasp.

1. Starting points: What epistemology is about

Theories, including epistemological theories, are supposed to be about something. They are supposed to explain or account for some range of phenomena. An important way in which our approach to epistemology differs from that of most contemporary English-speaking epistemologists is in terms of what we take to be the proper subject matter of epistemology—what we take to be the phenomena or evidence that an epistemological theory is supposed to account for or explain. Traditional epistemological theories aim to provide a theory that captures our considered epistemic judgments, in particular, our considered judgments about knowledge and justification. Our epistemological theory aims to uncover the normative assumptions of a branch of science. We disagree with most traditional epistemologists in terms of what epistemology is about. This difference couldn't be more fundamental.

1.1. The starting point of the standard analytic approach to epistemology

Standard Analytic Epistemology (SAE) names a contingently clustered class of methods and theses that have dominated English-speaking epistemology for much of the past century. Almost all the contemporary readings in the most popular epistemology textbooks are prime examples of SAE. Contemporary versions of foundationalism, coherentism, and reliabilism are exemplars of SAE. While we object to the methods of SAE, and therefore to the kinds of theories it leads to, our main goal in this chapter is to distinguish our approach from that of SAE. So let's begin with the starting points of SAE—what proponents of SAE take to be the fundamental phenomena or evidence of epistemology.

The goal of most philosophers engaged in SAE is to provide an account of knowledge and epistemic justification. What are the *success conditions* on such an account? In a typically clear and careful article, Jaegwon Kim identifies a number of criteria that any account of justification must meet in order to be successful. The most important of these conditions is what we will call the *stasis requirement*:

> Although some philosophers have been willing to swallow skepticism just because what we regard as correct criteria of justified belief are seen to lead inexorably to the conclusion that none, or very few, of our beliefs are

justified, the usual presumption is that our answer to the first question [What conditions must a belief meet if we are justified in accepting it as true?] should leave our epistemic situation largely unchanged. That is to say, it is expected to turn out that according to the criteria of justified belief we come to accept, we know, or are justified in believing, pretty much what we reflectively think we know or are entitled to believe. (Kim 1988, 382)

It is worth noting that this requirement—that the right account of justification "leave our epistemic situation largely unchanged"—is profoundly conservative. In particular, it is extraordinary that SAE should have *built right into it* a requirement that makes it virtually impossible that a successful epistemological theory would force us to radically alter our epistemic judgments.

Of course, proponents of SAE will not suggest that they are trying to provide an account of their naïve epistemic judgments, but of their considered epistemic judgments. One way to spell out the difference is in terms of reflective equilibrium. Nelson Goodman introduced reflective equilibrium as a process that involves aligning our judgments about particular instances with our judgments about general principles. "The process of justification is the delicate one of making mutual adjustments between rules and accepted inferences; and in the agreement achieved lies the only justification needed for either" (1965, 64). Narrow reflective equilibrium is the process of bringing our normative judgments about particular cases into line with our general normative prescriptions and vice versa. Wide reflective equilibrium differs from narrow reflective equilibrium by including our best theories in the mix. So wide reflective equilibrium is the process of bringing into alignment our best theories, as well as our normative judgments about particular cases, and our general normative prescriptions (Rawls 1971, Daniels 1979).

So according to the stasis requirement, if an epistemic theory forced us to radically alter our considered epistemic judgments (e.g., our epistemic judgments in reflective equilibrium), then ipso facto that theory is unacceptable. While some proponents of SAE might reject the stasis requirement (e.g., Unger 1984), we agree with Kim that stasis is a fundamental commitment of SAE. It is not, however, often explicitly stated. That is because the commitment to epistemic stasis is implicit in the practice of SAE. Much of SAE proceeds by counterexample philosophy: Someone proposes an account of justification, others propose counterexamples, and then the original account is altered or defended in the face of those counterexamples. What we find objectionable about this mode of argument is what proponents of SAE accept as a *successful* counterexample. To see this, let's consider the mother-of-all counterexamples in SAE, the Gettier Problem.

Before Gettier, it was generally thought that knowledge is justified true belief (JTB). Gettier (1963) describes a situation in which the JTB account is at odds with our considered knowledge judgments. One of Gettier's famous cases involves a man named Smith who has overwhelming evidence, and so justification, for believing that Jones will get a job and that Jones has ten coins in his pocket. On the basis of these beliefs, Smith infers that the man who will get the job has ten coins in his pocket. It turns out that unbeknownst to Smith, he will get the job, and he has ten coins in his pocket. His belief that the man who will get the job has ten coins in his pocket is true and justified. But Gettier insists that it is "clear" that Smith's belief is not knowledge (Gettier 1963, 122). For proponents of SAE, the Gettier examples are important because they show that the JTB account can't be right on the grounds that it does not "leave our epistemic situation largely unchanged." Rather than explore any more of the countless and wonderfully rococo counterexamples prevalent in the SAE literature, let's look at how some of these counterexamples end:

> However, it is perfectly apparent that I know nothing of the sort. (Lehrer and Paxson 1969, 235)

> Even if S correctly predicts that he is going to lose, we would deny that he knew he was going to lose if the only basis he had for this belief was the fact that his chances of winning were so slight. (Dretske 1971, 3)

> The situation is a peculiar one, and my intuitions, and I would suppose other people's, are not completely clear on the matter. But it seems, on the whole, that we ought not to speak of knowledge here. . . . (Armstrong 1973, 181)

> But, to make such an assumption is counterintuitive. In everyday situations we do not regard deception as precluding rationality. Likewise, we do not regard the fact that we have been deceived, or will be deceived, or would be deceived, as precluding rationality. (Foley 1985, 192)

> And, surely, we do not want to say that the fact that his friend has a generator in his basement *prevents* S from having knowledge that the company's generators are causing the lights to be on. (Pappas and Swain 1973, 66)

In the above passages (and we could have chosen literally hundreds of others), we are urged to share the philosopher's considered epistemic judgments about some imagined scenario. And we usually do. The problem, on our view, is that SAE rejects various accounts *solely on the grounds that they violate these judgments.*

The shockingly conservative nature of the method of SAE may only become clear when we compare it to methods in other fields of inquiry. The fact that relativity denies people's considered judgments about simultaneity is hardly a reason to reject it. If physics had been burdened with such a conservative method, we wouldn't have relativity, quantum mechanics (or perhaps even Copernicanism!). If biology had been taken over by such a conservative method, we wouldn't have Darwinism. If cultural studies had had such a conservative method, we wouldn't have postmodernism.

Okay, so sometimes conservatism is a good thing.

Behind this joke is an important point. The problem with conservative methods is not that they are conservative per se. Conservative methods work very well when applied to theories or propositions for which we have overwhelming evidence. It is perfectly reasonable to be conservative about the commitments of theoretical chemistry reflected in the periodic table, or about the core attachments of contemporary physics or biology. That doesn't mean we rule out the possibility that new developments will force us to abandon them. Conservatism isn't mulishness. Conservatism is appropriate in the case of the core commitments of these theories because we have so much evidence in their favor that in absence of extraordinary counterevidence, they deserve our allegiance. But while conservatism is fine for excellent theories, it is poison in domains where progress awaits deep and durable changes in method and outlook. The alchemist's attachment to conservatism was ill advised; it only protracted the alchemist's crippling (and it turns out, thanks to mercury and lead, fatal) ignorance. This raises an obvious concern for SAE, which we will explore more fully in chapter 7. No matter how polished or well thought-out our epistemic judgments, no matter how much in reflective equilibrium they might be, are we so confident in them that it is reasonable to make them the final arbiters of our epistemological theories?

1.2. The starting point of the philosophy of science approach to epistemology

We view epistemology as a branch of the philosophy of science. From our perspective, epistemology begins with a branch of cognitive science that investigates good reasoning. It includes work in psychology, statistics, machine learning, and Artificial Intelligence. Some of this work involves "predictive modeling," and it includes discussion of models such as linear models, multiple regression formulas, neural networks, naïve Bayes classifiers, Markov Chain Monte Carlo algorithms, decision tree models, and support vector machines; but much of this work comes from traditional psychology and includes the well-known heuristics and biases program launched by Kahneman and Tversky (Kahneman, Slovic, and Tversky 1982). It will be useful to give this wide-ranging literature a name. We call it *Ameliorative Psychology*. The essential feature of Ameliorative Psychology is that it aims to give positive advice about how we can reason better. We will introduce many findings of Ameliorative Psychology (particularly in chapters 2 and 9). But it will be useful here to introduce some of its noteworthy features.

In the course of this book, we will introduce a number of reason-guiding prescriptions offered by Ameliorative Psychology. This advice includes making statistical judgments in terms of frequencies rather than probabilities, considering explanations for propositions one doesn't believe, ignoring certain kinds of evidence (e.g., certain selected cues that improve accuracy only very moderately, and certain kinds of impressionistic information, such as opinions gleaned from unstructured personal interviews), and many others (Bishop 2000). These recommendations are bluntly normative: They tell us how we *ought* to reason about certain sorts of problems.

A particularly interesting branch of Ameliorative Psychology begins in earnest in 1954 with the publication of Paul Meehl's classic book *Clinical Versus Statistical Prediction: A Theoretical Analysis and a Review of the Evidence*. Meehl reported on twenty experiments that showed that very simple prediction rules were more reliable predictors than human experts. Since then, psychologists have developed many of these Statistical Prediction Rules (or SPRs). (In fact, in the past decade or so, there has been an explosion of predictive models in AI and machine learning.) There is now considerable evidence for what we call *The Golden Rule of Predictive Modeling*: When based on the same evidence, the predictions of SPRs are at least as reliable, and are typically more reliable, than the predictions of human experts. Except for an important qualification we will discuss in chapter 2, section 4.2, the evidence in favor of the Golden Rule is overwhelming (see Grove and Meehl 1996; Swets, Dawes, and Monahan 2000).

The Golden Rule of Predictive Modeling has been woefully neglected. Perhaps a good way to begin to undo this state of affairs is to briefly describe ten of its instances. This will give the reader some idea of the range and robustness of the Golden Rule.

1.   An SPR that takes into account a patient's marital status, length of psychotic distress, and a rating of the patient's insight into his or her condition predicted the success of electroshock therapy more reliably than a hospital's medical and psychological staff members (Wittman 1941).

2.   A model that used past criminal and prison records was more reliable than expert criminologists in predicting criminal recidivism (Carroll et al., 1988).

3.   On the basis of a Minnesota Multiphasic Personality Inventory (MMPI) profile, clinical psychologists were less reliable than an SPR in diagnosing patients as either neurotic or psychotic. When psychologists were given the SPR's results before they made their predictions, they were still less accurate than the SPR (Goldberg 1968).

4.   A number of SPRs predict academic performance (measured by graduation rates and GPA at graduation) better than admissions officers. This is true even when the admissions officers are allowed to use considerably more evidence than the models (DeVaul et al. 1957), and it has been shown to be true at selective colleges, medical schools (DeVaul et al. 1957), law schools (Swets, Dawes, and Monahan 2000, 18), and graduate school in psychology (Dawes 1971).

5.   SPRs predict loan and credit risk better than bank officers. SPRs are now standardly used by banks when they make loans and by credit card companies when they approve and set credit limits for new customers (Stillwell et al. 1983).

6.   SPRs predict newborns at risk for Sudden Infant Death Syndrome (SIDS) much better than human experts (Carpenter et al. 1977, Golding et al. 1985).

7.   Predicting the quality of the vintage for a red Bordeaux wine decades in advance is done more reliably by an SPR than by expert wine tasters, who swirl, smell, and taste the young wine (Ashenfelter, Ashmore, and Lalonde 1995).

8.   An SPR correctly diagnosed 83% of progressive brain dysfunction on the basis of cues from intellectual tests. Groups of clinicians working from the same data did no better than 63%. When clinicians were given the results of the actuarial formula, clinicians still did worse than the model, scoring no better than 75% (Leli and Filskov 1984).

9.   In predicting the presence, location, and cause of brain damage, an SPR outperformed experienced clinicians and a nationally prominent neuropsychologist (Wedding 1983).

10.   In legal settings, forensic psychologists often make predictions of violence. One will be more reliable than forensic psychologists simply by

predicting that people will not be violent. Further, SPRs are more reliable than forensic psychologists in predicting the relative likelihood of violence, that is, who is more prone to violence (Faust and Ziskin 1988).

Upon reviewing this evidence in 1986, Paul Meehl said: "There is no controversy in social science which shows such a large body of qualitatively diverse studies coming out so uniformly in the same direction as this one. When you are pushing [scores of] investigations, predicting everything from the outcomes of football games to the diagnosis of liver disease and when you can hardly come up with a half dozen studies showing even a weak tendency in favor of the clinician, it is time to draw a practical conclusion" (Meehl 1986, 372–73). Ameliorative Psychology has had consistent success in recommending reasoning strategies in a wide variety of important reasoning tasks. Such success is worth exploring.

The descriptive core of our approach to epistemology consists of the empirical findings of Ameliorative Psychology. And yet, Ameliorative Psychology is deeply normative in the sense that it makes (implicitly or explicitly) evaluative "ought" claims that are intended to guide people's reasoning. Let's look at three examples of the reason-guiding prescriptions of Ameliorative Psychology.

A well-documented success of Ameliorative Psychology is the Goldberg Rule (the third item on the above list). It predicts whether a psychiatric patient is neurotic or psychotic on the basis of an MMPI profile. Lewis Goldberg (1965) found that the following rule outperformed 29 clinical judges (where L is a validity scale and Pa, Sc, Hy, and Pt are clinical scales of the MMPI):

$$x = (L + Pa + Sc) - (Hy + Pt)$$

If $x < 45$, diagnose patient as neurotic.

If $x \geq 45$, diagnose patient as psychotic.

When tested on a set of 861 patients, the Goldberg Rule had a 70% hit rate; clinicians' hit rates varied from a low of 55% to a high of 67%. (13 of the 29 clinical judges in the above study were experienced Ph.D.s, while the other 16 were Ph.D. students. The Ph.D.s were no more accurate than the students. This is consistent with the findings reported in Dawes 1994.) So here we have a prediction rule that could literally turn a smart second-grader into a better psychiatric diagnostician than highly credentialed, highly experienced psychologists—at least for this diagnostic task. In fact, more than 3 decades after the appearance of Goldberg's results, making an initial diagnosis on the basis of an MMPI profile by using subjective judgment rather than the Goldberg Rule would bespeak either willful irresponsibility or deep ignorance. So here is a finding of Ameliorative Psychology: people (in an epistemic sense) *ought* to use the Goldberg Rule in making preliminary diagnoses of psychiatric patients.

Another example of Ameliorative Psychology making evaluative ought-claims is a 1995 paper by Gigerenzer and Hoffrage entitled "How to *Improve* Bayesian Reasoning Without Instruction: Frequency Formats" (emphasis added). As the title of the paper suggests, Gigerenzer and Hoffrage show how people charged with making high-stakes diagnoses (e.g., about cancer or HIV) can *improve* their reasoning. They suggest a reasoning strategy that enhances reasoners' ability to identify, on the basis of medical tests, the likelihood that an individual will have cancer or HIV. We will discuss these "frequency formats" in chapter 9, section 1. For now, it is enough to note that a finding of Ameliorative Psychology is that people *ought* to use frequency formats when diagnosing rare conditions on the basis of well-understood diagnostic tests.

Another particularly successful example of Ameliorative Psychology is credit scoring (the fifth item on the above list). Many financial institutions no longer rely primarily on financial officers to make credit decisions—they now make credit decisions on the basis of simple SPRs developed as the result of research by psychologists and statisticians (Lovie and Lovie 1986). Once again, this finding of Ameliorative Psychology seems to be normative through and through: When it comes to making predictions about someone's creditworthiness, one *ought* to use a credit-scoring model.

Not only does Ameliorative Psychology recommend particular reasoning strategies for tackling certain kinds of problems, it also suggests generalizations about how people ought to reason. (See, for example, the flat maximum principle, discussed in chapter 2, section 2.1.) On our view, the goal of epistemology is to articulate the epistemic generalizations that guide the prescriptions of Ameliorative Psychology. In this way, epistemology is simply a branch of philosophy of science. Just as the philosopher of biology might aim to uncover and articulate the metaphysical assumptions of evolutionary theory, the epistemologist aims to uncover and articulate the normative, epistemic principles behind the long and distinguished tradition of Ameliorative Psychology. (There are two objections philosophers are likely to immediately raise against our approach. We consider them in the Appendix, sections 1 and 2.)

Ameliorative Psychology is normative in the sense that it yields explicit, reason-guiding advice about how people ought to reason. Some might fix us with a jaundiced eye and wonder whether the recommendations of Ameliorative Psychology are really normative in the same way as the recommendations of SAE are normative. Admittedly, there does seem to be one telling difference. People outside academia have on occasion actually changed the way they reason about significant matters as a result of the recommendations of Ameliorative Psychology.

2. The end points: The theories generated by the two approaches

The two approaches to epistemology we have been considering differ in terms of what they take to be the appropriate subject matter of epistemology (our considered judgments vs. Ameliorative Psychology). Given that they differ so fundamentally regarding what epistemology is about, it is not surprising that they end up with quite different normative theories. Indeed, they end up with theories of different phenomena. The fundamental aim of SAE is to deliver an account of epistemic justification or knowledge (or one of their close relatives, e.g., warrant). The fundamental aim of our approach to epistemology is to provide an account of *reasoning excellence*. Is this really a deep difference? Yes, it is.

Justification, the target of theories of SAE, is a property of belief tokens. Judy might be justified in believing that George is a dolt, while Mary is not. So a theory of SAE will provide an account that distinguishes the justified belief tokens from the unjustified belief tokens (or, perhaps, the more justified belief tokens from the less justified belief tokens). Epistemic excellence, the target of our theory, we take to be a property of reasoning strategies. The primary normative assessments made by Ameliorative Psychology are of ways of reasoning. Ameliorative Psychology is in the business of telling us what are the best ways to go about (say) making tentative diagnoses of psychiatric patients (Goldberg Rule) or making judgments about a person's ability to repay a loan (credit-scoring models). So an epistemology that puts Ameliorative Psychology at center stage will yield a theory of reasoning excellence (see also Goldman 1979, Stich 1990).

While the notion of epistemic excellence might not have the common currency or the philosophical pedigree of notions like justification, rationality, or reason, it is a very useful concept to have at the center of one's epistemology. When a thoughtful person is faced with a reasoning problem, she will sometimes think about and try to figure out what is the best way to tackle this problem. We often have a sense (though perhaps sometimes a mistaken sense) that certain reasoning strategies are better than others for handling certain reasoning problems. For example, deciding whether a prisoner up for parole is a threat to society on the basis of his record in prison is better than flipping a coin (and, as it turns out, not as good as using a decision tree; see Quinsey, et al. 1998). So we understand that some reasoning strategies are better than others; and often there is a reasoning strategy that is the best available. Our epistemological theory aims to provide an account of what it is for a reasoning strategy to be excellent, or better than any of the alternatives.

If our theory and the theories of SAE are theories of different epistemological categories, one might wonder whether they can conflict. Perhaps by so radically altering what we take epistemology to be, we have changed the subject? We don't think this is a serious worry. A theory of justification will yield normative conclusions about *belief tokens*—whether they are justified or not (or the degree to which they are justified). A theory of epistemic excellence will yield normative conclusions about the epistemic quality of a *reasoning strategy*. But reasoning strategies typically produce belief tokens. So whenever a theory of reasoning excellence recommends a particular reasoning strategy for tackling a particular problem, it normally recommends a belief token, but at one remove. And this leaves open the possibility of conflict. It is possible for a theory of reasoning excellence to recommend a reasoning strategy to S that yields the belief that p, and for a theory of justification to conclude that S's belief that not-p is justified and that S's belief that p is not justified. Insofar as the two approaches to epistemology are meant to guide reasoning, it is possible for them to yield recommendations that are mutually incompatible (in the sense that both cannot be followed).

3. The structure of a healthy epistemological tradition

On our approach to epistemology, a healthy epistemological tradition must have three vigorous and interrelated components: theoretical, practical, and social. The practical or applied component of epistemology is an extension of what people do every day. Everyone who has ever thought about how to tackle a particular reasoning problem has engaged in applied epistemology. As is standard with an applied venture, some people do it better than others. Ameliorative Psychology is the science of applied epistemology. Much of the point of Ameliorative Psychology is to provide advice that will help people reason better about the world.

The second component of a healthy epistemological tradition is theory. We take theory and application to be mutually informing and supporting. Theory is extracted from practice. One of the goals—and one of the tests—of a theory of reasoning excellence is that it should be faithful to the practice of Ameliorative Psychology. When conjoined with the descriptive results of Ameliorative Psychology, the correct epistemological theory should yield the recommendations of Ameliorative Psychology. One of our primary goals in this book is to offer a theory that accurately depicts the normative machinery that guides the prescriptions of Ameliorative Psychology. But theory should do more than mimic. It should *explain* what makes some reasoning strategies epistemically better than others; it should also play a role in a full explanation for why good reasoning tends to lead to good outcomes. (To see how our theory addresses these explanatory challenges, see Appendix, section 8.) Further, a theory of reasoning excellence should be able to be applied back to Ameliorative Psychology. Practice informs theory; but good theory repays the kindness. When a disagreement erupts in the applied domain, and that disagreement is at bottom a theoretical one, a good theory should be able to clarify and, in some cases at least, resolve the issues. In chapter 8, we will apply our theory of reasoning excellence in an effort to resolve two disputes that have arisen in Ameliorative Psychology.

We have suggested that the theoretical part of a healthy epistemological tradition will be firmly connected to its applied components. As we have already suggested, by this yardstick, the standard analytic approach to epistemology does not seem to be a healthy tradition. As far as we have been able to tell, the theoretical musings of analytic epistemologists have not led to very much, if any, useful guidance about how people should reason. We will argue eventually that this prescriptive impotence is a natural consequence of the methods of Standard Analytic Epistemology. If this is right, it is a shame. It is the normative, reason-guiding promise of epistemology that makes it so much more than intellectual sport.

While a healthy epistemological tradition will provide useful reasoning guidance, good advice we keep to ourselves is no advice at all. Ameliorative Psychology is the science of applied epistemology, and theoretical epistemology is theoretical Ameliorative Psychology (i.e., a theoretical science). As with any science, it is important to think about what it would take for it to be a well-ordered social system (Kitcher 2001). An important aspect of epistemology's social presence is how it communicates its practical recommendations to the wider public. We don't have any detailed picture of what a socially well-ordered epistemology would look like. But we are confident that it would have at least two features. First, in order to achieve its ameliorative potential, epistemology should be organized so that it provides a way to effectively communicate its established findings, particularly its practical content, to a wide audience. Second, in order to minimize the risk of promulgating harmful or mistaken findings, epistemology should be organized so that whatever findings are communicated widely will have passed rigorous examination and empirical testing.

4. Seductive circularities and empirical hooks: Is a scientific investigation into normative epistemology possible?

We have argued that applied epistemology is a science, and that theoretical epistemology is a theoretical science. But we also seek an epistemic theory that is normative and reason guiding. How can a scientific epistemology also be a normative one? The standard worry with our approach is that it is somehow viciously circular. The objection goes like this: Suppose our epistemological theory begins with empirical claims about Ameliorative Psychology. Presumably, we have to make some decisions about which empirical claims to trust. So we have to decide which views are the epistemically good ones. But such decisions require a prior epistemological theory. So (the argument continues) one cannot begin one's epistemological speculations with empirical claims. (For a discussion of this objection, see Appendix, section 2.)

This is a very seductive argument. One problem with it is that it assumes the normative must come in a single dollop. So either one has a full-blown theory and can make normative judgments or one has no theory and can make no such judgments. If knowledge of the normative were an all-or-nothing affair, then a scientific epistemology, one that began with, say, Ameliorative Psychology, might be impossible. But it's not. In fact, Aristotle points the way to avoiding the theoretical stultification that comes with the dollop assumption.

Aristotle argued that at least some of the moral and the intellectual virtues are intimately related and mutually supportive (*Nicomachean Ethics*, Book VI). Aristotle's insight provides us with an empirical "hook" into our investigation of the normative. To see how this hook works, suppose we're faced with making parole decisions for people convicted of a violent crime. An important question to consider is whether the prisoner is likely to commit another violent crime. Suppose we decide to use the Shoe

Size Rule: If the prisoner's shoe size is a whole number (e.g., 9, 10, 11), he won't commit another violent crime; if it's not (e.g., 9½, 10½), he will commit another violent crime. The Shoe Size Rule is a poor reasoning strategy. And there is a tell-tale empirical mark of its being a poor reasoning strategy: In the long run, the Shoe Size Rule will lead to poor outcomes—or more precisely, it will lead to worse outcomes than better reasoning strategies. Now, this notion of bad outcomes is not particularly subtle or in need of philosophical elucidation. Reasoning poorly about this problem will lead to increases in murder and assault by paroled prisoners. Similarly, if medical doctors reason poorly about whether patients have brain damage, cancer, or HIV, patients will tend to have worse treatment outcomes. Again, this isn't a particularly subtle point. Poor reasoning in these matters will lead patients to make treatment decisions that will lead to unnecessary death, suffering, and illness. (More precisely, poor reasoning will tend to lead to worse outcomes for patients than will good reasoning.)

The Aristotelian Principle says simply that *in the long run, poor reasoning tends to lead to worse outcomes than good reasoning.* So the Aristotelian Principle allows us to empirically determine—though not with complete certainty—when one way of reasoning is better than another. Of course, there are no guarantees. It is logically possible for someone to have bad luck and for terrific reasoning to lead consistently to bad outcomes; and it is logically possible for someone to reason badly and yet, Magoo-like, to have consistently good outcomes. But seldom does anything good in life come with guarantees. To begin our empirical investigation into the epistemological, all we really need is the robust generalization we have called the Aristotelian Principle. It allows us to accept certain normative epistemological judgments as prima facie true and then explore more deeply the sorts of assumptions that drive such judgments. This is how we will start our investigations into the normative.

Why should anyone believe the Aristotelian Principle? It is an empirical, probabilistic claim and, as such, it is child's play to imagine environments that are so unfriendly as to make excellent reasoning a danger (e.g., a powerful evil demon sets out to punish excellent reasoners). But as a practical matter, we contend that any psychologically healthy, reflective person who has chosen to spend their life doing epistemology must accept the Aristotelian Principle. It is a necessary precondition for the practical relevance of epistemology. Recall that we opened this chapter by arguing that epistemology is important because it has real potential to improve people's lives. The Aristotelian Principle embodies this promise. If the Aristotelian Principle is false, if good reasoning doesn't tend to lead to better outcomes than bad reasoning, then epistemology can't be practically important. It would be like the New York Times crossword puzzle: an intellectual challenge, perhaps even an addictive one, but nothing more than an amusing pastime. More importantly, however, if the Aristotelian Principle is false, then we can't know how to lead our cognitive lives. Suppose we have to reason badly in order to achieve good outcomes. There are indefinitely many different ways to reason badly. And all of these ways of reasoning badly will typically lead to many, many different judgments about the world. Which way of reasoning badly will lead to good outcomes? Presumably we need to figure this out. But how are we supposed to figure that out? By reasoning well? Presumably not. But if by reasoning poorly, then once again, which way of reasoning poorly? And how are we supposed to figure that out? And so goes the infinite regress. . . .

If a useful epistemology is possible, then the Aristotelian Principle is true. But this raises an obvious and cynical worry: Is a useful epistemology really possible? There are at least two reasons for optimism. The first is that much of the world that is significant to us is stable enough for the quality of our reasoning to make a difference. We reason about medical diagnoses, policy choice, financial planning, criminal recidivism, etc. These (and many other) parts of the world have proven to be predictable enough for people to make judgments about them and make effective plans based on those judgments. The second reason to be optimistic about the Aristotelian Principle is that the human predicament comes with some stern and demanding contours. As people, we share substantial priorities. A good life, in general, will favor such things as health, shelter, satisfying, loving relationships, and the development of talents, interests, and other capabilities. Of course, there are myriad and surprising ways in which those facts can be realized. Our Aristotelian Principle does not depend on the Aristotelian view that the human ideal looks suspiciously like an ancient Greek philosopher (or a contemporary American one). A stable environment and the firm but multiply realizable boundaries of human welfare give us reason to be optimistic about the Aristotelian Principle and about the possibility of an effective, useful epistemology. Our goal in this book is to test this prospect.

5. Our uneasy relationship to tradition

When we began to study epistemology in graduate school, it seemed so full of promise. Who wouldn't want to divine the structure of knowledge? But

somewhere around the third epicycle on a counterexample involving reliable clairvoyants, back-up electrical generators, or an environment full of
objects that are phenomenologically identical but ontologically distinct,
SAE jumped the shark. ("Jumping the shark" is a specific allusion to the
episode—indeed, the moment—when Fonzie jumped the shark on the
sitcom Happy Days, in a shameless effort to resuscitate the failing sitcom.
It is a generic reference to any such moment in any TV series when it
becomes clear that the show is done for. People can disagree about when
or even whether a TV series has jumped the shark. The same goes for
advocates of particular philosophical movements.) At some point, we (and
we suspect at least some of our contemporaries) came to an uneasy and
perhaps not fully articulated realization that SAE is not what we signed up
for. It has taken us some time to put our finger on what we think the real
problem is. We think that the main problem with SAE is methodological:
its goals and methods are beyond repair. They guarantee that SAE will
never provide effective normative guidance, and so it will never achieve
the positive, practical potential of epistemology. In fact, we sometimes
despair about whether most contemporary epistemologists have lost sight
of this potential—and, indeed, of our obligation to seek it. We should
admit, however, that reliabilism has achieved some of epistemology's
reason-guiding potential. But as long as reliabilism remains wedded to the
goals and methods of SAE, it is doomed. That's because the real virtue of
reliabilism is not that it provides a perspicuous account of our concept of
justification. The real virtue of reliabilism lies in its reason-guiding (and
therefore action-guiding) potential.

Our perspective is uncompromisingly naturalistic. The standard philosophical literature is full of questions and concerns about naturalism:
What is the appropriate way to formulate it? Does it entail that all
knowledge is third person? Does naturalism undermine first-person au-
thority? Is a fully naturalistic epistemology compatible with internalism, or
with externalism? Does it rule out epistemology's normative function? Is
naturalistic epistemology even possible? Inevitably, these issues get integrated with metaphysical ones: Does naturalism entail materialism? Does
it entail reductionism? In the face of these worries, we can do no better
than to quote Elliott Sober: "Mark Twain once said that the trouble with
the weather is that everyone talks about it, but no one does anything about
it. I have had a similar gripe, from time to time, about the current vogue
for naturalism in philosophy" (1997, 549). In putting forth our positive
views, we intend to ignore concerns raised about naturalism except when
it suits our theoretical or narrative purposes. Questions about the nature

of naturalism are at this point premature. The right approach is to first build a naturalistic theory (or lots of them) and then noodle over what epistemological naturalism is like and what it entails.

There are a number of arguments from SAE that purport to show that naturalism in epistemology is impossible or self-refuting or self-undermining. We propose to ignore these arguments in putting forth our theory (although we do consider some of them in the Appendix). Some philosophers might wonder, with perhaps more than a hint of outrage, how we can justify blithely ignoring serious worries about our approach. Our decision to ignore such worries is a strategic one. Consider two points. First, arguments for rejecting a naturalistic approach to epistemology provide a positive reason for avoiding naturalism *only if* there is an alternative approach to epistemology that is more promising. But we contend that SAE embodies an approach that cannot fulfill the legitimate and essential practical ambitions of epistemology. In fact, given the failure of nonnaturalistic theories to offer anything in the way of useful reason guidance, it is high time to try something different. Our second point is that the history of science suggests that it is a mistake to wait for all objections to be met before proposing and defending a new, minority or unpopular theory. Naturalistic epistemology really *is* doomed if naturalists insist on attempting to defeat the Hydra-headed arguments for why it is doomed. When you're outnumbered and you want to show your theory is possible, proposing an actual theory is the best and probably only way to do it.

2

The Amazing Success of Statistical Prediction Rules

Judgment problems great and small are an essential part of everyday life. What menu items will I most enjoy eating? Is this book worth reading? Is the boss in a good mood? Will the bungee cord snap? These and other common judgment problems share a similar structure: On the basis of certain cues, we make judgments about some target property. I doubt the integrity of the bungee cord (target property) on the basis of the fact that it looks frayed and the assistants look disheveled and hungover (cues). How we make and how we ought to make such evidence-based judgments are interesting issues in their own right. But they are particularly pressing because such predictions often play a central role in decisions and actions. Because I don't trust the cord, I don't bungee jump off the bridge.

Making accurate judgments is important for our health and happiness, but also for the just and effective operation of many of our social institutions. Judgments about whether someone will become violent can determine whether that person loses their freedom by being involuntarily committed to a psychiatric institution. Predictions about whether a prisoner if set free will commit violence and mayhem can determine whether he is or is not paroled. Judgments about a student's academic abilities play a role in determining the quality of medical school or law school she goes to, or even whether she gets to study law or medicine at all. Judgments about a person's future financial situation can determine whether they receive loans to make large purchases; such judgments can also determine whether they receive the most attractive loans available. And most everyone who has ever held a job has had others pass judgments about their trustworthiness, intelligence, punctuality, and industriousness.

It is hard to overestimate the practical significance of these sorts of social judgments. Using reasoning strategies that lead to unreliable judgments about such matters can have devastating consequences. Unnecessarily unreliable judgments can lead to decisions that waste untold resources, that unjustly deprive innocent people of their freedom, or that lead to preventable increases in rape, assault, and murder. There is a difference between cancer and horseshoes, between prison and a good shave. For many reasoning problems, "close enough" isn't good enough. Only the best reasoning strategies available to us will do. Ameliorative Psychology is designed to identify such strategies, and the primary tasks of a useful epistemology are to articulate what makes a reasoning strategy a good one and to carry that message abroad so that improvements can be implemented. This chapter is the prologue to that epistemological message.

Who could possibly deny that those charged with making high-stakes decisions should reason especially carefully about them? Consider, for example, predictions about violent recidivism made by parole boards. Who could deny that members of parole boards should scrupulously gather as much relevant evidence as they can, carefully weigh the different lines of evidence, and on this basis come to a judgment that is best supported by the entirety of the evidence? Actually, we deny this. We contend that it would often be much better if experts, when making high-stakes judgments, ignored most of the evidence, did not try to weigh that evidence, and didn't try to make a judgment based on their long experience. Sometimes, it would be better for the experts to hand their caseload over to a simple formula that a smart 8-year-old could solve and then submit to the child's will. This is what Ameliorative Psychology counsels. (Of course, discovering such a formula takes some expertise.)

For the past half century or so, psychologists and statisticians have shown that people who have great experience and training at making certain sorts of prediction are often less reliable than (often very simple) Statistical Prediction Rules (SPRs). This is very good news, especially for those of us who like to do hard work without having to work hard. Of course, the philosophical literature is full of fantastic examples in which some simple reasoning strategy that no reasonable person would accept turns out to be perfectly reliable (e.g., "believe all Swami Beauregard's predictions"). But we are not engaged here in Freak Show Philosophy. Many SPRs are robustly successful in a wide range of real-life reasoning problems—including some very high-stakes ones. Further, the success of some SPRs seems utterly miraculous. (In fact, when we introduced one of the more shocking SPR results described below to a well-known philosopher of psychology who is generally sympathetic to our view, he simply didn't believe it.) But there are general reasons why certain kinds of SPRs are successful. We turn now to describing their success. Later, we'll try to explain it.

1. The success of SPRs

We have coined the expression 'Ameliorative Psychology' to refer to the various empirical work that concerns itself with passing normative judgments on reasoning strategies and prescribing new and better ways to reason. In this chapter, we will introduce what we take to be the two main branches of Ameliorative Psychology. In section 1, we will describe some of the shocking findings of the predictive modeling literature; and in section 2, we will try to explain some of these findings. In section 3, we will briefly explore the other main branch of Ameliorative Psychology—the psychological investigation into how people tend to reason about everyday matters.

1.1. Proper linear models

A particularly successful kind of SPR is the *proper linear model* (Dawes 1982, 391). Proper linear models have the following form:

$$P = w_1 c_1 + w_2 c_2 + w_3 c_3 + w_4 c_4$$

where c_n is the value for the nth cue, and w_n is the weight assigned to the nth cue. Our favorite proper linear model predicts the quality of the vintage for a red Bordeaux wine. For example, c_1 reflects the age of the vintage, while c_2, c_3, and c_4 reflect climatic features of the relevant Bordeaux region. Given a reasonably large set of data showing how these cues correlate with the target property (the market price of mature Bordeaux wines), weights are then chosen so as to best fit the data. This is what makes this SPR a *proper* linear model: The weights optimize the relationship between P (the weighted sum of the cues) and the target property as given in the data set. A wine predicting SPR was developed by Ashenfelter, Ashmore, and Lalonde (1995). It has done a better job predicting the price of mature Bordeaux red wines at auction (predicting 83% of the variance) than expert wine tasters. Reaction in the wine-tasting industry to such SPRs has been "somewhere between violent and hysterical" (Passell 1990).

Whining wine tasters might derive a small bit of comfort from the fact that they are not the only experts trounced by a mechanical formula. We have already introduced *The Golden Rule of Predictive Modeling*: When based on the same evidence, the predictions of SPRs are at least as reliable as, and are typically more reliable than, the predictions of human experts for problems of social prediction. The most definitive case for the Golden Rule has been made by Grove and Meehl (1996). They report on an exhaustive search for studies comparing human predictions to those of SPRs in which (a) the humans and SPRs made predictions about the same individual cases and (b) the SPRs never had more information than the humans (although the humans often had more information than the SPRs). They

> found 136 studies which yielded 617 distinct comparisons between the two methods of prediction. These studies concerned a wide range of predictive criteria, including medical and mental heath diagnosis, prognosis, treatment recommendations and treatment outcomes; personality description; success in training or employment; adjustment to institutional life (e.g., military, prison); socially relevant behaviors such as parole violation and violence; socially relevant behaviors in the aggregate, such as bankruptcy of firms; and many other predictive criteria. (1996, 297)

Of the 136 studies, 64 clearly favored the SPR, 64 showed approximately equivalent accuracy, and 8 clearly favored the clinician. The 8 studies that favored the clinician appeared to have no common characteristics; they "do not form a pocket of predictive excellence in which clinicians could profitably specialize" (299). What's more, Grove and Meehl argue plausibly that these 8 outliers are likely the result of random sampling errors (i.e., given 136 chances, the better reasoning strategy is bound to lose *sometimes*) "and the clinicians' informational advantage in being provided with more data than the actuarial formula" (298).

There is an intuitively plausible explanation for the success of proper linear models. Proper linear models are constructed so as to best fit a large set of (presumably accurate) data. But the typical human predictor does not have all the correlational data easily available; and even if he did, he couldn't perfectly calculate the complex correlations between the cues and the target property. As a result, we should not find it surprising that proper linear models are more accurate than (even expert) humans. While this explanation is intuitively satisfying, it is mistaken. To see why, let's look at the surprising but robust success of some *improper* linear models.

1.2. Bootstrapping models: Experts vs. virtual experts

A *proper* linear model assigns weights to cues so as to optimize the relationship between those cues and the target property in a data set. Improper linear models do not best fit the available data. Bootstrapping models are perhaps the most fascinating kind of improper linear models. These are proper linear models of a person's judgments. Goldberg (1970) constructed the classic example of a bootstrapping model. Many clinical psychologists have years of training and experience in predicting whether a psychiatric patient is neurotic or psychotic on the basis of a Minnesota Multiphasic Personality Inventory (MMPI) profile. The MMPI profile consists of 10 clinical (personality) scales and a number of validity scales. Goldberg asked 29 clinical psychologists to judge, only on the basis of an MMPI profile, whether a patient would be diagnosed as neurotic or psychotic. Goldberg then constructed 29 proper linear models that would mimic each psychologist's judgments. The predictor cues consisted of the MMPI profile; the target property was the psychologist's predictions. Weights were assigned to the cues so as to best fit *the psychologist's judgments* about whether the patient was neurotic or psychotic. So while a bootstrapping model is a proper linear model of a human's judgments, it is an improper linear model of the target property—in this case, the patient's condition.

One might expect that the bootstrapping model would predict reasonably well. It is built to mimic a fairly reliable expert, so we might expect it to do nearly as well as the expert. In fact, *the mimic is more reliable than the expert.* Goldberg found that in 26 of the 29 cases, the bootstrapping model was more reliable in its diagnoses than the psychologist on which it was based! (For other studies with similar results, see Wiggins and Kohen 1971, Dawes 1971.) This is surprising. The bootstrapping model is built to ape an expert's predictions. And it will occasionally be wrong about the expert. But when it is wrong about the expert, it's more likely to be right about the target property!

At this point, it is natural to wonder why the bootstrapping model is more accurate than the person on which it is based. In fact, it seems paradoxical that this could be true: If the bootstrapping model "learns" to predict from an expert, how can the model "know" more than the expert?

This way of putting the finding makes it appear that the model is adding some kind of knowledge to what it learns from the expert. But how on earth can that be? The early hypothesis for the success of the bootstrapping model was not that the model was adding something to the expert's knowledge (or reasoning competence), but that the model was adding something to the expert's reasoning performance. In particular, the hypothesis was that the model did not fall victim to performance errors (errors that were the result of lack of concentration or a failure to properly execute some underlying predictive algorithm). The idea was that bootstrapping models somehow capture the underlying reliable prediction strategy humans use; but since the models are not subject to extraneous variables that degrade human performance, the models are more accurate (Bowman 1963, Goldberg 1970, Dawes 1971). This is a relatively flattering hypothesis, in that it grants us an underlying competence in making social judgments. Unfortunately, this flattering hypothesis soon came crashing down.

1.3. Random linear models

Dawes and Corrigan (1974) took five bootstrapping experiments and for each one constructed a *random* linear model. Random linear models do not pretend to assign optimum weights to variables. Instead, random weights are assigned—with one important caveat: All the cues are defined so they are positively correlated with the target property. They found that the random linear models were as reliable as the proper models and more reliable than human experts. Recall we said that there was an SPR finding that was denied by a well-known philosopher of psychology. This is it. This philosopher is not alone. Dawes has described one dominant reaction to the success of random linear models: "[M]any people didn't believe them—until they tested out random...models on their own data sets" (Dawes 1988, 209, n. 17).

The resistance to this finding is understandable (though, as we shall later argue, misguided). It is very natural to suppose that people who make predictions are in some sense "calculating" a suboptimal formula. (Of course, the idea isn't that the person explicitly calculates a complex formula in order to make a prediction; rather, the idea is that there will be an improper formula that simulates the person's weighing of the various lines of evidence in making some prediction.) Since we can't calculate in our heads the optimum weights to attach to the relevant cues, it's understandable that *proper* models outperform humans. This picture of humans "calculating" suboptimal formulas, of implicitly using improper models, also fits with the optimistic explanation of the bootstrapping effect. A bootstrapping model approximates the suboptimal formula a person uses—but the bootstrapping model doesn't fall victim to performance errors to which humans are prone. So far, so good. But how are we to understand random linear models outperforming expert humans? After all, if experts are calculating some sort of suboptimal formula, how could they be defeated by a formula that uses weights that are both suboptimal and random? Surely we must do better than linear models that assign just any old weights at all. But alas, we do not. Without a plausible explanation for this apparent anomaly, our first reaction (and perhaps even our well-considered reaction) may be to refuse to believe this could be true.

1.4. Unit weight models

Among the successful improper linear models, there is one that tends to be a bit more reliable and easier to use than the others. Unit weight models assign equal weights to (standardized) predictor cues, so that each cue has an equal "say" in the final prediction. Our favorite example of a unit weight model is what we might call the "F minus F Rule." Howard and Dawes (1976) found a very reliable, low-cost reasoning strategy for predicting marital happiness. Take the couple's rate of lovemaking and subtract from it their rate of fighting. If the couple makes love more often than they fight, then they'll probably report being happy; if they fight more often than they make love, then they'll probably report being unhappy. Howard and Dawes tested their hypothesis on data compiled by Alexander (1971) in which 42 couples "monitored when they made love, when they had fights, when they had social engagements (e.g., with in-laws), and so on. These subjects also made subjective ratings about how happy they were in their marital or coupled situation" (Dawes 1982, 393). The results were interesting: "In the thirty happily married couples (as reported by the monitoring partner) only two argued more often than they had inter-course. All twelve of the unhappily married couples argued more often" (478). The reliability of the F minus F Rule was confirmed independently by Edwards and Edwards (1977) and Thornton (1977).

The F minus F Rule exhibits three advantages of unit weight SPRs. First, it requires attention to only a slim portion of the available evidence. We can ignore the endless variety of psychological and behavioral quirks and incompatibilities that married people can exhibit and instead focus on two relatively simple, straightforward (though personal) cues. Second, the

F minus F Rule is very simple to use. There is no need to try to weigh different complex cues against each other. For example, there is no need to guess whether the (presumably) negative sign that the partners have different approaches to finances is outweighed by the (presumably) positive sign that both had happily married parents. Third, the F minus F Rule is known to be quite reliable.

Given the success of unit weight models, Paul Meehl has said, "In most practical situations an unweighted sum of a small number of 'big' variables will, on the average, be preferable to regression equations" (quoted in Dawes and Corrigan 1974, 105). Dawes and Corrigan succinctly state the cash value of these results: To be more reliable than expert humans in the social arena, "the whole trick is to know what variables to look at and then know how to add" (1974, 105).

1.5. SPRs vs. Humans: An unfair test?

Before we turn to an explanation for the success of SPRs, we should consider a common objection against the SPR findings described above. The objection proceeds as follows: "The real reason human experts do worse than SPRs is that they are restricted to the sort of objective information that can be plugged into a formula. So of course this tilts the playing field in favor of the formula. People can base their predictions on evidence that can't be quantified and put in a formula. By denying experts this kind of evidence, the above tests aren't fair. Indeed, we can be confident that human experts will defeat SPRs when they can use a wider range of real world, qualitative evidence."

There are three points to make against this argument. First, this argument offers no actual *evidence* that might justify the belief that human experts are handicapped by being unable to use qualitative evidence in the above examples. The argument offers only a speculation. Second, it is possible to quantitatively code virtually any kind of evidence. For example, consider an SPR that predicts the length of hospitalization for schizophrenic and manic-depressive patients (Dunham and Meltzer 1946). This SPR employs a rating of the patients' insight into their condition. Prima facie, this is a subjective, nonquantitative variable because it relies on a clinician's diagnosis of a patient's mental state. Yet clinicians are able to quantitatively code their diagnoses of the patient's insight into his or her condition. The clinician's quantitatively coded diagnosis is then used by the SPR to make more accurate predictions than the clinician. Third, the speculation that humans armed with "extra" qualitative evidence can outperform SPRs has been tested and has failed repeatedly. One example of this failure is known as the *interview effect*: Unstructured interviews degrade human reliability (Bloom and Brundage 1947, DeVaul et al. 1957, Oskamp 1965, Milstein et al. 1981). When gatekeepers (e.g., hiring and admissions officers, parole boards, etc.) make judgments about candidates on the basis of a dossier and an unstructured interview, their judgments come out worse than judgments based simply on the dossier (without the unstructured interview). So when human experts and SPRs are given the same evidence, and then humans get more information in the form of unstructured interviews, clinical prediction is *still* less reliable than SPRs. In fact, as would be expected given the interview effect, giving humans the "extra" qualitative evidence actually makes it easier for SPRs to defeat the predictions of expert humans. To be fair, however, there are cases in which experts can defeat SPRs. We will discuss these exceptions below.

2. Why do SPRs work?

There is an aura of the miraculous surrounding the success of SPRs. But even if there is no good explanation for their relative success, we ought to favor them over human judgment on the basis of performance alone. After all, the psychological processes we use to make complex social judgments are just as mysterious as SPRs, if not more so. Further, there is no generally agreed upon explanation for why our higher-level cognitive processes have the success that they do. (Indeed, there is even disagreement about just how successful they are; see, for example, Cohen 1981 and Piatelli-Palmarini 1994.) It might be that given our current understanding, replacing human judgment with an SPR may inevitably involve replacing one mystery for another—but the SPR is a mystery with a better track record.

2.1. The flat maximum principle

Let's suppose we have an explanation for the success of *proper* linear models. It would be natural to suppose we still had a lot of work to do coming up with an explanation for the success of *improper* linear models. But that's not true. Interestingly enough, it turns out that anyone who explains the success of *proper* linear models for problems of human and social prediction gets for free the explanation of the success of *improper* linear models. That's because for certain kinds of problem, the success of improper models rides piggy-back on the success of proper models. Recall the passage quoted above in which Dawes reports that many people didn't believe his results concerning the success of improper linear models. Here it is in its entirety:

> The results when published engendered two responses. First, many people didn't believe them—until they tested out random and unit models on their own data sets. Then, other people showed that the results were trivial, because random and unit linear models will yield predictions highly correlated with those of linear models with optimal weights, and it had already been shown that optimal linear models outperform global judgments. I concur with those proclaiming the results trivial, but not realizing their triviality at the time, I luckily produced a "citation classic"—and without being illustrated with real data sets, the trivial result might never have been so widely known. (1988, 209, n. 17)

The reason some people argued that Dawes's results were trivial was because of a fascinating finding in statistics called *the flat maximum principle* (for a good nontechnical explanation, see Lovie and Lovie 1986; for a more technical introduction, see Einhorn and Hogarth 1975). (Einhorn and Hogarth in fact show there are not uncommon situations in which the improper unit weight models will be *more* reliable than the proper models. This is in part the result of the overfitting problem; i.e., the proper model "fits" some of the random, unrepresentative peculiarities of the data set on which it is constructed and is therefore less accurate on future data points than an improper model.)

The flat maximum principle says that for a certain class of prediction problems, as long as the signs of the coefficients are right, any linear model will predict about as well as any other. It is important to recognize that the flat maximum principle is restricted to certain kinds of problems. In particular, it applies only to problems in which the following conditions obtain:

1. The judgment problem has to be difficult. The problem must be such that no proper model will be especially reliable because the world is messy. Perhaps the best way to understand this is to visualize it. A linear model tries to draw a line through a bunch of data points. Suppose the points are quite spread out so that no single line can get close to all of them. Two things are intuitively obvious: (a) The best line through those points won't be *that* much better than lots of lines close to it. (b) The best line through those points might not be the best line through the next set of spread-out data points that comes down the pike. For example, consider the attempt to predict what an applicant's academic

performance in college might be. Even the best models are not exceptionally reliable. *No one* can predict with great accuracy who is and who is not going to be academically successful in college. A big part of the reason is colloquially expressed: Stuff happens. Two candidates who are identical on paper might have quite different academic careers for a multitude of unpredictable reasons.

2. The evidential cues must be reasonably predictive. The best cues for predicting academic performance (GPA, test scores) are reasonably predictive. Certainly, you'll do better than chance by relying on these cues.

3. The evidential cues must be somewhat redundant. For example, people with higher GPAs tend to have higher test scores.

Problems of social judgment—who is going to succeed in a job, who is going to commit another violent act, what football teams are going to win next weekend—tend to share these features. As a result, for problems of social judgment, improper models will be about as reliable as proper models.

Okay, so the success of improper linear models rides piggy-back on the success of proper linear models for problems of social prediction. So then what explains the success of proper linear models?

2.2. Condorcet to the rescue?

Condorcet's jury theorem, in its simplest form, says that if a jury is facing a binary choice and each jury member makes her decision independently and has a better-than-even chance of making the right decision, a simple majority of the jurors is likely to make the right decision, and this will tend toward certainty as the number of jurors tends toward infinity. We can think of the successful linear models we have introduced as a jury: The jury must make a binary decision about a target, and each jury member makes her decision on the basis of a single piece of evidence. Each piece of evidence correlates positively with the target; so each juror's decision is going to be right more often than not. And the linear model adds together each juror's judgment to come to a final decision about the target. The only difference between the different types of models is that some weigh certain lines of evidence more than others. Putting this in terms of our jury analogy, some models have more jurors focusing on certain lines of evidence than others. So given Condorcet's jury theorem, we should expect linear models to predict reasonably well. (Thanks to Michael Strevens and Mark Wunderlich for suggesting this explanation.)

The Condorcet explanation leaves open at least two questions. First, many successful linear models consist of a small number of cues (sometimes as few as two). But Condorcet's jury theorem suggests that high reliability usually requires many jurors. So the success of linear models still seems a bit mysterious. Second, why are linear models, particularly those with a very small number of cues, more reliable than human experts? After all, if human experts are able to use a larger number of reliable cues than simple linear models, why doesn't the Condorcet explanation imply that they will typically be more reliable than the models? We will address these questions in section 3. But for now, let's turn to a different explanation for the success of linear models.

2.3. An alternative hypothesis: The world we care about consists of mostly monotone interactions

Reid Hastie and Robyn Dawes have offered a different account of the success of linear models (2001, 58–62; see also Dawes 1988, 212–15). Their explanation comes in three parts. Since we embrace and elaborate on the third part of their explanation in section 3, we will focus only on the first two parts of their explanation here. The first part of their explanation for the success of SPRs is a principle about the relationship between proper linear models and the world: *Proper linear models can accurately represent monotone (or "ordinal") interactions.* We have already introduced linear models—they are models in which the judgment made is a function of the sum of a certain number of weighted variables. The best way to understand what monotone interactions are is to consider a simple example. Suppose a doctor has told you to reduce your body fat, and she recommends a special diet D and an exercise regime E. Now, let's suppose that D alone, without the exercise regime, is effective at reducing body fat. This would be the diet's *main effect.* Suppose also that the exercise regime alone, without the diet, is also effective at reducing body fat. Again, this would be the *main effect* of exercise. Now let's suppose Sam goes on the diet D and the exercise regime E. If Sam gets the benefits of both—the main effect of D and the main effect of E—then the interaction of D and E is monotone. If, however, Sam gets the main effects of both plus an extra benefit, then the interaction is not monotone. The extra benefit is often called an *interaction effect.*

If we continue this absurdly simplistic example, it will be easy to see why proper linear models can accurately represent monotone interactions.

Suppose that for a certain population of people, D will bring a loss of $\frac{1}{2}$ pound per week while E will bring a loss of $\frac{3}{4}$ pound per week. The following linear model will predict how much weight loss one can expect:

$$W = \frac{1}{2}d + \frac{3}{4}e$$

where W is the number of pounds lost, d is the number of weeks on the diet, and e is the number of weeks on the exercise regimen. It should be clear that a proper linear model will do a reasonably good job of predicting interactions that are not monotone, but for which the interaction effects are not strong.

The second part of the Hastie-Dawes explanation is a speculation about the world: *In practical social settings (where linear models have proven most successful), interactions are, near enough and in the main, monotone.* Those who study complex systems, nonlinear dynamics, and catastrophe theory will note that not all of the world we're interested in consists of monotone interactions. The idea is that as long as we are not looking for SPRs to predict the performance of nonlinear systems, linear models may perform well—better than human experts. By restricting the explanation of the success of linear models to practical, social settings, Hastie and Dawes can take advantage of the flat maximum principle. From the reliability of *proper* linear models, they can employ the flat maximum principle to infer the reliability of *improper* linear models as well.

We have doubts about the Hastie-Dawes explanation for the success of SPRs. Consider the linear model that represents the monotone weight loss interaction. The reason this linear model is reliable is that it accurately portrays the main causal agents and the relative influence of those agents in subjects' weight loss. But the robust reliability of SPRs can't depend on their reasonably accurate portrayal of causal reality. The reason is quite simply that many SPRs are not even close to accurate portrayals of reality. Consider a linear model that predicts academic performance on the basis of grade point average and test scores. The student's college GPA is not a primary cause of her graduate school performance; same with her test score. Rather, it is much more plausible to suppose that whatever complex of factors goes into a student's GPA and test scores is also heavily implicated in a student's success in graduate school. (Recall that the flat maximum principle is operative when the cues employed by a linear model are redundant.) So it seems unlikely that the success of SPRs depends on their mirroring or reflecting monotone interactions. (Thanks to Michael Strevens for this point.)

We need to be a bit careful here. We're not suggesting that we oppose or doubt the possibility of successful SPRs that identify causes. (Just the opposite.) Nor are we suggesting that successful SPRs do not depend for their success on causal regularities. (Again, just the opposite.) Our point is that even when we can't "read off" anything like the causal structure of the world from an SPR, it can still be highly reliable and worthy of being used. If that's so, then the success of SPRs can't depend on their representing (even approximately) the interactions that produce the item of interest.

3. The foibles of human prediction

In our philosophical circles, we're considered good athletes—well, okay, we used to be considered good athletes. Compared to our nonacademic friends, however, we have always aspired to athletic mediocrity. It may be that the success of SPRs is like our athletic success—apparent only when measured against earnest but rather undistinguished competition. (We could put the point more bluntly, but we're talking about our friends here.) The right question to ask might not be "Why are SPRs so good at prediction?" but rather "Why are we so bad at prediction?" There is a large and fascinating literature on this topic (Nisbett and Ross 1980; Gilovich 1991; Hastie and Dawes 2001). We can hit some of the high points of this literature by noting that in order to develop reliable reasoning strategies for problems of social judgment, it is typically necessary (a) to be able to determine which cues are most predictive, which requires detecting correlations between potential cues and the target property; (b) to be able to attend to and remember all those cues; (c) to be able to combine them appropriately; and (d) to get accurate feedback on one's judgments. As we shall see, we have considerable difficulty with each of these stages.

3.1. Covariation illusions

In order to reason well about social matters, we need to be able to reliably detect correlations. But in a classic series of studies, Chapman and Chapman (1967, 1969) found that we can be quite bad at this on tasks that represent the ordinary challenges facing us. We often don't recognize covariations that exist, particularly when they do not conform to our background beliefs; and we often report covariations where there are none, particularly when we expect there to be covariation. In the past, many psychologists used Draw-a-Person (or DAP) tests to make initial diagnoses.

It was thought that patients' disorders could be diagnosed from their drawings of people. For example, it was thought that paranoid patients would draw large eyes; the drawings of impotent patients would emphasize male genitalia or would be particularly macho. By the mid-1960s, it was well known that DAP tests were bunk. There are no such correlations. And yet clinicians continued to use them. Chapman and Chapman (1967) asked clinicians who used the DAP test to describe the features of patients' drawings they thought were associated with six diagnoses. Once they had these reports, Chapman and Chapman obtained 45 DAP drawings made by patients in a state hospital and randomly paired those drawings with the six diagnoses. Each drawing-diagnosis pair was then presented to introductory psychology students for 30 seconds, and then the students were asked to report which features of the drawings were most frequently associated with each diagnosis. Even though there were no systematic relationships in the data, subjects claimed to detect covariations. Further, they were virtually the same covariations the clinicians claimed to find in real data! It is plausible to suppose in this case that widely shared background assumptions (or perhaps just thoughtless stereotypes) led both expert clinicians and naïve subjects to "see" covariations in data that simply weren't there. Interestingly, when Chapman and Chapman built in massive negative covariations between the features of the drawings and the diagnoses subjects were likely to make, naïve subjects still reported positive covariations— though somewhat reduced in magnitude.

In another fascinating study, Chapman and Chapman focused on the famous Rorschach test. While most of the associations clinicians have believed they detected in Rorschach tests are actually not present, it turns out that two responses to the Rorschach test are correlated with male homosexuality. However, these responses are not particularly "face valid" (i.e., they do not strike most people as particularly intuitive). For example, male homosexuals are not more likely to identify in the Rorschach blots feminine clothing, anuses or genitalia, or humans with confused or uncertain sexes. In fact, homosexual men more frequently report seeing monsters on Card IV and a part-human-part-animal on Card V. (Again, Chapman and Chapman found that clinicians of the day believed there was a significant correlation between the "face valid" signs and homosexuality. Only 2 of the 32 clinicians they polled even listed one of the valid signs.) Naïve subjects (1969) were given 30 cards with traits (homosexual or nonhomosexual) on one side and Rorschach responses on the other (a valid sign, an invalid but "face valid" sign, or a filler sign) and were given 60 seconds to review each card. Even though the cards contained no correlations between the traits and the Rorschach responses, subjects reported frequent correlations between the "face valid" signs and homosexuality. This finding essentially replicates the DAP test result.

Next, Chapman and Chapman changed the cards so that the valid signs were associated more often with homosexuality than were the other signs. Even when the valid signs were associated with homosexuality 100% of the time, naïve observers failed to detect the covariation. So it's not just that subjects see correlations when there are none. In fact, we often don't see correlations that are actually there, and sometimes we see positive correlations when in fact the correlations are negative.

It should be noted that Chapman and Chapman did not draw particularly pessimistic conclusions from their experiments. Nor do we. In fact, when Chapman and Chapman took out the misleading invalid signs, subjects were capable of detecting the actual covariations in the data. Nisbett and Ross (1980) draw the following conclusion from these experiments:

> [R]eported covariation was shown to reflect true covariation far less than it reflected theories or preconceptions of the nature of the associations that "ought" to exist. Unexpected, true covariations can sometimes be detected but they will be underestimated and are likely to be noticed only when the covariation is very strong, and the relevant data set excludes "decoy features" that bring into play popular but incorrect theories. (97)

When it comes to social judgment, the evidential situation is likely to be quite complex—with many signs that are valid but counterintuitive and other signs that are "face valid" but not predictive. In such an environment, we are not likely to do a particularly good job of detecting covariations. And so, unless the theories, background assumptions, and stereotypes we bring to a particular prediction are accurate, we are not likely to be very good at identifying what cues are most likely to covary with and so predict our target property.

3.2. Limits on memory, attention, and computation

In reasoning about social matters, we often attend to a number of different evidential cues. But we have certain cognitive limits, including limits on memory, attention, and computation, that could well be implicated in the relative unreliability of our social judgments. For example, we aren't very good at keeping even medium-sized amounts of information available in attention or memory when solving a problem (Bettman et al. 1990). And this prevents us from making accurate predictions on the fly. On the received view, we attempt to arrive at a solution to a problem by searching the problem space. For many problems, the size of this space is cognitively unmanageable; the problem space contains more information than the electric flesh between our ears can handle at one time. Take the example of chess. If the goal is to checkmate your opponent, in the early stages of the game the solution search space is enormous. How do people make the problem tractable? They adopt a strategy that navigates a limited path through the search space, a heuristic that identifies a small number of plausible (rather than all possible) strategies to secure a solution (Newell and Simon 1972).

Daily life confirms that our memory is limited. (We seem to get more confirmation as we grow older!) It also confirms that our attention is limited. The so-called "central limited capacity of attention" principle has been a basic premise of the last 40 years of research on attention. In the classic divided-attention experiments, observed decrements in performance are explained in terms of limitations on internal processing (van der Heijden, 1998). If limitations on attention and memory produce regrettable performance in simple tasks, why should we suppose that we can, without fear of embarrassment, use the same feeble tools to accurately evaluate complex issues of social judgment?

Even if we knew what cues to look for and we could remember them and we could attend to them, we often find it very difficult to combine those cues effectively. Paul Meehl makes this point starkly by focusing on a familiar example:

> Surely we all know that the human brain is poor at weighting and computing. When you check out at a supermarket, you don't eyeball the heap of purchases and say to the clerk, "Well it looks to me as if it's about $17.00 worth; what do you think?" The clerk adds it up. There are no strong arguments from the armchair or from empirical studies ... for believing that human beings can assign optimal weights in equations subjectively or that they apply their own weights consistently. (Meehl 1986, 372)

Notice that in Meehl's grocery example, we know that a simple addition is the right calculation to apply, and the variable values (i.e., the prices) are usually stamped right on the products. But suppose that the computation required was much more complex. This of course would make matters even worse:

> Suppose instead that the supermarket pricing rule were, "Whenever both beef and fresh vegetables are involved, multiply the logarithm of 0.78 of the meat price by the square root of twice the vegetable price"; would the clerk

and customer eyeball any better? Worse, almost certainly. When human judges perform poorly at estimating and applying the parameters of a simple or component mathematical function, they should not be expected to do better when required to weigh a complex composite of those variables. (Dawes, Faust, and Meehl 1989, 1672)

So when it comes to problems of social judgment, we have trouble discovering the right correlations, remembering their values, attending to more than just a few of them, and combining the values appropriately to render a judgment. If this is right, if the basis of our social judgments are riddled with error and limitations, then why do most people seem to have so much success in the social world? The sobering answer is probably that most of us have less success in the social world than we think.

3.3. Lack of reliable feedback

Even if we don't start off making complex social judgments in a reliable fashion, we can at least hope to improve our judgments by receiving and acting on accurate feedback. If we can determine that a depressingly large number of our past judgments were mistaken (or even that a well-defined class of past predictions was mistaken), perhaps we can modify our reasoning strategies and so judge more accurately. (The fact that a person might have made such modifications might lead him to discount the pessimism we seem to be insisting upon here.) Unfortunately, there are a number of quite natural phenomena that keep us from getting accurate feedback on our past judgments and behaviors.

For many irrevocable decisions we make, the feedback we receive on our judgments is almost inevitably incomplete. Consider the grizzled philosopher who has played a major role in hiring a number of junior colleagues and who takes the interviews very seriously. Given the nature of the job market in philosophy, it's quite likely that his junior colleagues are, by and large, a pretty impressive lot. Given this feedback, he is likely to think quite highly of his ability to identify in interviews good young philosophers. The problem here is that the grizzled philosopher doesn't know whether his predictions would have turned out better or worse without the interviews. (And even if he did, it's unlikely he would have a large enough sample size to draw a reasonable conclusion.) Simply put, most gatekeepers don't have control groups to test the effectiveness of their reasoning strategies. After all, the set of junior colleagues who would have been hired without interviews (the control group) might have been even more terrific than his actual set of junior colleagues. The problem is not just that most gatekeepers don't have control groups—that is often a practical inevitability. The problem is that they don't recognize that this is a serious problem. Most gatekeepers should probably have much more diffidence concerning their powers of prediction—especially in a job market in which most job seekers are something more than competent.

Another problem is that the feedback we get, especially when it comes to social matters, is likely to be highly unrepresentative. Consider the finding that 94% of university professors believe they're better-than-average at their jobs (Gilovich 1991, 77). One reason for this may be that we typically get personal feedback from students who think we were terrific teachers (or at least who say we were terrific teachers). Seldom will students go out of their way to make contact with professors they thought were really mediocre (if for no other reason than, where would they begin?).

The problem of unrepresentative feedback can be made vivid with an example that is likely familiar to everybody. Think about someone who employs mildly (or outright) annoying interpersonal strategies, for example, dominating conversations or name dropping. How likely are you to tell this person that these behaviors are annoying? Some blunt folk might always do so. But most of us, probably as a result of some combination of politeness, pusillanimity, and prudence, let it slide. Of course, we recognize that this behavior is annoying (or worse), and we might judge the person to be annoying (or worse). But given the feedback he has received, he might well go forth into the world confident that he has once again been socially deft, charming, and deeply impressive. (We are inclined to suggest you perform a public service. Supply accurate feedback. Call a bore a bore, a jerk a jerk, a blowhard a blowhard. Just don't do it to us.)

Even when the feedback we get is representative and shows that our predictions are mistaken, we will often interpret such feedback in a way that supports our preconceptions. For example, Gilovich (1983) asked people who gambled on football games to tape-record their thoughts about the outcomes of their bets. One might expect the gamblers to remember their wins and repress their losses. In fact, just the opposite occurred:

> [T]hey spent more time discussing their losses than their wins. Furthermore, the kind of comments made about wins and losses were quite different. The bettors tended to make "undoing" comments about their losses—comments to the effect that the outcome would have been different if not for some anomalous or "fluke" element.... In contrast, they tended to make "bolstering" comments about their wins—comments indicating that the outcome either should have been as it was, or should have been even more extreme in the same direction.... By carefully scrutinizing and explaining

away their losses, while accepting their successes at face value, gamblers do indeed rewrite their personal histories of success and failure. Losses are often counted, not as losses, but as "near wins." (Gilovich 1991, 55)

One interesting feature of this common interpretative strategy is that the subject cannot be accused of ignoring negative evidence. In fact, the subject is attending more to the negative evidence than to the positive evidence. It's just that he interprets the positive evidence as positive, and the negative evidence as bad luck.

3.4. The basis of epistemic exceptionalism: The overconfidence feedback loop

Let's recap briefly. We aren't especially good at detecting the properties that covary with the target property we want to predict—especially when we have strong background opinions and when the informational situation is complex. We aren't especially good at recalling or attending to lots of different avenues of information. And often, the feedback we get about the quality of our judgments or behavior is unrepresentative (and we don't know it) or incomplete (and we don't see that this is a serious problem). As a result, it is not surprising that we aren't especially reliable in our judgments about complex social phenomena.

Against this background, the sluggish reception SPRs have received in the disciplines whose business it is to predict and diagnose is particularly puzzling. (Resistance to the use of SPRs is particularly strong when it comes to making social predictions. SPRs have found easier acceptance in non-psychiatric medical diagnosis.) In the face of a half century of studies showing the superiority of SPRs, many experts still base judgments on subjective impressions and unmonitored evaluation of the evidence. Resistance to the SPR findings runs deep and typically comes as a kind of *epistemic exceptionalism.* Those who resist the SPR findings take their reasoning powers to be exceptional, and so they defect from the judgments of SPRs when they find what they take to be exceptions to it. They are typically quite willing to admit that *in the long run,* SPRs will be right more often than human experts. But their (over)confidence in their subjective powers of reflection leads them to deny that we should believe the SPR's prediction *in this particular case.*

We suspect that epistemic exceptionalism, which we suggest has led to the sluggish reception of SPRs, is the result of two facts about people. When it comes to prediction, we find the success of SPRs hard to believe, and we find our lack of success hard to believe. The reason we find our own lack of success hard to believe is that most of the failures of our predictive capacities are hidden from us. We don't see what's gone wrong. We don't detect the right covariations, but we think we do. We can't attend to the relevant complexities, but we think we have. We aren't getting representative feedback on our predictions, but we think we are. As a result, we tend to be overconfident about the power of our subjective reasoning faculties and about the reliability of our predictions (Trout 2002). Our faith in the reliability of our subjective powers of reasoning bolsters our (over)confidence in our judgments; and our (over)confident judgments bolster our belief in the reliability of our subjective faculties (Arkes 1991; Sieck and Arkes [unpublished manuscript]). Let's focus on each side of this overconfidence feedback loop.

The first side of the overconfidence feedback loop consists in overconfidence in our judgments. This overconfidence leads too often to defection from a successful SPR. That we fall victim to an overconfidence bias is one of the most robust findings in contemporary psychology:

> [A] large majority of the general public thinks that they are more intelligent, more fair-minded, less prejudiced, and more skilled behind the wheel of an automobile than the average person.... A survey of one million high school seniors found that 70% thought they were above average in leadership ability, and only 2% thought they were below average. In terms of ability to get along with others, *all* students thought they were above average, 60% thought they were in the top 10%, and 25% thought they were in the top 1%! Lest one think that such inflated self-assessments occur only in the minds of callow high-school students, it should be pointed out that a survey of university professors found that 94% thought they were better at their jobs than their average colleague. (Gilovich 1991, 77)

The overconfidence bias goes far beyond our inflated self-assessments. For example, Fischhoff, Slovic, and Lichtenstein (1977) asked subjects to indicate the most frequent cause of death in the U.S. and to estimate their confidence that their choice was correct (in terms of "odds"). When subjects set the odds of their answer's correctness at 100:1, they were correct only 73% of the time. Remarkably, even when they were so certain as to set the odds between 10,000:1 and 1,000,000:1, they were correct only between 85% and 90% of the time. It is important to note that the overconfidence effect is systematic (it is highly replicable and survives changes in task and setting) and directional (the effect is in the direction of over rather than underconfidence). But overconfidence is eliminated or reversed when the questions are very easy. This phenomenon is known as the difficulty (or hard-easy) effect (Lichtenstein and Fischhoff 1977).

The second side of the overconfidence feedback loop consists of our overconfidence in the reliability of our subjective reasoning faculties. We are naturally disposed to exaggerate the powers of our subjective faculties. A very prominent example that we have already discussed is the interview effect. When gatekeepers avail themselves of unstructured interviews, they actually degrade the reliability of their predictions. Although the interview effect is one of the most robust findings in psychology, highly educated people ignore its obvious practical implication. We suspect that this occurs because of our confidence in our subjective ability to "read" people. We suppose that our insight into human nature is so powerful that we can plumb the depths of a human being in a 45-minute interview—unlike the lesser lights who were hoodwinked in the SPR studies. As we have said, a major reason our (over)confidence survives is because we typically don't get systematic feedback about the quality of our judgments (e.g., we can't compare the long-term outcomes of our actual decisions against the decisions we would have made if we hadn't interviewed the candidates). To put this in practical terms, the process by which most working philosophers were hired was seriously and, at the time, demonstrably flawed. This will be of no comfort to our colleagues, employed or unemployed. We expect, however, that the unemployed will find it considerably less surprising.

4. The tempting pleasures of broken legs

It doesn't matter how reliable a reasoning rule might be if a reasoner applies it poorly. There are two things the reasoner must do right. She must execute the strategy correctly (e.g., plug in the right values, perform the calculations properly), and she must apply the strategy to the right sorts of problems. It is not always easy to know whether it is appropriate to use a particular reasoning strategy in a particular case. This has come to be known as the broken leg problem, and here is a classical statement of it:

> Clinicians might be able to gain an advantage by recognizing rare events that are not included in the actuarial formula (due to their infrequency) and that countervail the actuarial conclusion. This possibility represents a variation of the clinical-actuarial approach, in which one considers the outcome of both methods and decides when to supercede the actuarial conclusion. In psychology this circumstance has come to be known as the 'broken leg'

> problem, on the basis of an illustration in which an actuarial formula is highly successful in predicting an individual's weekly attendance at a movie but should be discarded upon discovering that the subject is in a cast with a fractured femur (footnotes deleted). The clinician may beat the actuarial method if able to detect the rare fact and decide accordingly. In theory, actuarial methods can accommodate rare occurrences, but the practical obstacles are daunting. For example, the possible range of intervening events is infinite. (Dawes, Faust, and Meehl 1989, 1670)

The broken leg problem arises because a person who applies a reasoning strategy must judge whether it is appropriate to apply the strategy to this particular case. But there are bound to be difficult cases. The broken leg problem occurs when the person comes to believe she has strong evidence for defecting from the strategy.

4.1. Diagnosing the broken leg problem

The broken leg problem arises when a reasoning strategy that has been proven reliable on a particular class of problems is applied to a problem that is thought (rightly or wrongly) to be outside the range of problems for which the strategy is known to be reliable. For example, the VRAG (Violence Risk Appraisal Guide) test for violent recidivism was developed primarily as the result of research done on a population of violent Canadian psychiatric patients at the Oak Ridge Division of the Penetanguishene Mental Health Care Center (Quinsey et al. 1998, xi). When using the VRAG, one might reasonably wonder whether it is reliable on different subpopulations, such as non-psychiatric patients or criminals in the U.S. (In both cases, it is.) One way to pose the broken leg problem is to ask: Under what conditions is it reasonable to defect from a reasoning strategy that has been shown to be reliable for a particular class of problems?

The broken leg problem is a serious and pressing issue for any theory that embraces the findings of Ameliorative Psychology. On the one hand, it is absurd to suppose that one should never defect from a successful SPR. On the other hand, people have a hard time avoiding the temptations of defection. And excessive defection undermines reliability. After all, whenever an SPR is more reliable than human judgment and the expert and the SPR disagree, the SPR is more likely to be correct. In the long run, reliability is reduced if one insists upon consistently replacing more reliable reasoning strategies with less reliable reasoning strategies.

This intuitively powerful argument has been confirmed a number of times in the laboratory. There are a number of studies in which subjects are given SPRs and then are permitted to selectively defect from them (i.e., override them), sometimes after having been told that the SPR by itself has been shown to be more reliable than experts. Typically, subjects find more broken leg examples than there really are. As a result, the experts predict less reliably than they would have if they'd just used the SPR (Goldberg 1968, Sawyer 1966, Leli and Filskov 1984). (Interestingly, it doesn't usually seem to matter whether the subjects are experts or not.) Selective defection strategies generally have a poor track record (except when the defectors have expertise in a theory with significant predictive success).

The broken leg problem and the failure of selective defection strategies suggest that any epistemic theory that hopes to take full advantage of the prescriptive power of Ameliorative Psychology must do more than put forward and recommend reliable SPRs. It must include a psychological theory of human judgment that can anticipate the difficulties we will have implementing the best available reasoning strategies. It is an unfortunate fact about humans that we are too often tempted to defect from successful SPRs. A normative theory with prescriptive force needs to predict the ways in which we are likely to deviate from excellent reasoning and perhaps provide methods of preventing such unfortunate deviations. Of course, we don't pretend to have such a theory; accordingly, our discussion of this matter will be tentative and programmatic. But we take this to be a prime example of how a reason-guiding epistemology will essentially depend on, and be informed by, a mature empirical psychology.

4.2. Grounded and ungrounded SPRs

Let's make a rough distinction between two classes of SPRs. Grounded SPRs are SPRs for which we have a theoretical explanation for their success. Ungrounded SPRs are SPRs for which we do not have a theoretical explanation for their success. Basically, we understand why grounded SPRs work, but we don't understand why ungrounded SPRs work. There are two points to note about this distinction. First, it is not hard-and-fast, since we can have better and worse understanding of why an SPR works. Second, for any ungrounded SPR, there may well be a neat causal explanation for its success that we don't yet know. So the distinction is not meant to be a metaphysical one, but an epistemological one. It is a distinction based on the quality of our understanding of SPRs and the subject matters on which they are based.

Consider an ungrounded SPR—the F minus F Rule for predicting marital happiness (discussed in section 1). Why is this rule reliable?

A reasonable assumption is that the correlation between the combined set of predictor cues and the target property is sustained by an underlying, stable network of causes. This is not to say that there is a science that would treat such ensembles of cues as a natural kind; it *is* to say, however, two things. First, their arrangement has a natural explanation. The explanation may not be unified—indeed, it may be so tortured that it is little more than a description of causal inventory—but it is an explanation in terms of causes nonetheless. Second, these arrangements, in general, do not spontaneously vanish.

Whatever specific facts explain the success of SPRs, they are not metaphysically exotic. As predictive instruments, SPRs are not like the occasional "technical" stock market indicators offered by gurus who combine a motley of moon phases, glottal stops, and transfer credits to predict stock movements. The VRAG test for predicting violent recidivism is an ungrounded SPR. In its present form, it consists of twelve predictor variables, and each is scored on a weighting system of (+) or (−). The weights vary from a −5 to a +12. The VRAG requires such information as the person's: Revised Psychopathy Checklist Score, Elementary School Maladjustment Score, satisfaction of any DSM criteria for a personality disorder, age at the time of the index offense, separation from either parent (except by death) by the age of sixteen, failure on prior conditional release, nonviolent offense history score (using the Cormier-Lang scale), unmarried status (or equivalent), meeting DSM criteria for schizophrenia, most serious victim injury (from the index offense), alcohol abuse score, and any female victim in the index offense (Quinsey et al. 1998). Many of these categories are independently known to interact richly with social behavior. It is not as though the diagnostic problem of deciding whether this person is likely to commit a similarly violent crime is being determined by facts known to be ontologically unrelated to or isolated from social behavior, such as the psychic's interpretation of tarot cards.

Now let's turn our attention to grounded SPRs. Many good examples of grounded SPRs come from medicine. In the case of determining the extent of prostate cancer, for example, there is a four-variable SPR that takes into account patient age, PSA (prostate specific antigen) test value, the biopsy Gleason score (arrived at from a pathologist's assessment of tissue samples), and the observable properties of the magnetic resonance image. Each variable makes an incremental improvement in determining the patient's prognosis. But we understand very well why three of those variables help to reliably predict the target property. We don't understand much about what mechanisms account for age being a good predictor.

Recall that we said that there was an exception to the general failure of strategies of selective defection. Grounded SPRs provide that exception. Experts can sometimes improve on the reliability of SPRs by adopting a strategy of selective defection (Swets, Dawes, and Monahan 2000). But notice that the improved reliability comes about because the expert can apply her well-supported theoretical knowledge to a problem. When someone is in possession of a theory that has proven to be reliable and that theory suggests defecting from an SPR (particularly when the expert's judgment relies on a cue not used by the SPR), then a strategy of selective defection can be an excellent one.

Even when an expert is able to outperform an SPR because of her superior theoretical knowledge, there are two notes of caution. First, there is every reason to believe that a new SPR can be developed that takes the expert's knowledge into account and that the refined SPR will be more reliable than the expert. One way to think about this is that when an expert is able to defeat the best available SPR, this situation is typically temporary: There is likely another SPR that can take into account the extra theoretical knowledge being employed by the expert and that is at least as reliable as the expert. The second note of caution is that even in domains with grounded SPRs, selective defection is not *always* a good strategy. The reasoner who has adopted the selective defection strategy needs to be able to apply the relevant theoretical understanding well enough to reliably defect from the SPR. And this will not always be easy to do. Even when the reasoner knows what variables to look at, he might still have a hard time weighing and integrating different lines of information (see section 3, above).

What about the (unfortunately) more common ungrounded SPRs, such as the Goldberg Rule, the VRAG, and the F minus F Rule? For most of the variables that make up these rules, there is no well-confirmed theory that explains their incremental validity, even if we feel we can tell a good story about why each variable contributes to the accuracy of prediction. Broken leg problems are particularly acute when it comes to ungrounded SPRs. Since we don't know why, specifically, the SPR is reliable, we are naturally diffident about applying the SPR to cases which seem to us to have some relevantly different property. For example, as we have noted, the VRAG was originally developed for violent Canadian psychiatric patients. But in order to prove its worth, it was tested on other populations and shown to be robust. A reasoning rule, particularly an ungrounded rule, that is not tested on a wide variety of different subpopulations is suspect.

Once we know that an ungrounded rule is robustly more reliable than unaided human judgment, the selective defection strategy is deeply suspect. As far as we know, VRAG has not been tested on violent criminals in India. So suppose we were asked to make judgments of violent recidivism for violent criminals in India, and suppose we didn't have the time or resources to test VRAG on the relevant population. Would it be reasonable to use VRAG in this situation? Let's be clear about what the issue is. The issue is *not* whether VRAG in the new setting is as reliable as VRAG in the original setting (where it has been tested and found successful). *The issue is whether VRAG in the new setting is better than our unaided human judgment in the new setting.* Let's consider this issue in a bit of detail.

When trying to make judgments about a new situation in which we aren't sure about the reliability of our reasoning strategies, we are clearly in a rather poor epistemic position. It is useful to keep in mind that this is not the sort of situation in which *any* strategy is likely to be particularly reliable. But our unaided human judgments often possess a characteristic that ungrounded SPRs don't—a deep confidence in their correctness. When we consider whether to employ an SPR (like VRAG) or our unaided human judgment to a new situation, it will often seem more reasonable to employ our judgment than the SPR. But notice, we typically don't know why either of them is as reliable as it is in the known cases. So we are not deciding on the basis of a well-grounded theory that the new situation has properties that make our judgment more reliable than the SPR. Instead, we're probably assuming that our reasoning faculties are capable of adapting to the new situation (whereas the SPR isn't), and so our faculties are likely to be more reliable. But on what grounds do we make such an assumption? After all, in a wide variety of situations analogous to the new one (recall, we're assuming the SPR is robustly more reliable than human experts), the SPR is more reliable than the expert. Why should we think that the expert is going to do better than the SPR in a quite defective epistemic situation? Perhaps neither of them will do any better than chance; but surely the best bet is that the strategy that has proven itself to be more reliable in analogous situations is going to be more reliable in the new situation.

Our tendency to defect from a lovely SPR is related to our tendency to plump for causal stories. Consider a disturbing example of a catchy story being accepted as causal fact. For too long, infantile autism was thought to be caused by maternal rejection. The evidence? Parents of autistic children could readily recall episodes in which they had not been accepting of their child (Dawes 2001, 136). It is easy to piece together a story about how maternal rejection would lead to the characteristic social, emotional, and communication troubles associated with autism. But it is beyond appalling that such weak evidence could have been used to justify the view that mothers were causally responsible for their children's autism. As this case makes clear, stories are cheap. But even some of the most inaccurate stories are irresistible. When we tell a story, we begin to feel we understand. And when we think we understand, we begin to think we know when to defect from an SPR. Our unconstrained facility in generating stories, and our arrogance in accepting them, causes us to defect from far more accurate predictive rules. Consider another story. There are more "muscle car" purchases in the southeastern U.S. than in any other region. What explains this southeastern taste for Mustangs, Camaros, and Firebirds? Elements of an explanation immediately spring to mind. No doubt the Daytona and Winston-Salem stock car races influence local tastes. And (perhaps making a bit of a leap here), there's a good ol' boy hot-rod culture in the area— isn't there? As we fit these images into a more or less coherent assemblage, centered on a stereotype of rural poverty, poor education, and green bean casseroles, a gratifying sense of understanding washes over us. We become confident that we have hit upon an explanation. But as it turns out, the typical muscle-car purchaser also enjoys wok cooking and oat-bran cereal, uses fax machines, and buys flowers for special events (Weiss 1994, 62). Is the stereotype that motivates the story easily integrated with delectation of wok-prepared cuisine and floral sensibilities? It is hard to see how. Our "explanation" is really just a folksy story, creatively cobbled lore of familiar anecdotal cast. It is also dead wrong, and the sense of understanding it conveys, however comforting, is counterfeit. And yet it is hard to shake the story. Especially when it is fortified with apparently confirming evidence: The demographic map for muscle-car purchases looks very much like the demographic map for rates of response to junk mail. Those queried who aren't too shy sum it up very simply: It's what you'd expect from trailer trash (Weiss 1994).

As we have already admitted, sometimes reasoners should defect from SPRs, even ungrounded ones. One of our colleagues in psychology has developed an SPR for predicting recidivism for people convicted of child sexual abuse. When asked about the broken leg problem, the psychologist admitted that one should always correct the rule if it doesn't predict a zero chance of recidivism for dead people. There are very well-grounded causal hypotheses for why this sort of situation would call for defection. But in absence of a situation in which we have documented reasons (not merely easy causal stories) to believe that the "broken leg" property (e.g., death) is a powerful predictor of the target property (e.g., crime), defection is usually a bad idea. The best advice is probably that one should typically resist defecting well beyond what intuitively seems reasonable. As Paul Meehl has said, we should defect from a well-tested SPR when the "situation is as clear as a broken leg; otherwise, very, *very* seldom" (1957, 273).

4.3. *Three caveats on defection*

In light of the documented failure of selective defection strategies, we have suggested that overriding an SPR is a good idea only in very unusual circumstances. But we offer three caveats. First, for particularly significant problems in a new domain, it will often make sense to test the SPR against expert prediction on the new cases before making judgments. There is an attitude (and often explicit prescriptions) of caution when applying instruments or techniques to new domains, particularly high-risk domains. This attitude is evident in gene therapy and cloning. But when it's not possible to carefully determine which tool is better on the new domain, a conservative attitude to defection is warranted—particularly for domains without grounded SPRs. As we've already argued, in those domains, defection to human judgment is generally unreliable.

Second, it is important to keep SPRs current—especially those that tend to handle especially significant problems. The parts of the natural and social world to which SPRs are applied are dynamic. If SPRs detect people's dispositions, then we should attend to any of the social or psychological trends that change people's relevant behavioral dispositions. Many of these conditions change over time: Crime initiatives in law enforcement, federal housing subsidies, emergency health care policies, and yes, even people's knowledge that statistical prediction rules, and more broadly actuarial methods, are being used to categorize them in various ways (see Hacking 1999). In order to ensure that the SPRs perform with optimal accuracy, SPRs must be regularly updated with fresh outcome information. In fact, it will often be more important to keep an SPR current than it will be to put effort into determining the conditions under which it is best to defect from it.

And third, after defecting from an SPR on the grounds of a broken leg problem, it is important to go back to the SPR next time (unless there is another such problem). Applying successful SPRs is an epistemically excellent tendency to cultivate. Defecting from an SPR frustrates and undermines the formation of such positive habits. If defecting from an SPR undermines our long-term commitment to using it, then defection is a risky proposal, even when one is faced with a genuine broken leg problem. Ideally, we should take the proven exceptions and build them into a better SPR, if this can be done simply enough that people can use it.

5. Conclusion

Two central lessons of Ameliorative Psychology are that when it comes to social judgment, (a) proper unit weight models outperform humans in terms of reliability and (b) improper unit weight models (of which the Goldberg Rule and the F minus F rule are examples) often perform nearly as well as proper models and therefore better than humans. So why the resistance to these findings? We suspect that part of the reason people resist this "practical conclusion" is that the SPR results are noxious to our conception of ourselves as good reasoners. Further, they undermine our hope—so evident in the a priorism of so much contemporary epistemology— that we can be experts at recognizing good reasoning without massive empirical aid. (The SPR results do not, of course, suggest that we are naturally atrocious at recognizing good reasoning. It just suggests that we aren't *experts*; we aren't so good that we couldn't learn a lot from Ameliorative Psychology.) Once our dreams of native epistemological expertise are dashed, we can no longer take seriously the idea that we should attempt to build a theory of good reasoning without attending to empirical matters.

The fact that people are slaves to the temptation of broken legs suggests a deep problem with the methods of Standard Analytic Epistemology. SAE makes our considered epistemic judgments the final arbiters of matters epistemic. But it is precisely these epistemic judgments that so often fall to the temptation of broken legs. We have seen this countless times in discussions with philosophers. When confronted with 50-years worth of evidence suggesting that short, unstructured interviews are worse than useless, we are now accustomed to philosophers dismissing these findings ultimately because, well, they just don't fit in with their considered judgments. Now the defender of SAE might reply that there is no principled reason why SAE is committed to excessive defection—for the evidence here presented can now help to guide our judgment. Our reply is that, after 50 years, it hasn't. Avoiding defection isn't a matter of simply knowing the threat; it is a matter of avoiding it in the first place. And we can't avoid it if we have a philosophy that presses our faces into temptation's fleshy cargo.

3

Extracting Epistemic Lessons from Ameliorative Psychology

Ameliorative Psychology offers a number of useful normative recommendations about how people (or at least some people) ought to reason. One of our main goals in this book is to articulate the epistemological framework that guides these recommendations. Perhaps the most obvious feature of this normative framework is that it is not primarily a theory of epistemic justification, as understood by contemporary epistemologists. Justification is a property of belief tokens. Ameliorative Psychology does not dwell on individual belief tokens. It is in the business of telling us what are the best ways to go about (say) making tentative diagnoses of psychiatric patients (Goldberg Rule) or making judgments about a person's ability to repay a loan (credit-scoring models). Ameliorative Psychology assesses reasoning strategies. At the center of the epistemological framework guiding the prescriptions of Ameliorative Psychology is the notion of *epistemic excellence* as applied to reasoning strategies.

What features of a reasoning strategy contribute to its epistemic excellence? As far as we know, Ameliorative Psychologists have not explicitly tried to extract and carefully articulate their normative assumptions. (It is not uncommon for scientists to usefully employ a theoretical notion without having fully articulated it.) By looking at some of the successes and failures of Ameliorative Psychology, we can identify three factors that tend to contribute to the quality of a reasoning strategy. The epistemic quality of a reasoning strategy is a function of its reliability on a wide range of problems; the strategy's tractability (that is, how difficult it is to employ); and the significance of the problems it is meant to tackle. Let's briefly examine how these three basic notions manifest themselves in the Ameliorative Psychology literature.

1. Robust reliability

Ameliorative Psychology identifies successful reasoning strategies in terms of their reliability. Goldberg's Rule is better than clinical judgment, at least in part, because it is more reliable. But reliability is not enough. It is important for a reasoning strategy to be *robustly* reliable—reliable on a wide range of problems. We noted this in our discussion of the VRAG (Violence Risk Appraisal Guide) test for predicting violent recidivism (in chapter 2, section 4.1). The VRAG was originally developed on a group of Canadian psychiatric patients. But the VRAG is powerful, and can be recommended, because it is reliable on a much larger set of people. In other words, the VRAG is robustly reliable.

The importance to Ameliorative Psychology of reasoning strategies of robust reliability is evident in the objections leveled against certain proposals. Consider Gigerenzer's *recognition heuristic* (Gigerenzer, Todd, and the ABC Group 1999). Which city has more inhabitants, San Diego or San Antonio? United States students answered this question correctly 62% of the time. German students, on the other hand, answered the question correctly 100% of the time (Goldstein and Gigerenzer 1999). Goldstein and Gigerenzer (1999) took the 22 largest cities in the U.S., randomly paired them, and asked U.S. students to pick the larger (in terms of inhabitants). Then they took the 22 largest German cities, randomly paired them, and asked the students again to pick the larger. The U.S. students did better on the German cities (median 71% versus median 73%). And when Goldstein and Gigerenzer ran this same experiment on German students, they found that the Germans were more accurate on the U.S. cities. They call this the *less-is-more effect*: Under certain circumstances, less knowledge can yield more reliability. What explains the less-is-more effect? Goldstein and Gigerenzer hypothesize that when subjects are somewhat ignorant about a subject, it allows them to employ the *recognition heuristic*: If S recognizes one of two objects but not the other, and recognition correlates positively (negatively) with the criterion, then S can infer that the recognized object has the higher (lower) value. So consider again the San Diego vs. San

Antonio problem. The German students tended to recognize the former city but not the latter, so they used the recognition heuristic and inferred (correctly) that San Diego was larger. The U.S. students recognized both cities and so did not use the recognition heuristic; they made a judgment on the basis of the knowledge they had about the respective cities. In the case of San Diego vs. San Antonio, the recognition heuristic was more reliable.

The obvious worry about the recognition heuristic is that its reliability depends on whether recognition really does correlate with the target criterion. This limits the heuristic's range (i.e., the range of problems on which it will be reasonably reliable). But it also makes it difficult to discover the heuristic's range. (This problem is raised in various ways by many commentators on Todd and Gigerenzer's target BBS article [2000].) The problem can be clearly seen in the application of the recognition heuristic to the area of investment. Borges, Goldstein, Ortmann, and Gigerenzer (1999) tested a number of different investment strategies against the recognition heuristic (investments were selected on the basis of name recognition). For the six-month period of study, the recognition heuristic outperformed the other strategies (Borges et al. 1999, 65). Borges et al. suggest that ordinary people (using the recognition heuristic) can perhaps do better on the stock market than mutual fund managers and market indices: "In investments, there may be wisdom in ignorance" (1999, 72). But this conclusion is dubious. In such a short amount of time, an investment strategy's results are likely owed to the period of the study rather than the power of the strategy. Put another way, a six-month period is unlikely to reliably discriminate between winning and losing strategies. To perform a valid test of whether the recognition heuristic is better than other investment strategies, we would need to compare those strategies on rolling six-month periods over a long period of time (i.e., decades). As applied to investment, there is reason to suspect that the recognition heuristic is not robust—it will not reliably identify winners in a wide range of market environments.

2. The costs and benefits of reasoning

Some of the best Ameliorative Psychology concerns itself with discovering ever cheaper and easier ways of tackling reasoning problems. There are obvious pragmatic benefits to employing simple reasoning strategies, particularly when quick action is imperative. But simpler reasoning strategies can also bring epistemic benefits. By reducing the price we pay for truths, simple reasoning strategies allow for the possibility of purchasing more truths or more significant truths at the same price. Let's look at some examples in which the drive to construct high-reliability, low-cost reasoning strategies is evident in Ameliorative Psychology.

Gigerenzer and Goldstein (1999) propose a reasoning strategy they call *Take the Best*, which they praise as a "fast and frugal" heuristic. One way they argue for the high quality of Take the Best is by comparing it to more expensive reasoning strategies (e.g., Bayesian models). They argue that in many sorts of cases, Take the Best is considerably more frugal than other strategies (in the sense that it uses fewer cues in coming to its judgment), while at the same time being about as reliable (or more reliable) than costlier strategies (Gigerenzer and Goldstein 1999, 87). Another example involves the flat maximum principle (see chapter 2). Lovie and Lovie argue that one of the benefits of the flat maximum principle is that it "allows a relatively low cost choice" between different SPRs of approximately equal reliability (1986, 167). Often in Ameliorative Psychology, a concern for tractable, easy-to-use reasoning strategies (or SPRs) is evident when it comes to high-stakes predictions. For example, in assessing the benefits of SPRs over clinical prediction, Dawes, Faust, and Meehl point to their lower opportunity costs: "Even when actuarial methods merely equal the accuracy of clinical methods, they may save considerable time and expense. For example, each year millions of dollars and many hours of clinicians' valuable time are spent attempting to predict violent behavior. Actuarial prediction of violence is far less expensive and would free time for more productive activities, such as meeting unfulfilled therapeutic needs" (1989, 1673). Developing simpler, easier-to-use reasoning strategies is important in the prediction of violence (see, e.g., Swets, Dawes, and Monahan 2000) and in the prediction of serious disease, such as Sudden Infant Death Syndrome (see, e.g., Carpenter et al. 1977, Golding et al. 1985).

3. Significance

The world is full of correlations, and so it is very easy to come up with SPRs; what's difficult is coming up with *useful* SPRs. For example, the Mayo Clinic has records for thousands of subjects who have taken the MMPI (Meehl 1990, 207). It turns out that there are significant correlations between subjects' gender and answers on 507 (out of 550) of the items. Some of these items include "I think Lincoln was greater than

Washington," and "I sometimes tease animals." We don't know by what unholy mixture of causes gender is related to attitudes toward Lincoln, but the correlations are very small—they are significant because of the enormous statistical power purchased by the large sample size. Were you to predict respondent sex on the basis of one of these answers, you might get it right 51% of the time. Such an SPR would be useless for at least three reasons. First, it would be a feeble SPR—a two-choice randomizer would perform almost as well without devoting any resources whatever to the problem. Second, even if the Lincoln-gender correlation were larger, we seldom find ourselves in a position in which we know a person's attitude toward Lincoln and have to predict their gender on that basis. And third, even if we did find ourselves in a situation in which we could use the Lincoln Rule, it is not likely to be especially relevant to our lives. The problem of predicting gender from attitudes toward dead Presidents is just not likely to be a significant problem for most reasoners.

The world is full of correlations that are practically useless for most people most of the time. The number of SPRs that are actually prescribed by Ameliorative Psychology is a tiny fraction of the SPRs that could in principle be suggested. A distinctive mark of SPRs recommended by Ameliorative Psychology is that they tackle significant problems. There are SPRs for passing judgments about matters like medical and psychiatric diagnoses, proneness to violence, academic success, and bankruptcy. Some strategies are concerned with less momentous matters, such as the outcomes of football games. But by and large, Ameliorative Psychologists tend to focus attention on significant kinds of reasoning problems. In this way, a commitment to seek out significant truths is apparent in Ameliorative Psychology.

4. A practical framework for improved reasoning

While we have not yet fully spelled out the normative framework that supports the prescriptions of Ameliorative Psychology, we have described a broadly cost-benefit approach to epistemology that takes significant truths to be a primary benefit. Even with this sketchy theoretical framework in hand, we can begin to piece together a unified approach to thinking about applied epistemology, or the ways in which people's reasoning can be improved.

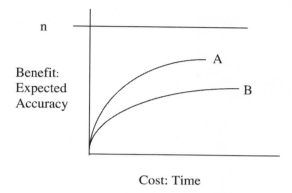

Figure 3.1.   Cost-benefit curves for Test Strategies A and B.

Applied epistemology is essentially about second-order reasoning strategies. It concerns thinking about how we can better think about the world. Our view takes applied epistemology to involve a cost-benefit approach to thinking about how we ought to allocate cognitive resources and replace old reasoning strategies with new ones. Getting clear about the nature of the costs and benefits of reasoning is a tricky issue, one we will address in chapter 5. For now, we can introduce this cost-benefit approach with an artificial but familiar epistemic challenge: an aptitude test. Suppose a test has two different parts, and a Test Taker is disposed to apply different reasoning strategies to each part of the test. We can define a crude notion of epistemic benefits in this particular setting in terms of correct answers, and we can define a notion of epistemic costs in terms of elapsed time. Very roughly, Test Taker's reasoning on the test is better to the extent he gets more right answers in a shorter amount of time. (This view has obvious problems; we introduce it here only for illustrative purposes.)

Suppose Test Taker is using strategy A on the verbal section of the test and strategy B on the quantitative section of the test. We can represent these two strategies using cost-benefit curves that plot the total number of right answers the strategy can be expected to generate per unit of time. We will assume that n is the total number of problems on each section of the test (see Figure 3.1). The cost-benefit curves have a particular kind of shape—a rapid increase with a steady leveling off. This leveling off represents a reasoning strategy's *diminishing marginal utility*: Increasing

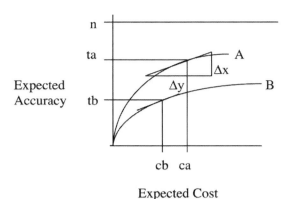

Figure 3.2.   Optimizing resource allocation: Equalizing
marginal expected accuracy.

resources expended on the reasoning strategy brings steadily fewer benefits. This is why cost-benefit curves are typically hump shaped rather than
straight or upward sloping. Reasoning, like most of life, is full of examples
of diminishing marginal returns. For instance, if we were to spend eigh-
teen more years lovingly polishing this book, it would end up being only
slightly better than it is.

From a cost-benefit perspective, then, the obvious question to ask is:
What is the best way to distribute Test Taker's finite resources to these two
reasoning strategies? The most effective allocation, the one that would
maximize expected reliability (or accuracy) would be the one that made
the *marginal expected reliability* (MER) of both reasoning strategies equal.
The marginal expected reliability of a reasoning strategy given some quantity of resources expended on that strategy is basically the benefit one gets
from the last resource expended on that reasoning strategy. If on Figure
3.2, the cost expended on A is ca, then the MER of that reasoning strategy
at that cost is given by the tangent of the cost-benefit curve at ca: $\Delta x/\Delta y$. If
Test Taker has (ca + cb) resources, then to maximize his right answers, he
should devote ca resources to strategy A and cb resources to strategy B. At
those points, the MER of both cost-benefit curves is identical. If Test Taker
were to devote fewer than ca resources to A and greater than cb resources
to B, he would lose net reliability—he'd lose more truths sliding down A's
cost-benefit curve than he would gain by moving up B's cost-benefit curve.

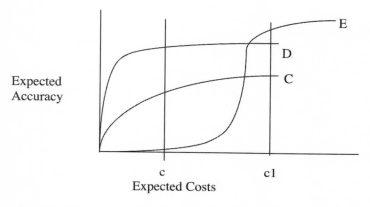

Figure 3.3.   Resource-dependence of accuracy.

The same general point would hold if Test Taker were to devote greater resources to A and fewer to B.

In order to think clearly about applied epistemology, it is important to recognize that reliability is a resource-dependent notion. How reliable a reasoning strategy is depends on the resources expended on it. This insight is built right into the cost-benefit curves: A reasoning strategy's reliability is a function of the amount of resources devoted to it. To see why the resource dependence of reliability is important to applied epistemology, consider the example depicted in Figure 3.3. Suppose there are three strategies available to Test Taker for solving the quantitative problems on the aptitude test. Among these three strategies, which is the most reliable? That's a poorly framed question (sort of like, "Is Larry taller than?"). At low costs (e.g., at c), D is the most reliable strategy; at high costs (e.g., at c1), E is the most reliable strategy. In this case, there is no strategy that is more reliable at all costs. There is, in short, no strategy that dominates all other strategies. Now suppose also that the line at c represents the maximum resources Test Taker can employ on these problems. So for all attainable possibilities, strategies C and D dominate strategy E. Further, strategy D dominates strategy C. Given this set of options, it is clear that D is the epistemically best strategy Test Taker can employ. If he is currently using strategy C or E, by switching to D, he can attain the same level of reliability more cheaply, or he can attain greater reliability at the same cost. (There is a problem here about individuating reasoning strategies. At c on

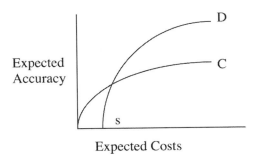

Figure 3.4.   Start-up costs.

Figure 3.3, it's not clear it makes sense to say that E is even implemented. The question of whether a reasoning strategy has in fact been implemented at a particular point along the cost-benefit curve is a tricky one, and one that probably does not always admit of a definite answer. It can only be adequately addressed by examining the details of how it is employed by a reasoner in a particular context.)

There is one more item to note when doing applied epistemology. So far, our discussions of the cost of reasoning strategies have focused on the resources (represented by the time) it takes to execute a reasoning strategy. But we have ignored a very important class of costs—start-up costs. These are costs associated with adopting new reasoning strategies. Such costs include search costs (the cost of searching for more reliable reasoning strategies) and implementation costs (the cost of learning to use, and then deploying, a new strategy). Our discussion of replacing C with D has assumed that D incurs no start-up costs. But this is unrealistic. So let's suppose that there are start-up costs (s) associated with replacing C with D, as depicted in Figure 3.4. Now, even though D dominates C when start-up costs are ignored, it doesn't when they're not. In fact, Test Taker might become a worse reasoner by replacing D with C. One obvious way this might happen is if paying the start-up costs for adopting D is simply beyond Test Taker's means. In that case, he has traded in a reasoning strategy (C) that gives him some right answers for another (D) that he can't even use—so he gets no right answers.

Start-up costs tend to be a conservative epistemic force—they give default or current reasoning strategies a built-in advantage when it comes to epistemic excellence (Sklar 1975). A number of philosophers accommodate start-up costs in their accounts of belief-change. For example, the so-called conservation of belief is the tendency for people to not change their beliefs without substantial reason (Harman 1986). One reason for this conservatism is start-up costs. But it is important to understand that the relative importance of start-up costs is associated with the time frame in which we make our epistemic judgments. For example, suppose Sam is faced with a stack of 200 applications that must be ranked within 24 hours, and he is comfortable with his current reasoning strategy. The start-up costs associated with any alternative reasoning strategy for ranking those 200 dossiers in the next 24 hours may be so high that Sam can't do better than use his current strategy. In other words, by the time Sam found a better strategy and learned how to use it, he would not have the resources to actually rank the dossiers. So even if some other strategy is clearly more reliable than the one Sam uses, that's no help if Sam can't find, learn, and execute the strategy in a timely fashion. But now suppose we take a longer view. Suppose we ask what strategy Sam should use on the dossiers he will face every year for the next 30 years. In this case, the start-up costs associated with adopting a new strategy might be easily borne. Further, the start-up costs might be insignificant next to the long-term execution costs of the competing strategies. If the new strategy were significantly easier to use than the old, in the long run, it might be cheaper to pay the start-up costs and adopt the new strategy.

We now have in hand some very basic tools of applied epistemology—cost-benefit curves, start-up costs, and marginal expected reliability. This approach to applied epistemology provides new insights and useful categories for understanding reasoning excellence. One insight yielded by this cost-benefit approach to epistemology is that there are four (and only four) ways one can become a better reasoner. This fourfold, exhaustive characterization of "improved reasoning" is (we believe) original, and it raises practical possibilities for improved reasoning that have been largely overlooked in the epistemological literature.

A good way to introduce the Four Ways is to focus on Test Taker's approach to the aptitude test. Three of the four ways one can become a better reasoner are represented in Figure 3.5. This figure represents four possible outcomes of replacing one reasoning strategy with another. The horizontal dimension represents the costs of the new strategy as compared to the old one (higher vs. same or lower); and the vertical dimension represents the benefits of the new strategy at that cost compared to the old one (greater vs. same or less). The first two ways one can become a better reasoner involve adopting new reasoning strategies that bring greater benefits—more right answers (or, in more realistic cases, more significant truths). Let's consider some illustrations of the Four Ways to better reasoning.

	Cost: Same (or lower)	Cost: Higher
Benefit: Greater	(1) Always leads to better reasoning *Start up costs	(2) Sometimes leads to better reasoning *Start up costs *Opportunity costs
Benefit: Same (or less)	(3) Sometimes leads to better reasoning *Start up costs *Opportunity costs	(4) Always leads to worse reasoning

Figure 3.5. Four possible outcomes of replacing one reasoning strategy with another.

4.1. Resource reallocation

The first way to improve one's reasoning is not depicted on Figure 3.5. It is possible for one to become a better reasoner without adopting any new first-order reasoning strategies, without changing our strategies for reasoning about the world (i.e., our first-order strategies). We can, instead, change our (second-order) strategies for allocating resources to our first-order strategies. For example, suppose Test Taker devotes a lot of time to the quantitative section of the aptitude test, thereby leaving insufficient time to do well on the analytical section. If Test Taker's cognitive resources are allocated in such a way that the MERs of all his reasoning strategies are not all equal, then he could improve his reasoning (i.e., generate a greater number of right answers) by transferring resources from reasoning strategies with lower MERs to reasoning strategies with higher MERs. He might reason better (i.e., get more correct answers) by simply spending less time on the quantitative section and more time on the analytical section of the test. (For a similar discussion, see Goldman 1999, 87–94.)

The Test Taker example does not do justice to the potential practical importance of the insight that one can become a better reasoner simply by reallocating resources. That's because our toy Test Taker model presupposes that the only way to improve our reasoning is by reallocating resources so as to get more truths. But excellent reasoners reason reliably about *significant* matters. So we can reason better by reallocating resources in such a way that we end up with more significant truths—even if the total number of truths we end up with is not much changed.

Some people might object that they don't need to be reminded to spend resources on problems that matter. Still, the advice we offer here is not idle. Whether a reasoning problem is significant is an empirical question, and there is now considerable empirical evidence that identifies some of the factors that most affect people's happiness. The burgeoning research area of "affective forecasting" has amply demonstrated the radically mistaken character of people's predictions concerning what will make them (and others) happy. For example, once a person is a decile or so above the poverty level, money contributes little to happiness (Diener and Oishi 2000). Yet, people who pursue money in the belief that it will increase their happiness express greater frustration than their peers (Myers 2000). Money is only the tip of the illusion. People believe that winning the lottery, getting tenure, and moving to a sunnier climate will make them happier. They believe they (and others) will be made substantially less happy in the long run by a paraplegia-inducing spinal cord injury and getting denied tenure, and in the short run by having a painful colonoscopy of longer rather than shorter duration. The scientific evidence shows that they are wrong on all counts. Our attachments to these personal forecasts can be extremely costly and personally damaging (Kahneman 2000). These results are counterintuitive, but fortunately, science (unlike some branches of philosophy) isn't about respecting our intuitions.

The very happiest of people—those ranking in the top 10% of global satisfaction with their lives—have a number of things in common, but none of these is especially specific, occult, or exotic. They do not exercise more than others, experience more "good" events, nor are they wealthier or more religious. Their common "secret" is disarmingly simple: They tend to be more social, with stronger social and romantic relationships than the less happy groups (Diener and Seligman 2002). When monitored over electronic pagers, people report the most enjoyment not when eating chocolate mousse as they recline in a chaise lounge on a Caribbean beach (or any of its slothful, self-indulgent correlates), but when they are unselfconsciously absorbed in a mindful challenge (Csikszentmihalyi 1999).

Given its attention to significance, our epistemological theory has the resources to guarantee that our normative recommendations will be informed by the lessons of hedonic psychology. Good reasoners adopt reasoning strategies that operate reliably on significant problems, including problems that are important to our well-being. We have already discussed how all manner of false belief and personal conceit will intervene to tempt defection from excellent reasoning strategies. But our best psychological theories can predict these siren songs, and our theory can recommend a resolute course of action in reply. As a result, our theory will be able to recommend that people allocate cognitive resources to reasoning strategies that tackle problems that are most likely to promote their well-being and away from reasoning strategies that tackle problems that are likely to undermine their well-being. Our theory has the wherewithal to make such recommendations even if the prescribed change of focus does not lead to a greater number of truths.

4.2. Adopting a more reliable (but no more expensive) reasoning strategy

The simplest and most straightforward way to improve reasoning is to replace a reasoning strategy with one that is no more expensive and is more reliable at that price (top left quadrant of Figure 3.5). Such a change always leads to better reasoning. For example, Test Taker should always adopt a strategy that leads him to answer more questions correctly on the (say) quantitative portion of the test in a shorter (or equal) amount of time. A number of SPRs we have considered improve reasoning in this way. For example, Goldberg's Rule is so easy to use that it is almost surely less expensive (both in cognitive and monetary terms) than clinical prediction. There are a number of SPRs for assessing infants' risk for SIDS (Sudden Infant Death Syndrome) that are also likely to be less expensive than clinical prediction (Carpenter et al. 1977, Golding et al. 1985). Credit-scoring models are also likely to be less expensive than using bank managers to make credit decisions, although it is hard to know this for sure since such models are a closely guarded secret (Lovie and Lovie 1986; Stillwell et al. 1983). These SPRs are more reliable than clinical prediction. (Further, when SPRs are used by institutions, they can often be handed over to a computer program, which can make them inexpensive indeed.)

4.3. *Adopting more reliable, more expensive reasoning strategies*

One might adopt a reasoning strategy that brings more benefits but is more costly than the old strategy. Such a change will sometimes (but not always) lead to better reasoning (top right quadrant of Figure 3.5). Suppose Test Taker is currently expending c resources on reasoning strategy D; but he has the time and energy to employ c1 resources on these problems (Figure 3.6). At this expenditure of resources, E is the most reliable reasoning strategy available. Now should Test Taker quit D (at cost c) in favor of E (at cost c1)? The answer is, of course, it all depends. If he were to switch to E, he would increase his reliability on these particular reasoning problems. But whether this change leads to better overall reasoning all depends on whether the gain in reliability in this portion of the test more than offsets the loss of reliability that results from spending fewer resources on the other portion of the test. Although this may seem odd to say, the most *locally* reliable reasoning strategy is not always the best *overall* reasoning strategy. That's because given resource limitations, the optimization of global reliability often *requires* that local reliability not be optimized.

All reasoning strategies have opportunity costs (i.e., what is forgone by not devoting resources to the best available alternative). The devotion of cognitive resources to one problem typically prevents or hinders us

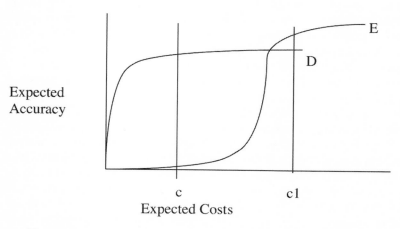

Figure 3.6.   Opportunity costs of adopting a new reasoning strategy.

from spending time and energy on something else. Our point here is akin to one made years ago by Simon (1982) about satisficing and about bounded rationality in general: sometimes it is better to adopt reasoning and decision procedures that are good and cheap rather than great and expensive. We take Simon's point to be that from the perspective of prudential rationality, one ought not always use the ideal (in the sense of "maximally accurate") reasoning strategy. If given the choice between reasoning in an ideal fashion about X or using the same energy to reason very well (but less than ideally) about X and take your kid fishing, most problems we face aren't so significant that it would be worth it to miss out on the fishing trip. But there is a stronger point to make. When a reasoner has a choice between two tractable reasoning strategies (i.e., reasoning strategies she can actually employ), sometimes the reasoner ought to adopt the cheaper and less reliable strategy—*even from a purely epistemic perspective.* This will occur when the opportunity cost comes in the form of a forsaken epistemic benefit. In these cases, part of the cost of devoting those resources to one problem is not having made any headway on some other problem.

There are many examples of highly reliable reasoning strategies that come with high costs. For example, any epistemological theory that recommends Bayes' Rule for updating belief is recommending a reasoning strategy that is more reliable but also more expensive than ones a reasoner is likely using. Another high cost prescription is that reasoners' knowledge should be closed under entailment (Cherniak 1986). Many have made the point that strategies that are in practice impossible to implement cannot enhance epistemic excellence. But given our discussion of opportunity costs, there's a brash lesson to draw: A reasoning strategy that is more costly and reliable, but not so costly that it can't be used, still does not necessarily enhance epistemic excellence. By expending more resources on a new and improved reasoning strategy, one inevitably takes resources that could be used elsewhere. And if those extra resources could be better used elsewhere, then one could be a better reasoner if one retained the less reliable reasoning strategy and used the extra resources more effectively.

Ameliorative Psychology recommends a number of reasoning strategies that would likely be more expensive to implement and execute than the reasoning strategies most people currently employ. For example, deciding to use frequency formats or a consider-the-opposite strategy (see chapter 9) comes with nonnegligible start-up costs. And even if we ignore start-up costs, they are likely to be more expensive to execute than most reasoners' default strategies. As a result, it is not inevitable that such reasoning strategies will make someone a better reasoner—even though such strategies are more reliable than reasoners' actual reasoning strategies and can in practice be implemented and executed.

4.4. Adopting less reliable (but cheaper) reasoning strategies

Let's now acknowledge the mirror image of the point just made: the cost-benefit approach to epistemic excellence suggests that it is possible to become a better reasoner by adopting new reasoning strategies that are less reliable than current strategies (lower left quadrant of Figure 3.5). How can this be? The answer lies in our discussion of opportunity costs. Consider again Figure 3.6. Suppose that Test Taker is expending c_1 resources on strategy E for solving quantitative problems on the test. For these problems, there is no other reasoning strategy available that would be more reliable. Nevertheless, Test Taker is expending a lot of cognitive effort (c_1) on the quantitative problems. By expending much less effort (c), he can be almost as reliable on these problems. Further, he frees up resources to tackle new problems or to tackle other problems more effectively. So by adopting a new reasoning strategy that leads to decreased *local* reliability, he can reallocate resources so as to increase *global* reliability.

The possibility that epistemic excellence might be served by replacing a reasoning strategy with another that is less reliable and easier to use might seem paradoxical. But a cost-benefit perspective on epistemology leads us naturally to recognize this apparently paradoxical possibility. One might suspect that this insight is unlikely to have much practical applicability. But the practical import of this prospect becomes evident when we consider (again) that excellent reasoners reason reliably about *significant* matters. Suppose a reasoner employs a consider-the-opposite strategy for a very wide range of reasoning problems. This strategy involves explicitly considering reasons for why one's judgment might be wrong; it has been shown to decrease overconfidence (Plous 1993, 228). Suppose further that although the consider-the-opposite strategy makes the reasoner more reliable, he employs it so often that it has turned him into an unhappy, neurotic nebbish, impossible to get along with. Even the most trivial judgments get the full consider-the-opposite treatment. Such a person could well become a better reasoner (and a happier person) by restricting the use of the consider-the-opposite strategy to just those problems for which it is important not to be overconfident. (Don't apply consider-the-opposite to the issue of whether you changed the roll of toilet paper; do apply it to the issue of whether you turned off the safety switch at the nuclear power plant.)

5. Conclusion

In this chapter, we have introduced the three central features of the epistemological framework that guides the prescriptions of Ameliorative Psychology (robust reliability, a cost-benefit approach to reasoning, and the importance of significance), and we have introduced a framework for thinking about applied epistemology that drops out of Ameliorative Psychology. We recognize that much of our discussion has been too abstract, and as a result, some might view it as not terribly useful. For those who are inclined to react in this way, we would ask for patience. In chapters 8 and 9, we will draw out some practical implications of our view. But first, let's try to develop in a bit more detail the account of epistemic excellence that guides the prescriptions of Ameliorative Psychology.

4

Strategic Reliabilism:
Robust Reliability

A meliorative Psychology provides countless examples of reasoning strategies that we ought to adopt. In making these recommendations, it is guided by substantive epistemological assumptions. The epistemological theory underlying Ameliorative Psychology is a view we call Strategic Reliabilism: Epistemic excellence involves the efficient allocation of cognitive resources to robustly reliable reasoning strategies applied to significant problems. Strategic Reliabilism gives a systematic voice and a theoretical foundation to the long-standing success of SPRs while at the same time avoiding the most serious objections to traditional process reliabilism (as we will argue in the Appendix, section 10).

1. Real reliability scores

A reasoning strategy is a rule for making judgments on the basis of certain cues. We can characterize the Goldberg Rule (but not necessarily all reasoning strategies) in terms of four elements: (a) the *cues* used to make the prediction; (b) the *formula* for combining the cues to make the prediction; (c) the *target* of the prediction (i.e., what the prediction is about); and (d) the *range* of objects (states, properties, processes, etc.), defined by detectable cues, about which the rule makes judgments that are thought to be reliable.

Cues: 4 MMPI personality scales (Pa, Sc, Hy, Pt) and one validity scale (L)
Formula: If $[(L + Pa + Sc)-(Hy + Pt)] < 45$, diagnose patient as neurotic;
   otherwise diagnose patient as psychotic
Target: Neurosis or psychosis
Range: All psychiatric patients (assumed to be either psychotic or neurotic)

A reasoning strategy's real reliability score is its ratio of true to total judgments in the limit on its expected range of problems. When tested on a set of 861 patients, the Goldberg Rule had a 70% hit rate; that is, the ratio of its true predictions to total predictions was .7. So the Goldberg Rule's observed reliability score on this particular set of problems was 70%. On the assumption that this set of problems is representative of the rule's entire range of problems, this *observed* reliability score can be said to approximate (to a high degree of confidence, given the sample size) the rule's *real* reliability score.

But things are not so simple. Notice an important fact about the real reliability score of any empirical reasoning rule: It is essentially dependent on contingent factors. In one environment, the real reliability score of a reasoning strategy might be high, whereas in another environment, it might be low. This is the problem of environmental disparity. To see this problem clearly, consider another example. The *academic success prediction rule* (ASPR) works as follows: It makes relative predictions about applicants' disposition to succeed in college by taking high school rank and aptitude test score rank, weighing them equally, and then predicting that the best students will be those with the highest scores. So if Smith's high school rank is 87 and her test score rank is 62, Smith gets a 149; if Jones's scores are 75 and 73 respectively, he gets a 148; and so the ASPR predicts that Smith will be more academically successful, as measured by GPA and prospects for graduation, than Jones. We can characterize ASPR as follows:

Cues: High school rank, test score rank
Formula: Target is an increasing function of (hs rank + ts rank)
Target: Disposition to succeed academically in college
Range: All high school applicants to U.S. colleges and universities

A rule's range is just a bunch of objects (states, properties, processes, etc.) about which the rule allows us to make a judgment (e.g., all U.S. males, all U.S. children under 10 with reading disorders, NFL football games, etc.). A typical range can be subdivided into many different natural discriminable partitions. A *natural* partition will divide the objects in the range in terms of properties that could in principle be causally related to the target property. This restriction is meant to rule out partitions that involve mere-Cambridge properties (e.g., the property of being closer to Des Moines than to Chicago), grue-ified properties (e.g., the property of being green before 2010, blue afterward), or other artificial means of carving out partitions for a range. A *discriminable* partition of a rule's range is a partition based on some feature that can in principle be detected by a reasoner prior to the rule's formulation. There are typically going to be many different ways to divide a rule's range into discriminable subgroups. For example, ASPR's range can be subdivided in terms of many properties of the applicants (age, geography, quality of high school, etc.). Thus, the requirement that partitions be discriminable limits the potentially infinite number of possible partitions of a rule's range. (One reason to insist on only discriminable partitions is to avoid objections that might try to partition a rule's range into those cases in which the rule gives an accurate judgment from those in which the rule does not give an accurate judgment. Permitting such partitions would undermine our view. Rules could be made to be perfectly reliable if their ranges were to be defined as consisting of only those cases for which they are accurate. But rules whose conditions of application cannot be detected cannot be used, and so they should not play a role in a reason-guiding epistemology.)

The problem of environmental disparity arises when a rule is not consistently reliable across discriminable partitions of a rule's range. Suppose for example that ASPR performs differently when it is applied to native English speakers and nonnative English speakers. In particular, when applied to native speakers it has a reliability score of 70%, but when applied to nonnative speakers it has a reliability score of only 60%. Let's suppose that S and S1 have adopted the ASPR for making predictions about the future academic success of high-school applicants. Even if S and S1 are disposed to apply the ASPR to the same kinds of problems—to all high school applicants to U.S. colleges and universities—they might find themselves in quite different circumstances. Suppose S is a recently hired admissions officer at a small, prestigious eastern liberal arts college; and S1 is a recently hired admissions officer at a small community college in a Texas border town. Because of their systematically different environments, it is possible that ASPR's reliability score for S would not be ASPR's reliability score for S1. There are many familiar examples of environmental disparity. For example, concluding that a lake trout is safe to eat will depend on the lake it comes from and perhaps also on the trout's age. Many examples come from strategies involved in interpreting behaviors across different cultures. While most of us would interpret being spit on by a priest in a Christian church to be a very bad sign, we have been told that being spit on by a priest in Senegal is a very good sign (one of purification).

The problem of environmental disparity is troubling for our view because it makes it hard to figure out just what a rule's real reliability score is supposed to be. Is ASPR's real reliability score 67% because that's its score (let's suppose) on all high school applicants? Or is it different for different people? We will argue that real reliability scores attach to reasoning strategies, or more specifically, to an individual's use of a reasoning strategy. So we will argue that if S and S1 are in different environments, their use of ASPR might well have different real reliability scores.

To handle the problem of environmental disparity, let's introduce the notion of a reasoning strategy's *expected range* for a subject in an environment. The intuitive notion is straightforward: Given a person's disposition to apply a certain reasoning strategy R, there is a certain distribution of problems she can expect to face, given her environment. How exactly this expected range is to be defined will depend on the particulars of the case. We can often expect counterfactual-supporting generalizations to play an important role in defining the expected range of a reasoning strategy for a subject in an environment. For example, small, prestigious, eastern liberal arts colleges tend to attract a certain distribution of students, while small community colleges in southern border towns tend to attract a different distribution of students. There is a quite powerful, complicated web of causal connections that maintains and explains those distributions. Once we know what a reasoning strategy's expected range is (for a person in an environment), we can approximate the strategy's real reliability score. We test the strategy on a representative sample of problems in the expected range. The strategy's observed reliability score in that range will approximate the reasoning strategy's real reliability score for that person in that environment.

But what about those cases in which there are no generalizations one can reasonably make about the expected range of problems for a particular reasoner in an environment? Perhaps the person moves quickly through relevantly different environments based on whim or unpredictable contingencies. In such cases, what is our theory to say? To handle these sorts of cases, we need to introduce the notion of a robustly reliable reasoning strategy. Intuitively, a robust reasoning strategy is one that is reliable across a wide range of environments. If there is really no reason to think S is more likely to face some natural partitions of the rule's range rather than others, then the only reasoning strategy that is reliable on S's expected range of problems will be a robust reasoning strategy. Let's turn to this important notion.

2. Robust reliability

A rule is *robustly* reliable to the extent that (a) it makes accurate predictions for the various natural partitions of the rule's range and (b) it has a wide range. Robustness is a matter of consistency and scope. First, a rule's robustness is a function of the extent to which its reliability score is *consistently reliable* across various discriminable partitions of the rule's range. A rule that is reliable for some problem-types in its range but not for others is not robust. And a rule's robustness is a function of the scope of its range. The wider the range of the rule, the more robust it is. Both features of robustness are matters of degree; and so robustness is a matter of degree as well.

There are at least three reasons epistemology should recommend *robust* reasoning strategies—strategies that are resilient (retain high truth ratios) under changes in cognizers and environments. First, as more rules are tested and recommended, the probability increases that a rule will seem more reliable than it really is. An epistemological theory that values robustness is best positioned to catch a rule whose real reliability score is relatively low but whose observed reliability score is high by chance. One way to identify lucky rules is to export them to a somewhat different domain and see whether they hold up under the strain. This is essentially the familiar admonition in science that one should test hypotheses on diverse evidence. A second reason robustness is important is that more robust rules can be easier to implement. Other things being equal, applying one rule to a wide range of problems is easier than keeping in mind and applying many rules (with their varying application conditions) to those problems. A third reason to prefer robust rules is that they can be recommended for general use, regardless of the vagaries of an individual's environment.

Assessing whether a reasoning strategy is robust can be trickier than it appears. Consider Gigerenzer's *recognition heuristic*, which we introduced in chapter 3: If S recognizes one of two objects but not the other, and recognition correlates positively (negatively) with the criterion, then S can infer that the recognized object has the higher (lower) value. It has been applied to problems of city size and investment (Gigerenzer, Todd, and the ABC Group 1999). Is the recognition heuristic robust? This is not a well-framed question. Recall that a reasoning strategy is defined in terms of cues, a formula (or algorithm), a target property, and a range. The robustness of a reasoning strategy is a function of the scope of its range and how accurate the strategy is on natural partitions within the rule's range. Unless we specify the appropriate range of the recognition heuristic, we cannot assess its robustness. If the range of the heuristic is city size problems, then it will not be robust because of its rather narrow scope. If its range is investment strategies, we suspect that it will not be robust because of its failure to be reliable on many discriminable subsets (or partitions) of that range, e.g., rolling 6-month periods from 1960 to 2000 (see chapter 3, section 1). So the recognition heuristic provides a nice example of the ways in which reasoning strategies can fail to be robust.

It is perhaps worthwhile to note that second-order reasoning strategies can be, and can fail to be, robust. Recall that Grove and Meehl (1996) surveyed 136 studies which had 617 distinct comparisons of the reliability of SPRs and clinical prediction (see chapter 2, section 1.1). They concluded that 64 studies favored the SPR and 8 favored the clinician (with the other 64 showing approximately equivalent accuracy). Grove and Meehl then examined the cases in which the clinicians were more accurate and wondered whether they could fathom some coherent set of problems on which human experts are more reliable than SPRs. Here is their conclusion:

> The 8 studies favoring the clinician are not concentrated in any one predictive area, do not overrepresent any one type of clinician (e.g., medical doctors), and do not in fact have any obvious characteristics in common. This is disappointing, as one of the chief goals of the meta-analysis was to identify particular areas in which the clinician might outperform the mechanical prediction method. (Grove and Meehl 1996, 298)

Grove and Meehl are after a kind of (second-order) robustness here. They want to know whether there is some set of problems for which clinical prediction is robustly more reliable than SPRs. Since they couldn't find any such pocket of expertise, they conclude that "the most plausible explanation of these deviant studies is that they arose by a combination of random sampling errors (8 deviant out of 136) and the clinicians' informational advantage in being provided with more data than the actuarial formula" (1996, 298).

3. The importance of real reliability scores

As a practical matter, real reliability scores are less useful than they might seem to be—even for a reliabilist view like ours. The reason is that what we're typically interested in when we're doing *applied* epistemology is not a reasoning strategy's absolute reliability score, but its score relative to other strategies for solving the same (or some of the same) problems (and sometimes for solving different problems). And we acquire evidence that can justify our confidence that one strategy's reliability score really is higher than another's, *even without knowing exactly what either strategy's real score is.* For example, we have a *lot* of evidence for thinking that Goldberg's Rule is more reliable than any alternative rules we know about for distinguishing between psychotics and neurotics among psychiatric patients on the basis of MMPI profiles. This evidence is based on the relevant rules having been applied literally thousands of times to various populations of psychiatric patients. Further, the Goldberg Rule is easier to use than most of its competitors, and there is no special reason to suppose the causal structure of the relevant parts of the world is about to change in a way that would undercut the rule's reliability. This overwhelming evidence is all we really need to make a reasonable epistemic recommendation.

We do not need to know precisely what a strategy's real reliability score is in order to do good applied epistemology. But we should not derogate real reliability scores too much. Real reliability scores are a theoretical and unobservable posit of our epistemological theory. They play a vital role in at least two places. First, a reasoning strategy's observed reliability score is supposed to approximate its real score. So when figuring out a strategy's observed score—its track record—we are inevitably guided by our notion of its real reliability score. (This is why, for example, we don't assign observed reliability scores after testing an empirical reasoning strategy on just one problem.) A strategy's real reliability score is like the statistical notion of a "real value," such as a population mean. We explain features of the sample from a population in terms of a "real value" of the population, a value that the population has independent of attempts to measure it. The second role real reliability scores play in epistemology is as (part of) the ultimate ground of our epistemic judgments. The ultimate reason Goldberg's Rule is the best strategy we can use on the MMPI prediction problems is that its real reliability score is higher than alternatives (and it is at least as easy to use as its alternatives). Our epistemic recommendations are based (in part) on the quality of the reasons we have for believing claims about the real reliability scores of various reasoning strategies.

4. A circularity objection

A standard concern about naturalistic approaches to epistemology is that they are viciously circular. We want to distinguish between two circularity arguments. First, one might argue that any naturalistic theory is inevitably viciously circular because such theories rely on empirical hypotheses which require for their justification epistemological assumptions. We will consider this objection in the Appendix, section 2. A second type of circularity objection raises worries about the application of a naturalistic theory. In particular, in applying Strategic Reliabilism, we must employ an explicitly epistemic notion (i.e., overwhelming evidence that one strategy is more reliable than another). One might argue that this is a problem.

The second circularity objection is not concerned about whether a naturalistic theory, like Strategic Reliabilism, might in some sense be viciously circular. (That is the charge leveled by the first objection.) Strategic Reliabilism says a reasoning strategy's quality is a function of its reliability score, robustness, the significance of the problems it targets, and how difficult it is to implement. As Strategic Reliabilists, we can take these facts to be independent of our epistemic access to them. But when it comes to implementing Strategic Reliabilism, we are up to our ears in epistemic notions. In order to apply our epistemological theory, we will typically have to rely on observed reliability scores (and the quality of our evidence for them). But this is not a vicious circularity. *Any* epistemological theory that offers epistemic guidance will appeal to empirical notions in its application. Unless an epistemological theory is meant to be useless to real reasoners, it is hard to see how its application can avoid defeasible judgments based on explicitly epistemic notions. (This argument is made persuasively in Stich 1990, 145–149.)

5

Strategic Reliabilism: The Costs and Benefits of Excellent Judgment

Many virtues are involved in excellent reasoning, and an important one involves the efficient allocation of one's cognitive resources. The excellent reasoner will occasionally spend time and energy pondering the potential revision of her reasoning strategies, revising them when advisable, and applying reasoning strategies to problems that are most likely to yield significant truths. Any epistemological theory that aspires to guide reason must recognize that we are limited creatures, and as such we have to make choices about how to spend our cognitive resources.

Many epistemological theories ignore cost-benefit considerations. For example, the theories of Standard Analytic Epistemology provide accounts of what makes a belief justified. But there are infinitely many justified beliefs one might adopt at any particular time (e.g., I am not the number 1, I am not the number 2 . . .). Without some further guidance about which of the infinitely many justified beliefs one ought to adopt, such theories cannot be reason guiding in any positive sense. They can offer negative guidance—by telling us what we ought not believe (i.e., we ought not adopt unjustified beliefs). But this is surely disappointing. It appears that the normative force of theories of SAE is exhausted by something like the following prescription: "Adopt only a subset of the infinitely many beliefs that are justified for you." For such theories not to offer anything in the way of useful, positive guidance is surprising, especially given the loud and oft-repeated insistence on the part of proponents of SAE that Epistemology is Normative.

Of course, defenders of SAE can argue that issues of resource allocation are not fundamentally epistemological considerations, but are instead pragmatic considerations. On this view, from a purely epistemological perspective, it is immaterial whether one has a justified belief about the length of one's left index fingernail or about whether one has time to cross the tracks before the train comes. While this move is certainly available, taking it means that one's epistemological theory will be empty of positive, reason-guiding recommendations. It is not possible to offer an effective reason-guiding epistemology that ignores resource allocation considerations.

Strategic Reliabilism addresses resource allocation considerations within a cost-benefit framework. But there are serious reasons to worry about the feasibility of a cost-benefit approach to epistemology. First, there are serious general objections to cost-benefit analyses; and second, it is not clear how we can identify the costs and benefits of reasoning. Our goal in this chapter is to tackle these two worries. Against the first, we grant that many of the deep general concerns about cost-benefit analysis are legitimate. Nonetheless, we argue that flawed cost-benefit analyses can be very useful, especially if we are clear about the ways in which such analyses are flawed. Against the second point, we argue that there are measurable proxies for the costs and benefits of reasoning we can employ in a cost-benefit approach to epistemology. Such analyses are flawed, but as we argued against the first point, flawed cost-benefit analyses can be very useful.

1. The virtues of flawed cost-benefit analyses

In most general terms, cost-benefit analysis is a reasoning strategy that permits us to estimate the desirability of various tradeoffs available to us. The most familiar form of cost-benefit analysis places a dollar value on the costs and benefits of each available option. This procedure is supposed to allow any person or institutional body to identify the option that promises the greatest total benefit. For example, in deciding whether to expand a successful company's production capacity, cost-benefit analysis would have us compare the expected profits to be gained by expansion with current expected profits. The objection to this standard approach to cost-benefit analysis is as obvious as it is serious: It relies on money as its only measure of value. A deeper and more interesting objection is that there is no "neutral" measure of value for comparing very distinct sorts of goods. Values are incommensurable. We cannot reduce all value to money, and there is no realistic way to assign commensurable units of value to freedom, happiness, personal security, or a (relatively) pristine Grand Canyon. These objections show that it is not possible to measure the net benefits (or costs) of different options against each other. We are sympathetic to many of these objections to cost-benefit analysis (Anderson 1993, Sen 2000). Still, we would argue that flawed cost-benefit analyses can be very useful and important.

A cost-benefit approach to a problem can be very useful even if it is plagued by theoretical problems. It permits us to estimate the desirability of various tradeoffs available to us, no matter what kind of value we place on them. In doing so, it can be useful for helping us to avoid making decisions that do not reflect our own values. Explicitly engaging in cost-benefit analysis, even a flawed analysis, allows us to slow down, cool off, compare the value we assign to certain outcomes, and determine what strategies we ought to adopt to achieve them. The primary virtue of cost-benefit analyses, even when flawed, is that they can help us to set and adjust our priorities in ways that better reflect our values.

We can distinguish between two kinds of flawed but useful cost-benefit approaches to problems, incomplete cost-benefit analyses and unreduced cost-benefit analyses. An incomplete cost-benefit analysis focuses on only a subset of the values at stake in a decision. For example, cost-benefit analyses that focus only on money as a unit of value are typically incomplete. An unreduced cost-benefit analysis focuses on a realistic set of values that are at stake in making a decision, but it does not attempt to reduce those values to standard units of costs and benefits. To make our case that these sorts of flawed cost-benefit analyses can be useful in helping us to set and reset our priorities, let's consider some examples.

Many companies offer their employees (sometimes quite generous) retirement packages; but a surprising percentage of people don't participate in them. Many of these people would benefit from an unreduced cost-benefit analysis of the choice of whether to invest in such a retirement account. Such an analysis would not even attempt to reduce all the costs and benefits of the options to a single value (like current dollars). Consider the benefits of current spending (on, say, a larger mortgage on a larger home) and the potential future costs of inadequate retirement funds (lower standard of living, dependence on kin or children). While these costs and benefits cannot be reduced to a single unit of value, we suspect that if people thought clearly and coolly about the various options, they might be surprised to find that they would explicitly reject the values implicit in their actual decisions.

   Let's consider an example of some radically incomplete cost-benefit analyses that as a historical matter affected public-policy decision making for the better: attempts to put a monetary value on human lives. In late seventeenth-century Britain, William Petty "argued in favor of measures to ward off or mitigate the effects of the plague on the grounds that by spending a few thousand pounds the king might protect an investment many times greater in the lives of his subjects" (Porter 1994, 214–15). By the early part of the twentieth century, professional actuaries working for insurance companies had taken over the business of placing monetary values on human lives. In *The Money Value of a Man* (1930), Louis Dublin and Alfred Lotka attached a dollar figure to human lives, basing their calculations on the expected net present value of future earnings. Their analyses explicitly recognized that they could not put a monetary figure on the "intangibles of life" but instead viewed humans (and in particular, men) as just so much equipment:

> Man has much in common with the industrial aids, machines, manufacturing plants, and so forth, of which he makes use to conduct the business of life. Like them he has a "cost of installation," . . . running expenses, interest on capital invested, and the loss of a certain proportion of children that do not live to attain adult age, just as in manufacturing processes allowance must be made for losses by "spoilage" of material that never reaches the "finished" stage. (1930, 44, quoted in Porter 1994, 216)

This kind of cost-benefit analysis inevitably strikes us as appallingly crass. But besides figuring out how much life insurance to sell people, these analyses were also typically put to political use:

> None of these calculations . . . was part of a formal assessment of costs and benefits. They were intended not to guide policy in detail, but to soften slightly those famously hardheaded administrators and businessmen who were reluctant to invest dollars, pounds, and francs in what would come to be known as human capital. The sentimental and self-regarding emotions could be left out because the numbers were already large enough to draw attention, and that was their only real purpose . . . [W]hile these formulas may not have been very accurate, they were surprisingly precise. . . . This was almost indispensable if calculation was to figure significantly in decisions vulnerable to public criticism. (Porter, 217)

The cost-benefit analyses suggested that the preventable suffering and death of poor laborers was bad for business. We might view it as wearily predictable that it was profit that spurred captains of industry to support the public works projects that prevented the deaths of many of our ancestors. And one would be right to object that the cost-benefit approach is no guarantor of a positive outcome. The morally right policies were implemented because of contingent facts about the profit structure of local industrial economies rather than because of the intrinsic moral worth of human laborers. But while we may be appalled that ethical considerations did not move the captains of industry quicker, we can be glad that cost-benefit considerations kept them from moving slower still.

The cost-benefit analyses that convinced "hardheaded administrators and businessmen" that they were underestimating the monetary value of their "human capital" was radically incomplete. It focused only on economic considerations. But the right course of action was so clearly right that any number of different cost-benefit analyses—even those informed by values we might find crass or repugnant—delivered the correct result. When the world is obliging in this way, incomplete cost-benefit analyses can lead us to effectively revise our priorities and actions.

Flawed cost-benefit analyses are useful because they dramatize the opportunity costs of a favored course of action. For example, after airplane crashes, there are often voices pressing for greater air safety regulations. While such regulations might make air travel safer, they might also have the effect of making travel more dangerous. That's because the increased regulations may increase the price of flying and so lead more people to drive—which is a more dangerous form of transportation (Sunstein 2000, 1073). (Further, given its relative safety, making air travel a tiny bit safer may well be less cost effective than, say, repaving the Pennsylvania Turnpike.) Now it may be that we are willing to accept a greater number of total traffic injuries and fatalities in exchange for slightly safer (and more expensive) air travel. But by engaging in cost-benefit analysis—even one that only considers the rather crass value of money spent per death prevented—we can recognize that the decision to make air travel slightly safer has this effect. Even a flawed cost-benefit analysis can help us to expose the aims and values implicit in our decisions; and this exposure can lead us to change, challenge, or clarify our values and priorities. Perhaps we so dread the terrifying nature of airplane deaths that we are willing to accept an increased probability of injury or death for a decreased probability of a terror-filled death. But only by exposing this value underlying our decision can we even begin to question it. Even a flawed cost-benefit analysis can help us set priorities and effectively marshal our scarce resources so as to improve our decision making (Sunstein 2000).

As citizens of a democracy, we have an interest in how members of governmental safety boards (e.g., OSHA, EPA, etc.) decide how to allocate scarce resources to improve occupational and other federal safety standards. In making such decisions, it is useful to know that (according to the Consumer Product Safety Commission) banning unvented space heaters is among the cheapest ways to save lives, costing $100,000 per prevented death. Limiting exposure to asbestos in the workplace is considerably more expensive, at 8.3 million dollars per prevented death (OSHA). And the cost of listing wood-preserving chemicals as hazardous waste is estimated by the EPA to be 5.7 trillion dollars per prevented death (Sunstein, 2000). By being clear about what measures are likely to save the greatest number of people (or minimize the number of people getting sick), we can better make decisions that accurately reflect our values.

2. A cost-benefit approach to epistemology

Before tackling the difficulties associated with a cost-benefit approach to epistemology, it might be valuable to note that cost-benefit considerations are a familiar, even banal, feature of perceptual and cognitive psychology. From early psychophysics to contemporary cognitive psychology, psychologists often explain successes, as well as routine breakdowns, in terms of specific allocations of attention and memory across perceptual modalities and cognitive capacities. For example, many of our reflexes are best understood as cognitive instantiations of a complex cost-benefit analysis. The ducking reflex occurs whenever you see a rigid object translating toward your head. Those who don't duck, to quote Quine, "have a pathetic but praiseworthy tendency to die before reproducing their kind" (1969, 126). This reflex has accommodated a complex payoff matrix. When a rigid object is moving toward your head, the potentially serious consequences of not avoiding it call for a fast and mandatory reflex. So you duck, even when the trusted friend who threw the object tells you that it won't hurt you. Low risk and low benefit outcomes do not produce comparably reliable behavior. We are skeptical that this kind of adaptationist story will work for all of our cognitive mechanisms. But adaptationist explanations are quite plausible for reflexes, and such explanations tend to rely explicitly on cost-benefit considerations (e.g., Parker 1974; Maynard Smith 1978).

Processes of greater cognitive depth also reveal tradeoffs between costs and benefits. Consider memory. Our recall performance suffers terribly when resources get allocated to competing tasks. In the classic experiments on divided attention, people were presented with two spoken messages. The participants could not identify the contents of both messages, recalling one well and only the most basic characteristics of the other (e.g., that it changed from speech to tone, etc.). Consider a timely example. Talking on a cellphone (either handheld or hands-free) while driving resulted in twice as many failures to detect a simulated traffic signal and slower reactions to those signals when they were detected (Strayer and Johnston, 2001). These effects of divided attention exert a powerful influence on our daily activities, which often involve doing two or more things at once. In short, strategies involving divided attention bring predictable costs. (This point is embodied in the wise advice of a parent: "Don't smooch while driving—you'll do both badly.") We can drive safely or talk on the cellphone. We can read or listen to someone addressing us. The choice to do one, the other, or both should be based on an analysis of the costs and benefits of the various distributions of cognitive resources (Payne, Bettman, and Johnson 1993).

Now it's time to pay the piper. If applied epistemology involves a kind of cost-benefit analysis, then we need to clearly identify the costs and benefits of reasoning. But this is hard to do for three reasons. First, it is not clear how to reduce the myriad benefits of reasoning to countable units. Second, it is not clear how to reduce all the various costs of reasoning to countable units. And third, it's doubtful that we can reasonably interpret a smooth cost-benefit curve for a reasoning strategy. Let's consider these issues in turn.

2.1. Epistemic benefits

One might think that the benefits of reasoning will be a function of the accuracy of our judgments. Yes, but it will be a very complicated function. Accuracy by itself is cheap. What's dear when it comes to reasoning is accuracy about *significant* problems. We will discuss the issue of significance in detail in chapter 6. Significance on our view is a property of a problem for a person—so a reasoning problem can be more or less significant for a person. The excellent reasoner will tend to focus on significant reasoning problems, even if those problems are difficult to solve. As a result, the excellent reasoner will often decide to execute a reasoning strategy that is not among the most reliable strategies available to her. Suppose an excellent reasoner is charged with making decisions about whether a potential parolee is likely to commit another violent crime. She will adopt the best reasoning strategy she can for that problem, even though tackling an easier problem ("At every 10-second interval, how many people are there in this room?") will get her more true judgments. So in practice, the call for the excellent reasoner to tackle *significant* problems will mean that she will not maximize accuracy in her judgments. She will not come to maximize the overall reliability (or truth-ratio) of her beliefs.

Significance also has a role to play in the decision to act on judgments. Certain significant problems are such that certain sorts of errors are more costly than others. In these cases, one might come to a judgment but act "as if" that judgment were mistaken. For example, in an environment in which social institutions have broken down and a significant minority of the population are armed, the epistemically excellent reasoner might well judge of any particular person who is not obviously armed that he or she is probably not armed. But she might act on the assumption that everyone is armed. (This sort of example is different from the ducking reflex. With the reflex, it isn't obvious whether the ducker acquires a belief. Further, even if she does, it isn't the result of higher-order processing over which she has any control. Applied epistemology is relevant only to those reasoning problems about which one has some control over how to reason.)

Our account of significance will not yield a notion of epistemic benefit that can be represented by units along a single dimension. The fact that we can't accurately assign units of epistemic benefit to a reasoning strategy might seem like a serious problem for any cost-benefit approach to epistemology. And it would be if cost-benefit analyses had to exhaustively identify the benefits of good reasoning along a single dimension. But as we have already argued, even deeply imperfect cost-benefit analyses can be useful. So we propose to identify the benefits of a reasoning strategy in terms of its reliability. We can measure the reliability of a reasoning strategy; and this tracks reasonably well (in most cases) the real benefits of reasoning. Reliability is a measurable surrogate that stands in for a reasoning strategy's epistemic benefits.

Some might worry about such an obviously flawed cost-benefit approach playing such a central role in applied epistemology. Two points should help assuage this worry. First, we begin our cost-benefit analysis by recognizing that what we're counting as the benefit of reasoning is only a stand-in, and more importantly, by recognizing the *way* in which this stand-in is flawed (i.e., it ignores significance). Given that we include in our theory an account of significance, the applied epistemologist can readily identify those cases in which reliability is likely to closely gauge the real benefits of reasoning and those cases in which it is not likely to closely gauge the real benefits of reasoning. As a result, we can decide to trust some particular analysis (when the surrogate tracks the real benefits), and we can decide to ignore or amend another analysis (when the surrogate does not track the real benefits). The second reason not to worry too much about this flaw in our cost-benefit approach arises out of our view about what is the central task of applied epistemology: to suggest reasoning strategies that are tractable, robustly reliable, and focused on problems that tend to be highly significant. We can explore each of these three factors independently: We can begin by noting what sorts of problems tend to be highly significant for people, and then we can search for reasoning strategies that are both tractable and robustly reliable on those problems. (In fact, this is essentially what we do in chapter 9.)

2.2. Cognitive costs

We have so far assumed that there are "resources" available for solving voluntary reasoning problems and that these resources can be moved around easily from one reasoning strategy to another. (In economic parlance, we're assuming these resources are "fungible.") But that is not so. There are a number of quite different kinds of resources required for solving voluntary reasoning problems—time, attention, and short-term and long-term cognitive capacity. Different reasoning strategies will place more pressure on some of these resources than others. And some of these resources handle the strain better than others. One reasoning strategy might be easy to use because the effort is spread out across various capacities that work together easily. Another strategy might be just as easy to use (measured, say, in terms of how many basic operations it employs), but it might be very hard to implement because its demands overwhelm a single capacity (e.g., short term memory) or are spread out across capacities that interfere with each other's effective operation. It is doubtful that there is any way to sensibly reduce these various demands on our various capacities to a single notion of cognitive cost that can be represented by units along a single dimension.

As was the case with cognitive benefits, the fact that we can't accurately assign units of epistemic cost to a reasoning strategy is not a particularly serious problem for our cost-benefit approach to epistemology. The notion of epistemic cost does map onto a notion we are able to use to good effect—the notion of some strategies being harder or easier to use than others. Indeed, given that people are less likely to use a reasoning strategy as it gets more complicated (Nisbett 1993), there is good reason to stick to as simple a strategy as possible. We can measure the time it takes people to implement the strategy; and this tracks reasonably well (in most cases) the real costs of reasoning. So this measurable quantity can serve as an imperfect stand-in for the notion of cognitive costs.

2.3. Curves and processes

A cost-benefit curve characterizes the trajectory of performance and so allows you to predict it. At the same time, the fact that a line connects two points does not necessarily imply that there are mechanisms determining arbitrarily selected values on the line. If it did, a cardinality argument could be constructed that there are infinitely many mechanisms, or that the mechanisms that exist are infinitely sensitive. And this is not a general assumption we would want to embrace. But we can very roughly represent the reasoning strategy's performance in terms of a smooth curve as long as the curve is a product of documented performance or outcomes, and we have no reason to think that the reasoning strategy would exhibit wildly discontinuous performances on some task.

3. The cost-benefit imperative

Our cost-benefit approach to epistemology takes elapsed time to be a surrogate for epistemic costs and reliability to be a surrogate for epistemic benefits. This approach has at least two important virtues. The first is that our surrogates (time and reliability) are *measurable*. This means that the central components of applied epistemology (or at least their rough approximations) can be *empirically determined* in the following sense: (a) The cost-benefit curve is determined by observed outcomes in performance; and (b) the curve can then be successfully used as a basis for predictions of performance. So the central theoretical components of applied epistemology— or at least rough approximations of them—can in principle be tested for accuracy, rather than for their ability to stand up to imagined counterexamples. The second virtue of our approach is that our surrogates roughly track the properties of interest (the costs and benefits of reasoning). As a result, the central tool of applied epistemology is reasonably accurate.

At this point, one might point out that successful SPRs have typically been introduced without the explicit use of the formal machinery of cost-benefit analysis we have introduced here. So one might wonder whether

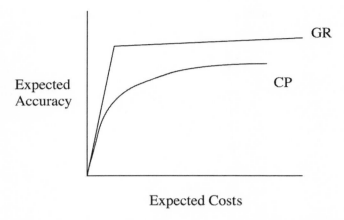

Expected
Accuracy

Expected Costs

Figure 5.1.   Costs and benefits of the Goldberg Rule vs. clinical prediction.

this machinery is really required to address the efficient allocation of cognitive resources. Are we shooting a mosquito with a bazooka? We don't think so, for two reasons. First, cost-benefit curves are good teaching tools. When repairing individual reasoning strategies, it is helpful for the individual to see, in stark and unapologetic terms, how poorly they are performing, even by their own lights. And nothing does that like a curve—even if the curve does not capture everything of value. Cost-benefit curves are at once painfully accessible and mercifully impersonal. Consider the Goldberg Rule we introduced in chapter 2. This rule predicts whether a psychiatric patient is neurotic or psychotic on the basis of an MMPI profile. When tested on a set of 861 patients, the Goldberg Rule had a 70% hit rate; clinicians' hit rates varied from a low of 55% to a high of 67%. We can set out the choice between the Goldberg Rule and clinical prediction in terms of what their cost-benefit curves might look like (see Figure 5.1).

The cost-benefit curve for the Goldberg Rule is very steep and hits its near-maximum reliability after a rather modest expenditure of resources. That's because it doesn't require many resources to achieve a high degree of accuracy; spending more resources (by checking whether one has plugged in the proper values and done the arithmetic correctly) is likely to bring very small increments in reliability. Clinical prediction requires greater resources than the Goldberg Rule but never achieves its reliability. This point can be made vivid with a curve.

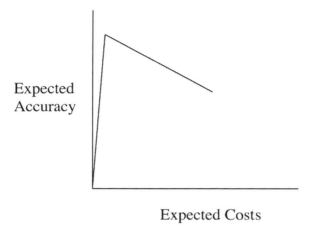

Figure 5.2.   Cost-benefit curve for the Goldberg Rule
(with selective defection).

There is a second way that an explicit cost-benefit approach can be useful. It can help to bring a certain kind of discipline to reasoners. Recall the selective defection findings. Those who are given the Goldberg Rule and allowed to selectively defect from it end up reasoning less reliably than the rule itself; and many who know about the interview effect nonetheless insist on doing unstructured interviews and drawing conclusions from them. This hapless defection is typically undesirable. If we have two strategies for solving a problem and one is more reliable, it is folly to use the less reliable strategy to correct the more reliable one. There are some very limited situations in which defection is warranted (see our discussion in chapter 2). We can represent the costs and benefits of selective defection with a cost-benefit curve, which might have something like the shape shown in Figure 5.2. This curve suggests that with minimal cognitive resources (i.e., those resources necessary to find the relevant scores, do the simple arithmetic, and determine whether the sum is or is not greater than 45), the reasoner can attain a 70% accuracy rate. But by devoting more resources to the problem (i.e., by using information from the MMPI profile to try to improve on the Goldberg Rule's prediction), the reasoner degrades his reliability. This finding—that there is a point beyond which the additional effort associated with considering more information degrades performance—was also found in the interview effect (chapter 2). So when our cognitive limitations tempt us with a reasoning strategy that is both subjectively seductive and systematically defective, it is time to lean on a cognitive prosthetic. Cost-benefit analysis is that cognitive prosthetic.

We understand the temptations of defection. We know what it's like to use a reasoning strategy of proven reliability when it seems to give an answer not warranted by the evidence. It feels like you're about to make an unnecessary error. And maybe you are. But in order to make fewer errors *overall*, we have to accept that we will sometimes make errors we could have corrected—errors that we recognized as errors before we made them but made them nonetheless (Einhorn 1986). (Of course, the point is that in these situations, more often than not, what we think will be an error in fact won't be.) People often lack the discipline to adhere to a superior strategy that doesn't "feel" right. Reasoning in a way that sometimes "feels" wrong takes discipline. And one way to impose that discipline is to think about applied epistemology in terms of costs and benefits. All reasoning strategies will lead to error (costs). When it comes to deciding whether to defect from an SPR, the net benefits of defection (more errors with greater effort) are typically outweighed by the net benefits of diffident acquiescence to the SPR. When it comes to learning to reason better, discipline is essential; and we can think of no more effective way to impose that discipline than with a cost-benefit approach to applied epistemology.

Robyn Dawes (2001) notes that piloting an airplane by sight can give you the powerful impression that you are flying right-side up when you are actually upside down. So pilots learn to fly by instruments. This takes some doing, but pilots are repaid with longer lives. To the extent that individuals appreciate the benefits of averting costly error, they need to fly by cost-benefit instruments. Adhering to a cost-benefit analysis may feel wrong, but then again so does flying by instruments at first.

We fear this discussion may have made us appear like unduly strict disciplinarians, so let us end on a gentler note. It would be irresponsible for any applied epistemology that announces the importance of efficiency to ignore the controllable inefficiency of reasoners. And we worry about just how far discipline can really go in saving reasoners from ill-fated temptation. For certain sorts of reasoning problems, applied epistemology might well recommend strategies—reasoning or otherwise—that are designed to develop and foster healthy reasoning dispositions. Why labor in the construction of reasoning rules designed to correct our errant cognitive impulses when we can cultivate actors who are not seduced by those detrimental impulses in the first place? This point is reflected in good advice for parents: It is probably less costly to cultivate your child's many interests—keeping them very busy and focused on satisfying activities—than to teach them how to control or correct their drug addictions later. Similarly, when thinking about the various ways people reason badly, it may be easier to cultivate new habits than to revise how we reason. If S's reasoning rashly discounts the future, rather than force her to adopt new reasoning strategies, it might be more effective to set up an automatic withdrawal from her bank account into a retirement fund that comes with stiff penalties for early withdrawals. Suppose S is tempted to become an active stock-market trader because he takes a short-term rise in his portfolio to be evidence of his financial cleverness. Rather than fill his head with a lot of theories and statistics, it is probably easier to force him to focus on time horizons of at least 10 years in the stock market and thereby avoid the temptation of active trading. And what about an academic department tempted by the interview effect? Take the money the department spends to send interviewers to conferences and transfer it into research accounts for junior faculty. The result will likely be better hires and happier, more productive junior faculty.

6

Strategic Reliabilism: Epistemic Significance

Reasoning to true beliefs is easy, if all you want is true beliefs. An individual will reason to many true beliefs if he spends time and resources reasoning about how many Goodyear Blimps are in his field of vision every second of the day ("No blimps. No blimps. One blimp! No blimps.") But as his hygiene and relationships suffer, it would not be correct to say he is an excellent reasoner. Excellent reasoners reason reliably to *significant* truths, not just to any old truths (Kitcher 1993, 2001). Many accounts of significance will be compatible with the epistemic machinery of Strategic Reliabilism we have provided in the previous two chapters. On our view, significance is nonaccidentally related to the requirements of human well-being. These requirements can be surprising and are not always open to casual inspection or introspection (as we argued in chapter 3 and will argue in section 2, below). So our account of significance, like the empirical discipline of moral psychology, must await further scientific discoveries. It is fitting, then, that our account of significance is programmatic. We will offer a framework for understanding significance that tolerates our incomplete knowledge of the conditions for human well-being.

1. The role of significance in Strategic Reliabilism

It is easy to despair of coming up with a notion of significance that might be useful for epistemology. Take a reasoner in a context who is trying to figure out what is the most significant problem she faces. Will a general theory of significance provide useful information about this case? If it is an easy case, the answer will be so obvious that a theory of significance will be superfluous. If she is concentrating very hard on the mind-body problem while driving up to a railroad crossing with the sound of a train in the distance, we don't need any fancy theories to tell us which problem is more significant. In many hard cases, the answer will be nonobvious because the reasoner doesn't know enough about the idiosyncratic details of his situation to know which problem is the most significant. For example, a reasoner's boss might ask him to develop a business plan; it might not be clear whether he should be developing what he thinks is the best plan or whether he should be developing what he thinks his boss thinks is the best plan. In this case, no theory of significance is going to be useful because what the reasoner lacks isn't a sense of what problems are generally significant. The reasoner lacks knowledge about what his boss really wants, and that knowledge won't be provided by a theory of significance. We might despair because no significance-based epistemology is going to be able to provide advice that is specific to a reasoner's particular situation that is both nonobvious and definitive. So one might reasonably conclude that while significance is an important notion, there is nothing much useful for an epistemological theory to say about it.

We endorse the premises of the above argument: Issues of significance arise in particular cases. And an epistemological theory that includes an account of significance will not be able to be applied directly and fruitfully to many particular cases. In other words, we should not expect a recipe book that will allow a reasoner to identify beforehand all and only the significant problems that confront her. It does not follow, however, that epistemology need not concern itself with significance. Let's step back and investigate the *role* significance ought to play in a normative epistemology.

The primary aim of epistemology, from our perspective, is to provide useful, general advice about reasoning. Such advice is inevitably going to depend on fairly *general* judgments of epistemic significance. These judgments will typically involve claims about what *kinds* of problems are likely to be significant for *reasoners in general*. For example, in their day-to-day lives, people often rely on causal reasoning. We can avoid pain and misery if we can accurately predict the causal outcomes of various actions—our own, those of others, and those of nature. That's not to say that *every* reasoning problem that calls for causal reasoning is significant. But many of the significant problems that people generally face involve causal reasoning. As a result, a significance-based epistemology can recommend that we be prepared to expend a fair amount of time and energy improving our reasoning about causal matters. This general truth about significance also has important implications for the practice of epistemology. In filling out the practical, prescriptive content of a significance-based epistemology, we can focus our attention on uncovering biases to which people are most prone in reasoning about significant matters. We can then offer well-tested correctives to those biases, or we can suggest new, replacement strategies for reasoning about those matters.

2. A reason-based approach to significance

The fundamental difficulty in developing an account of significance is what we might call the thick-thin problem. On the one hand, we need an account of significance that is thick enough to forbid an "anything goes" attitude toward significance. For example, no matter how intrinsically compelling one might find the problem of (say) establishing the length of one's left thumbnail at every five second interval, that interest, by itself, does not make that problem particularly significant. (That's not to say, of course, that we can't imagine a fanciful scenario in which close thumbnail monitoring is a highly significant problem. But for most of us most of the time, it's not.) So we need an account of significance that is thick enough to yield the result that a problem might be relatively insignificant even if someone has a powerful subjective desire to tackle it. But on the other hand, we need an account of significance that is thin enough to license some dramatic interpersonal differences in what problems are significant. For example, establishing whether the short-tailed shrew is the smallest North American mammal with poisonous saliva might be a very significant problem to a biologist whose professional reputation depends on her knowledge of North American shrews. For most of the rest of us, however, this is not an especially significant problem. So the thick-thin problem is that the constraints on significance must allow for some substantive interpersonal and interinstitutional differences about what problems are significant without licensing an "anything goes" subjectivism.

Our view holds that *the significance of a problem for S is a function of the weight of the objective reasons S has for devoting resources to solving that problem.* This view assumes that we have objective reasons of various sorts for action and that we can weigh these reasons against one another. We are aware that these are bold and controversial assumptions. But given our broadly Aristotelian approach to epistemology, we don't think it's possible to think fully and clearly about epistemology without also bringing in views about other normative domains. So we will unabashedly take the assumption that there are objective reasons for action—they stand regardless of whether a subject recognizes them or (after reflection) accepts them as legitimate (see Railton 1986; Boyd 1988). This reason-based account of significance has the resources to handle the thick-thin problem. Some reasons (such as those that arise from basic moral obligations) are universal. They place firm restrictions on the sort of problems that can be significant. But other reasons (such as those that arise from one's social or professional obligations) might be quite different for different people. These sorts of reasons permit fairly dramatic differences in the sorts of problems that different people might find significant.

The two most intuitively compelling kinds of objective reasons are also the most important for our purposes. We take it that people have objective moral reasons and objective prudential reasons for action. So consider the reasoning problem faced by a doctor who is diagnosing whether a patient has a serious disease on the basis of various test results. This problem is highly significant for the doctor because she has objective moral and prudential reasons for reasoning very carefully and well about such a problem. These reasons are objective because they stand regardless of whether she recognizes them or, upon reflection, accepts them. This is particularly plausible in a case (like this one) in which the objective reasons the doctor has for devoting resources to this problem are connected (at least in part) to the *consequences* of her reasoning. Accurately diagnosing a patient is a high-stakes proposition, both for the patient and for the doctor. The potential costs of an inaccurate diagnosis are huge, as are the potential benefits of an accurate diagnosis. When someone's objective reasons for tackling a problem are a function of the consequences of getting or not getting an accurate result, it's intuitively plausible that these reasons stand even if the doctor doesn't recognize or care about them. And since these reasons are weighty, the problem is significant for the doctor (not to mention her patient!).

It would be a mistake, however, to think that all the objective reasons we could have for action involve only consequences. Individuals can have reasons for tackling certain problems because they have pursued or accepted the moral and professional duties (along with the attendant benefits) of certain social or professional roles. For example, regardless of the consequences, doctors have a duty (a moral and professional duty) to devote resources to thinking clearly about their patients; police officers have a duty to devote resources to thinking clearly about solving and preventing crime; university professors have a duty to devote resources to thinking clearly about how to effectively teach their students—and some have a duty to devote resources to thinking clearly about short-tailed shrews or the mind-body problem.

Objective reasons include more than moral, prudential, or social-role sorts of reasons. For example, people can have legitimate (and objective) epistemic reasons for tackling a certain problem. We take it that discovering the truth about the basic physical or social structure of the world is intrinsically valuable. So even if we can't be sure that it will lead to any practical results, the physicists at CERN and Fermilab have epistemic reasons (beyond their prudential reasons) for spending cognitive resources on trying to discover the Higgs boson.

Let's consider three worries about this reason-based account of significance. The first worry concerns insignificant problems. For those of us who have no legitimate reasons and no personal interest in constantly monitoring our fingernail length or the number of Goodyear Blimps in our field of vision, our view is that such problems are insignificant. But the thick-thin problem arises when we ask: What about the subject who *is* interested in tackling such navel-gazing reasoning problems? Doesn't this interest, by itself, give the subject some objective reason to tackle the problem? Yes. We can grant the following general principle: *If S desires to do X, that gives S some (objective) reason to do X.* But notice, this principle is silent about the *strength* of this objective reason. On the assumption that S has no other reasons—moral, prudential, epistemic, aesthetic, etc.—to pursue this problem, it would seem that this problem, while not completely insignificant, is of very, very little significance. If S is devoting resources to monitoring his fingernail length rather than (say) the safety of his child, this is a pathology that goes well beyond concerns with poor reasoning. But on our view, devoting resources to a barely significant problem instead of a significant problem is a case of poor reasoning—and possibly worse.

A second worry about our view concerns "lost cause" problems. Consider the problem of whether the current health care system in the U.S. is just and efficient. Given our health care system's barriers to participatory influence, it might be that an individual has no power to change or help change the system. Is this apparently "lost cause" a significant problem for the person? If the person is interested in the problem, then (as in the navel-gazing cases) that makes the problem at least a little bit significant. But on what grounds might it be more than barely significant? One might have prudential reasons to think about the health care system in order to understand it well enough to make good use of it. But let's suppose this consideration isn't relevant to the reasoner. There are still two classes of objective reason that could make "lost cause" problems significant. First, we have a civic or political duty to be well informed on important topics of the day (i.e., topics that are important to people's well-being). How does this duty work? The only way positive change can occur in a democracy is if those with minority opinions don't give up when they don't foresee beneficial changes coming in the short term. But the possibility of positive change also requires that those who aren't informed on important subjects pay attention to them. This seems to us to be the basis of the civic or political duty that makes thinking about the moral status of our society's institutions significant—even when we have vanishingly small prospects for changing them. Another set of objective reasons that might ground the significance of these "lost causes" involves considerations of virtue. Following up on our generally Aristotelian approach to epistemology, it seems plausible to suppose that there is a nonaccidental connection between being an excellent reasoner and an excellent person. We venture to guess (and we take this to be a testable assumption) that spending resources thinking seriously about whether one's society is just is a feature of an excellent character and a flourishing life. Indeed, it's not too much of an overstatement to say that Western philosophy originated, in the person of Socrates, in precisely this kind of serious reflection on "lost causes."

The third worry about our view concerns "negatively" significant reasoning problems. Reasoners may have objective reasons for *not* devoting resources to particular sorts of problem. For example, we suspect that a psychologically healthy person will not regularly calculate and recalculate what are his narrow self-interests—particularly if such constant recalculation alienates him from activities he finds satisfying and casts his friends as potential competitors. We take it that this can be a "negatively" significant reasoning problem. This is a separate category from significant and insignificant problems. "Negatively" significant problems are those for which one has positive reason (not based on opportunity costs) to avoid. We have discussed (in chapter 3) some of the counterintuitive findings of "hedonic psychology." These findings suggest that focusing cognitive resources on certain kinds of problem are likely to lead to frustration and loss of happiness. To take one perhaps unsurprising example, people who pursue money in the belief that it will increase their happiness express greater frustration than their peers (Myers 2000). We suspect (although we have only anecdotal evidence for this hypothesis) that "philosophy graduate student disease" (the constant monitoring of one's actual or perceived "smartness" status) involves the devotion of resources to a negatively significant problem.

Our general account of epistemic significance resides, ultimately, in judgments about what conduces to human well-being. If we view humans as part of the natural order, then the conditions that contribute to human well-being are open to scientific investigation. Some might worry that these conditions are too variable to be studied systematically and generalized about scientifically. There is, however, reason for optimism. While the conditions of human well-being may be tied to norms that differ across individuals and across cultures, the challenges of generalizing across varied groups and individuals have been surmounted in other sciences, such as developmental and evolutionary biology. There is ample empirical evidence that the basic conditions of human well-being involve health, deep social attachments, personal security, and the pursuit of significant projects (Diener and Seligman 2002; Myers 2000). Just as certain personality types engage in activities that make them less happy, there are economic, social, and political institutions that have a systematic and adjustable influence on people's happiness (Diener 2000; Diener and Oishi 2000; Frey and Stutzer 2002; Lane 2000). For example, income, unemployment, and inflation all have marked and sustained influences on happiness (Frey and Stutzer 2002). Interestingly, all three partly result from institutional planning—of tax policy, monetary policy, and available services—and so can be regulated to a certain extent by government action. To continue the theme, certain objective economic conditions, such as destitution, are incompatible with well-being (Dasgupta 1993). These empirical findings about the conditions that influence happiness and welfare set limits on what can count as a significant problem. Some of the most significant problems we face concern how to renovate maladaptive social institutions that undermine our happiness and well-being, and how to implement new social, political, and economic institutions and procedures that are most likely to promote well-being and control the sources of avoidable unhappiness.

3. The potential unavailability of objective reasons

The significance of a problem is determined by the strength of the reasons one has for devoting resources to it. But often people through no fault of their own don't have access to those reasons. We often reasonably believe that a problem is significant when it's not. Trying to predict what gift a spouse would enjoy for an anniversary might seem a fairly significant problem, deserving to be pondered in considerable detail. But it's probably not if the spouse runs off with the neighbor a week before the anniversary. Further, often people through no fault of their own will be correct about whether a problem is significant but wrong about why. Stich offers the example of the person who reasons to a true belief about when her plane leaves but who doesn't know the plane is doomed to crash (1990). The problem of finding out when the flight left was significant, but not for the reason she thought. The fact that the significance of particular problems will sometimes (or perhaps regularly) be unavailable to reasoners might seem like a serious problem for our view. We claim to be offering a normative epistemological theory that provides reasoning guidance. A central aspect of our theory is that reasoners should focus on significant problems. But we admit that reasoners will often not know which are the significant problems. So how can our theory offer people useful reasoning advice?

Even though a reasoner might not have a good sense of what problems are most significant for him to tackle, this does not undermine our theory. First, any theory that takes significance to be important will have this problem; and any theory that does not take significance to be important will be incapable of making positive normative recommendations. So this worry is an unfortunate feature of the human condition, not a weakness of our view. Second, recall the role that significance is supposed to play in our epistemological theory. It directs reasoners to be prepared to spend more resources improving or replacing reasoning strategies that *as a general rule* tend to have in their range significant reasoning problems. (It might also direct reasoners to avoid spending resources on problems that are negatively significant.) So the notion of significance plays a regulative role in guiding the research of a prescriptive epistemology. A priority for epistemology is to develop excellent reasoning strategies (i.e., reliable and tractable for ordinary reasoners) that can be used on significant problems. The fact that individual reasoners will sometimes be quite mistaken about which problems facing them are the significant ones does not undermine the epistemological project of recommending excellent reasoning strategies (i.e., strategies that are robustly reliable, tractable, and applicable to significant problems).

The call to allocate our cognitive resources to significant problems places specific demands on the excellent reasoner. The most important demand concerns setting priorities. The priorities of the excellent reasoner (and more generally, of the wise person) are set so that they may serve as a means to human flourishing. Sometimes the excellent reasoner must replace hot, spontaneous judgment with the cool administration of our epistemic priorities. We might prioritize our projects so that they keep us happily occupied. We might place a priority on family and friends because their well-being matters to us. But when our interests are stable and healthy, we don't have to explicitly arrange these priorities—our interests spontaneously direct us to significant problems. Our decision to have children is more often the spontaneous result of a loving relationship than it is the issue of a cold calculation that it will pay off in the long run. A toned body can just as easily be the result of pleasant sport as it can be the joyless consequence of scheduled maintenance. And like the beautiful dust on a butterfly's wings, these spontaneous interests result from natural ends that subtly sculpt our lives. When determining the significance of the problems we face, we should attend to these contours.

We should emphasize that a successful epistemological tradition will not demand that the responsibility for reasoning excellence be shouldered entirely by individuals. The well-ordered social presence of a reason-guiding epistemology should promote the proper distribution of epistemic responsibility. Institutions can make it more likely that individuals will act responsibly, through for example, proper training, institutional procedures, a well-designed system of incentives, or formal or informal sanctions.

The objection we are considering is an instance of a more general worry about our theory. Strategic Reliabilism is a theory that sets forth the conditions of reasoning excellence. This theory also holds out the promise of an applied component, which will include reasoning advice we have strong empirical reason to think is good reasoning advice. At the moment, the practical content of Strategic Reliabilism is limited by the current state of our well-tested, empirical knowledge about what sorts of reasoning strategies are robustly reliable, tractable, and focused on significant matters. Although limited, our view still recommends a number of specific strategies that most people should adopt (e.g., frequency formats for diagnosis problems, the consider-the-opposite strategy to counteract overconfidence, and others to be discussed in chapter 9). But we cannot guarantee that people will follow this advice—some will not follow our advice because they have never been introduced to it, others because they decide to ignore it. But these possibilities are no objection to our theory. Our theory provides useful advice—but that doesn't mean it provides advice that everyone can always use no matter what. An analogy might be helpful. The owner's manual for a car provides useful advice. It doesn't follow that everyone regardless of their skill or knowledge can use that advice profitably. There is another aspect to the owner's manual analogy. If there exists only one copy of a Chevy Vega owner's manual and it is locked in a vault in Detroit, it is not *available* enough to be genuinely useful to Vega owners (who are likely to need genuine help). Similarly, if the advice of Strategic Reliabilism is to be restricted to highly specialized journals, then it will not be available enough to be genuinely useful. That is why our view takes seriously the idea that epistemology, like any science, ought to be a well-ordered social system (Kitcher 2001). A well-ordered social system for epistemology would have at least two features. First, in order to achieve its ameliorative potential, epistemology should be organized so that it provides a way to effectively communicate its established findings, particularly its practical advice, to appropriate audiences. Second, in order to minimize the risk of promoting harmful or mistaken findings, epistemology should be organized so that whatever findings are communicated widely have passed rigorous empirical scrutiny.

Recognizing the importance of significance in epistemology opens up a pair of empirical issues that are perhaps deserving of more study: First, what sorts of problems are significant that people tend to think are not significant and so perhaps reason poorly or not enough about? For example, people tend to unduly discount the future, as when they overvalue small current increments of money compared to their compounded value in the future. And second, what sorts of problems are not significant (or perhaps "negatively" significant) that people tend to believe are significant and so perhaps spend too much time and energy on? For example, people tend to unduly focus on vivid low probability risks at the expense of pallid but much higher probability risks. Given the empirical nature of significance, no theory can guarantee that significant problems are psychologically available to us. The best our theory can do is to ensure that it recommend strategies that will improve our reasoning about matters of significance.

4. Conclusion

Properly understanding the notion of epistemic significance is a core problem for any epistemological theory that claims to be able to guide reason. Any epistemological view that gives a central place to the notion of significance is bound to be deeply empirical. We cannot know a priori what sorts of problems are significant. Perhaps this explains why so much traditional epistemology neglects the notion of significance (but see Firth 1998). It would make epistemology dependent on contingent facts about what sorts of problems tend to be significant and insignificant. In its attempt to avoid empirical matters, SAE avoids issues of significance. But it is important to keep in mind that the call to allocate our cognitive resources to significant problems applies not only to individuals, but also to disciplines like physics, chemistry, and indeed epistemology itself. We have in fact identified some problems we think are important in epistemology that have been mostly ignored by contemporary epistemologists— for example, determining what sorts of reasoning problems are likely to be significant or negatively significant, identifying excellent (tractable and reliable) reasoning strategies for such problems, and setting up social institutions that can communicate established findings responsibly. It may seem the pinnacle of arrogance for us to declare which problems are significant for epistemology. Perhaps. But arrogance has many forms, from boastful certainty to aloof self-satisfaction. Would it be less arrogant for us to suppose without any explicit defense that the current priorities of our discipline just happen to be fine? Or that the current allocation of resources in our discipline is optimal in terms of giving us the best chance to achieve the normative goals of epistemology?

7

The Troubles with Standard Analytic Epistemology

The nonsocial components of our approach to epistemology have a particular structure. Epistemology begins with a descriptive core, which naturally yields various epistemic prescriptions; these prescriptions are supported by the Aristotelian Principle (good reasoning tends to lead to good outcomes) and are guided by some general normative assumptions. On our view, the descriptive core of epistemology consists of the empirical findings of Ameliorative Psychology. An example of an epistemic prescription that flows naturally from Ameliorative Psychology would be, "Use Goldberg's Rule to make preliminary diagnoses of psychiatric patients." And we have argued that Strategic Reliabilism articulates the general assumptions that guide the prescriptions of Ameliorative Psychology. But there is a different way to do epistemology. For much of the past century, epistemology in the English-speaking world has employed the tools of analytic philosophy. Contemporary theories of Standard Analytic Epistemology include versions of foundationalism (Chisholm 1981, Pollock 1974), coherentism (BonJour 1985, Lehrer 1974), reliabilism (Dretske 1981, Goldman 1986), and contextualism (DeRose 1995, Lewis 1996).

While proponents of SAE don't agree about how to define naturalistic epistemology, most agree it can't work. What makes our approach naturalistic is that it begins with a descriptive core and works out from there. (We take this to be sufficient for an approach to be naturalistic; we don't know whether it is also necessary.) The standard objection to this version of naturalism is that epistemology is essentially prescriptive, and a descriptive theory cannot yield normative, evaluative prescriptions. Our aims in this chapter are three. First, we will argue that the theories of SAE are structurally analogous to our own naturalistic approach. They have at their core a descriptive theory, and from that descriptive theory, proponents of SAE draw normative, epistemological prescriptions. Second, we will argue that the prospects for the theories of SAE overcoming the is-ought gap are not good. And finally, we will argue directly for the superiority of Strategic Reliabilism over any extant theory of Standard Analytic Epistemology.

1. The descriptive core of the theories of Standard Analytic Epistemology

As we noted in chapter 1, proponents of Standard Analytic Epistemology aim to provide an account of knowledge and epistemic justification. One of the main success conditions on such an account is the *stasis requirement*: The correct account of knowledge or justification will "leave our epistemic situation largely unchanged. That is to say, it is expected to turn out that according to the criteria of justified belief we come to accept, we know, or are justified in believing, pretty much what we reflectively think we know or are entitled to believe" (Kim 1988, 382). If an account of justification must satisfy the stasis condition in order to be successful, then such an account can be successful only if (a) for every belief B, clearly in the extension of the predicate 'is justified' as used by proponents of SAE, the account yields the result that B is justified, and (b) for every belief N, clearly not in the extension of the predicate 'is justified' as used by proponents of SAE, the account yields the result that N is not justified. (A similar condition can be defined for a successful account of knowledge.)

The commitment to epistemic stasis is embodied in the *method* of SAE. Philosophers accept or reject an epistemological theory on the basis of whether it accords with their considered judgments. Gettier's (1963) paper is a classic because it describes clear and compelling examples in which the justified true belief (JTB) account of knowledge is at odds with our considered judgments about knowledge. Our central worry about SAE arises from the fact that its epistemic theories are so often rejected *solely on the grounds that they violate our considered epistemic judgments*. Why should we place so much trust in our well-considered judgments? We need some reason for thinking that our well-considered epistemic judgments are correct. The Aristotelian Principle provides us with part (but only part) of the story about how we can test the deliverances of those judgments under the heat of careful experimentation rather than in the relaxation of the philosophical salon. Perhaps our armchair judgments will survive those fires. But before offering the world recommendations about how we should reason or what we should believe about important matters, it seems prudent to check.

Suppose God gave us the theory of justification that best satisfied the stasis requirement. What sort of information would such a theory give us? What would that theory be about? We can approach this as a problem of reverse engineering: Given how SAE works, what is its likely output? Some might note close analogies between epistemology and science. In SAE and science, articles are written primarily for and by people who have received distinctive educations and who have a highly specialized set of skills. While there is not much empirical work on the subject, it seems plausible to suppose that this education significantly affects the concepts, categories, and inferential patterns one uses in thinking about the world. So far, so good. In the natural sciences, however, hypotheses are typically tested against the world. But in SAE, hypotheses are tested against the well-considered judgments of other (similarly trained) philosophers.

Given how SAE works, it seems doubtful that it is geared to informing us about how regular folk think about justification. One needn't be a sociologist to realize that philosophers as a group are a relatively small and idiosyncratic sample of folks (Goldman 1999a). Philosophers' median education and intelligence are surely well above average. We speculate that philosophers' median scores on various MMPI scales (e.g., social alienation, hypersensitivity, social introversion) might be above average as well. Of course, proponents of SAE might view this as being all to the good. They might argue: "We don't want to offer a description of the epistemic practices of common folk. We're examining the concepts of experts. If you want to know what the right concept of bird is, ask an ornithologist. If you want to know what the right concept of justification is, ask an epistemologist." If this is the sort of move a proponent of SAE might make, we need to ask: What exactly is an epistemologist an expert about?

If we take the Aristotelian Principle to heart, if we believe that good reasoning tends to lead to better outcomes than bad reasoning, then we might wonder whether SAE tells us about how a wide variety of people who lead flourishing lives—people in a wide range of stations, in different cultures, in different times—have reasoned about important matters. But this is a deeply empirical matter, and one that the conservative method of SAE does not seem especially well designed to illuminate. If, however, epistemologists themselves tend to lead particularly successful lives, then perhaps providing people with their epistemic autobiographies would be useful. It is not obvious, however, that when socioeconomic factors are controlled for, epistemologists as a group lead more or less meaningful or flourishing lives than other folk.

So what is SAE geared to tell us about? We suggest that it tells us about the reflective epistemic judgments of a group of idiosyncratic people who have been trained to use highly specialized epistemic concepts and patterns of thought. By 'highly specialized' we mean that people who have not received the relevant training would find at least some of those concepts and patterns of thought strange, foreign, or unfamiliar. The conservative goals and methods of SAE are suited to the task of providing an account of the considered epistemic judgments of (mostly) well-off Westerners with Ph.D.'s in Philosophy. This is a thoroughly descriptive endeavor. Such an account aims to describe the clear application conditions of an expression as it is used by a particular group of people. It is an open question whether SAE *also* provides knowledge of normative matters. But this possibility should not hide the heretofore unrecognized naturalistic essence of SAE.

A particularly dramatic way to see that the core of SAE is a descriptive theory of analytic epistemologists' own epistemic judgments is to consider how SAE might be different if it were conducted by a very different group of people. In a fascinating study, Weinberg, Nichols, and Stich (2001) found that people in different cultural and socioeconomic groups make significantly different epistemic judgments. A group of Western subjects and non-Western subjects were given the following Gettier-style example:

> Bob has a friend, Jill, who has driven a Buick for many years. Bob therefore thinks that Jill drives an American car. He is not aware, however, that her Buick has recently been stolen, and he is also not aware that Jill has replaced it with a Pontiac, which is a different kind of American car. Does Bob really know that Jill drives an American car, or does he only believe it?

REALLY KNOWS   ONLY BELIEVES

A large majority of Western subjects gave the answer sanctioned by SAE ("only believes"), but a majority of East Asians and a majority of subjects from India gave the opposite answer ("really knows") (2001, 443).

Weinberg et al. considered an anti-reliabilist type of example in which a reasoner, as a result of being hit on the head with a rock, unwittingly acquires a reliable belief-forming mechanism for determining ambient temperature. They found significant differences in the judgments of Western and East Asian subjects. A majority of both groups of subjects, however, thought that the reasoner did not have knowledge of the ambient temperature (2001, 439–440).

Another fascinating finding involved giving high socioeconomic status (SES) subjects and low SES subjects the following case:

> It's clear that smoking cigarettes increases the likelihood of getting cancer. However, there is now a great deal of evidence that just using nicotine by itself without smoking (for instance, by taking a nicotine pill) does not increase the likelihood of getting cancer. Jim knows about this evidence and as a result, he believes that using nicotine does not increase the likelihood of getting cancer. It is possible that the tobacco companies dishonestly made up and publicized this evidence that using nicotine does not increase the likelihood of cancer, and that the evidence is really false and misleading. Now, the tobacco companies did not actually make up this evidence, but Jim is not aware of this fact. Does Jim really know that using nicotine doesn't increase the likelihood of getting cancer, or does he only believe it?

REALLY KNOWS   ONLY BELIEVES

There were statistically significant differences between high and low SES subjects. Low SES subjects were evenly divided on whether Jim really knows or only believes that using nicotine doesn't increase the likelihood of getting cancer. High SES subjects were much more likely to say that Jim only believes it (82%) (2001, 447–48).

The possibility that there is considerable variation (not only across cultures but also within cultures) in people's epistemic judgments makes it plausible to believe that we learn about the epistemic judgments of an idiosyncratic group of people when we do SAE. This is as descriptive a fact as there could possibly be. Indeed, it suggests that SAE is actually an odd kind of cultural anthropology: building theories that describe how privileged (mostly) Westerners with Ph.D.s in Philosophy engage in epistemic assessment. Weinberg, Nichols, and Stich call this endeavor "ethno-epistemology" (454). If SAE is but anthropology, it is unclear on what grounds its proponents can reasonably make universal normative claims about the nature, origin, and limits of human knowledge. To make universal claims—to claim SAE is more lofty than anthropology—has the uncomfortable feel of brute cultural imperialism.

Now it may turn out that there is less diversity in people's epistemic judgments than the fascinating studies by Weinberg, Nichols, and Stich suggest. But even if the diversity findings collapse, this, by itself, won't help show that SAE is normative. Even if SAE describes a universal practice, rather than a culturally situated one, that doesn't make SAE normative. The diversity findings simply allow us to put our point dramatically: SAE appears to describe the idiosyncratic epistemic practices of a particular group of people. But even if the world came to be populated only by analytic epistemologists, the central endeavor of SAE would still be essentially descriptive.

As a descriptive attempt to capture the epistemic judgments of philosophers, we have powerful reasons to think that the methods of psychology are superior to those of SAE. Insofar as the core of the theories of SAE is descriptive, they are very likely to be *bad* descriptive theories. This point is not essential to our argument. But it is worth noting that psychologists develop models of our concepts all the time. These models mimic our categorization judgments. (These models can mimic concepts with "fuzzy boundaries" and indeterminate instances.) If philosophers want an account that mimics their epistemological judgments, all we would need is a psychologist who is willing to model our judgments (e.g., Smith and Medin 1981, Keil 1989). Indeed, if philosophers really want to begin their epistemological musings with a descriptive core that accurately accounts for their judgments about knowledge or justification, they could save a lot of time, energy, and expense by employing a few psychology graduate students.

2. Standard Analytic Epistemology: Throwing stones in glass houses

The descriptive core of SAE is a theory that captures the considered epistemic judgments of philosophers. Some proponents of SAE believe that those judgments are best captured by a coherentist theory, others believe that they are best captured by a foundationalist theory, others believe that they are best captured by a reliabilist theory, etc. The obvious challenge for these theories is: How are they to extract normative consequences from a descriptive theory? While we intend to argue that the prospects for the theories of SAE overcoming the naturalist challenge are not good, we do not contend that the theories of SAE *cannot* overcome it. We recognize that there may be a way we have not properly identified for proponents of SAE to respond successfully to the naturalist challenge. However, proponents of SAE have wielded arguments against naturalistic epistemology that can be readily adapted to show that their own preferred theories cannot be normative. We emphasize again that we do not endorse these arguments. Our point here is that proponents of SAE have for too long been throwing stones at naturalistic epistemology from glass houses.

Michael Williams argues that the normative nature of epistemology makes it impossible to fully "naturalize" it:

> [Epistemic claims] depend on meeting certain norms or standards which define, not what you *do* do, but what you *must* or *ought* to do. To characterize someone's claim as expressing or not expressing knowledge is to pass judgment on it. Epistemic judgments are thus a particular kind of value-judgment. It is far from obvious that investigations with such a strongly normative component can be fully 'naturalized.' (Williams 2001, 11)

Williams's argument applies equally to the theories of SAE: As we have just argued, when it comes to epistemic judgments, the theories of SAE define what we "*do* do" not what we "*must* or *ought* to do." They don't tell us how to reason or believe; they merely tell us how we *do* make epistemic judgments (and by "we," we mean the tiny fraction of the world's population who has studied SAE).

According to Richard Feldman, psychology and philosophy must at best co-exist because psychology can't ask or answer the relevant normative questions:

> The original epistemological questions seem to be perfectly good questions, well worthy of our attention. It is difficult to see, then, why the availability of this other field of study [psychology], concerning how we reason, is a suitable replacement for the evaluative questions that are at the heart of epistemology. (Feldman 2003, 168)

Feldman's point can be made against the theories of SAE: "It is difficult to see, then, why the availability of this other field of study" (namely, SAE, which aims to describe how some people make evaluative judgments) "is a suitable replacement for the evaluative questions that are at the heart of epistemology." The proponent of SAE is replacing normative questions about how to evaluate reason and belief with descriptive questions about how proponents of SAE evaluate reason and belief. To suppose that answers to the descriptive questions are also answers to the normative questions is to take a big leap.

Lawrence BonJour argues that any epistemology subsumed by psychology does not have the resources to evaluate, positively or negatively, beliefs about alleged occult phenomena of various sorts, such as astrological or phrenological beliefs. For just as naturalized epistemology can say nothing positive about the justification of science or common sense, and is thus impotent in the face of skepticism, so also it can say nothing distinctively negative about the justification of these less reputable sorts of belief. (BonJour 2002, 244)

We can once again turn the tables on the proponent of SAE. A theory that accurately describes how a certain group of people make certain evaluative judgments "can say nothing positive about the justification of science or common sense, and is thus impotent in the face of skepticism, so also it can say nothing distinctively negative about the justification of" occult, astrological, or phrenological beliefs. Of course, such a theory might tell us how some people evaluate those beliefs. But that's not the same as actually evaluating those beliefs.

In a similar vein, Alvin Plantinga notes that Quinean naturalism in epistemology cannot be normative:

[T]he most extreme version of naturalism in epistemology eschews normativity altogether, seeking to replace traditional epistemology (with its concern with justification, rationality, reasonability, and their normative colleagues) by descriptive psychology; this seems to be Quine's suggestion. [fn deleted] (Plantinga 1993, 45)

By now, we're confident our argumentative strategy is wearing thin, but here it is anyway: SAE "eschews normativity altogether, seeking to replace traditional epistemology (with its concern with justification, rationality, reasonability, and their normative colleagues) by descriptive psychology"— a psychology that describes how certain people make certain sorts of judgments.

Proponents of SAE have argued for decades that radically naturalistic theories of epistemology cannot succeed because they cannot be normative. Our aim has been to turn the tables on proponents of SAE. We distance ourselves from these arguments. Merely pointing out that a theory faces the problem of bridging the is-ought divide does not by itself damn that theory. And this is a good thing for proponents of SAE. We all start our normative musings with psychology. Proponents of SAE start by describing a certain group's epistemological judgments, and we start with what we have called Ameliorative Psychology. (We argue that the former is probably very bad psychology, but that is not essential to the case we're building here.) When it comes to bridging the is-ought gap, everybody has work to do.

3. How SAE might try to get normative prescriptions from its descriptive core

Let's suppose that a breakthrough in SAE results in wide agreement that (say) a certain kind of foundationalism captures perfectly well the considered epistemic judgments of proponents of SAE. Does anything follow about how we *ought* to reason or about what beliefs we *ought* to adopt? The proponent of SAE might argue that in the given scenario, it follows that our cognitive efforts should be aimed at adopting empirical beliefs that are basic or that are appropriately related to basic beliefs—related in the way described by the account that accords with our considered epistemic judgments. But why? It doesn't matter how deeply philosophers may have considered and refined their epistemic judgments. We still need to know what's so great about philosophers' considered epistemic judgments.

Proponents of SAE might respond to this challenge as follows: "We can connect the descriptive results of SAE with normative prescriptions by noting that normative, epistemic claims are *a priori*. It is natural, therefore, to suppose that figuring out the truth about epistemology will involve the close analysis of our epistemic concepts. To characterize SAE as a descriptive endeavor (as you have done) might be correct, but it is misleading. The theories of SAE aim to describe an essentially normative concept (or set of concepts). And that's why SAE is normative. To put it crudely, discovering conceptual truths involves the accurate description of concepts. So discovering conceptual truths about the epistemological involves the accurate description of epistemological concepts. And this is precisely what SAE does. And so even though this endeavor is descriptive (it involves describing our concepts), it nonetheless yields normative, a priori prescriptions. It tells us what it *really is* for a belief to be justified, and so what we *ought to* believe."

Let's grant for the sake of argument that epistemic claims are a priori (BonJour 2002). It doesn't follow that SAE is the proper way to discover such a priori truths. Given that proponents of SAE disagree with each other about the nature of justification and that not all of these views can be true, we can distinguish between a priori beliefs (that are true or false) and a priori knowledge. We are willing to grant for the sake of argument that the theories of SAE give us a priori beliefs. But why suppose that they give us a priori knowledge? We cannot always assume that a priori truths can be easily read off of our deeply considered judgments. The history of mathematics shows how difficult it can be to come to grips with a priori truths. The long-held belief that the sum of the internal angles of any triangle equals 180 degrees may have been a priori, but it was never knowledge. If proponents of SAE have not properly grasped the concepts of epistemic evaluation, then no amount of careful armchair contemplation and analysis is going to succeed in uncovering a priori epistemological truths.

The diversity findings of Weinberg, Nichols, and Stich discussed in section 2 bring home the possibility that proponents of SAE are busy analyzing the wrong epistemic concepts. If there are significant intercultural and intracultural differences in our epistemic concepts, then not all of these groups will be able to read off a priori truths from an accurate account of their use of epistemological expressions (unless, of course, one defends a crude kind of epistemological relativism). It may be that philosophers actually have the right concepts. But we need some reason to think so.

Our naturalistic perspective suggests another way to think about the possibility that proponents of SAE are focused on concepts that will not yield a priori knowledge. We share a common, folk understanding of physics (Carey 1985, Spelke 1994). Our primitive physical concepts are swamped by the perceptual accessibility of superficial features of objects. Our folk judgments treat pulleys as objects that use rope and eyelets, inclined planes as tilted surfaces, and screws as a stem with twisted threads. Our folk understanding of the world does not allow us to see the basis of the screw in the inclined plane, as physics experts do (Chi, Glaser, and Rees 1982). Possession of a good theory allows us to classify certain problems as tokens of a type (e.g., problems soluble by energy equations and problems soluble by Newton's laws of motion). But our folk notions of physics have a powerful hold on us. For example, when novices are asked to explain what forces are acting on a flipped coin, they typically identify a diminishing upward force as the coin ascends, no forces (or balanced forces) when the coin reaches its peak, and then increasing downward forces as the coin drops (Clement 1982). These subjects employ a "folk" theory that is quite reminiscent of Aristotelian physics. The flipped coin acquires "impetus," which explains its upward motion; but the impetus is soon sapped by gravity, at which point the coin falls. This way of understanding the problem—as involving two forces, the impetus upward and gravity downward—is so natural that even many who have taken Newtonian mechanics will describe the flipped coin in these terms. But from the perspective of Newtonian mechanics, ignoring air resistance, the only force acting on the coin is gravity, even when the coin is moving upwards. And that force, for all practical purposes, is constant.

Suppose the naïve physicist were to sit down and carefully analyze his concept of impetus. He refines, codifies, and harmonizes his impetus judgments with great care and Austinian attention to linguistic detail. Now he constructs an account that captures, with total accuracy, his application of his concept of impetus. As an attempt to tell us the truth about something other than his own linguistic predilections, lovingly detailing his naïve concept of impetus is a waste of resources. (Actually, we can grant that understanding the notion of impetus as it was employed by ancient and medieval physicists can be of significant value in understanding the history of science.) The attempt to clarify the central concepts of highly successful scientific theories—gene, function, superposition, force—can be of great value. What's interesting and important about these notions, and what draws our attention to them, is that they do (or presume to do) real explanatory, predictive, and practical work in a successful theory about how some aspect of the world works. Providing a careful account of a concept can yield worthwhile results—but only when the concept is embedded in a high-quality theory. And it is here where the challenge to SAE can be put in sharp relief by comparing it to Ameliorative Psychology. Unlike the normative judgments of Ameliorative Psychology, philosophers' considered epistemic judgments have been incubated in happy isolation from what we have learned about how best to reason about significant matters.

As far as we can see, there is only one line of argument for the idea that the theories of SAE are capable of yielding correct epistemic judgments (a priori or not). The proponent of SAE must make a case for a special kind of *expertise* for himself in matters of reasoning and belief. This claim to expertise would presumably depend on the claim that the methods of SAE have allowed philosophers to home in on what knowledge or justification really is. Just as medical doctors spend years studying what disease really is and so end up with an expertise in matters of disease that others lack, philosophers with the appropriate training have an insight into knowledge and justification that others lack. But if proponents of SAE are experts about epistemological matters, then it is reasonable to suppose that they have some kind of documented success. As far as we know, however, SAE does not have a documented track record of success in epistemological matters. (In fact, in the past half-century or so, SAE has not converged on an ever smaller set of plausible theories but has instead spawned brand new theories about the nature of justification [e.g., reliabilism and contextualism]. This suggests that SAE is failing even to approach realizing the limited, descriptive goal of capturing the judgments of philosophers.) Besides the lack of a documented record of success, philosophers are not the only ones who study what's involved in good reasoning. Ameliorative Psychologists can also reasonably claim to have some expertise in what's involved in good and bad reasoning. Further, as we have already noted, these scientists have many documented successes in helping people and social institutions reason better about matters of great importance.

Proponents of SAE have many of the social trappings of expertise. But as far as we can tell, proponents of SAE are experts about a purely descriptive domain: their own epistemological views (and the views of others who have been similarly trained). Unless proponents of SAE can offer some evidence for thinking that they have some kind of expertise that makes their judgments about epistemic matters more worthy of trust than the judgments of East Asians, Ameliorative Psychologists, or plumbers, we just don't see how the proponent of SAE is going to overcome the naturalist challenge.

4. How does Strategic Reliabilism handle the naturalist challenge?

Many readers will quite reasonably point out that we have leveled an extremely difficult challenge to the proponent of SAE. What's more, our view faces the same challenge, and we would not claim to have fully and adequately addressed it. So what do we say about the naturalist challenge? From our perspective, the Aristotelian Principle provides at least part of the motivation for bridging "is" (successful outcomes) and "ought" (how we ought to reason). At least part of the story for why the dictates of Strategic Reliabilism are normatively binding is that following the prescriptions of Strategic Reliabilism will tend over the long run to lead to better outcomes than violating those prescriptions. The appeal to the Aristotelian Principle might strike some, particularly those who are wedded to the methods of analytic philosophy, as mildly disappointing. Surely it would be more dramatic, more fitting, to claim that we have direct access to the normative domain. Surely it would be more profound, indeed more *philosophical*, to aver that we have plunged deep, deep into our own consciousness, engaged in tortured investigations that tested the limits of our will and intellect, and resurfaced to report on the intricate structure of the normative realm. But alas, no. Our access to the normative comes from what we can infer about the regularities in the world that are responsible for the success of certain reasoning strategies. It is indirect and empirical—and so subject to standard skeptical concerns. But our access also relies on the powerful methods of contemporary science. While neither perfect nor unassailable, such methods seem to us to be at least as good as any other on offer, and better than most.

5. The relationship between Strategic Reliabilism and the theories of Standard Analytic Epistemology

As must be clear by now, we do not believe that constructing theories that render judgments of justification on belief tokens is a fruitful endeavor in epistemology. Strategic Reliabilism identifies excellent reasoning strategies, and it does not require that we render a verdict of "justified" or "unjustified" for every belief token produced by a reasoning strategy. In fact, we find the temptation to construct a theory to separate out the "justified" from the "unjustified" oddly Scholastic—designed for a kind of prim conceptual tidiness rather than for useful guidance. Still, given the dominance of Standard Analytic Epistemology, it is reasonable to wonder about its relation to Strategic Reliabilism.

Strategic Reliabilism is not a theory of justification. However, a high-quality theory can often be shown to be preferable to other theories by couching it in its opponents' vocabulary. Strategic Reliabilism recommends reasoning strategies. And reasoning strategies typically produce beliefs. So Strategic Reliabilism recommends beliefs at one remove. In the spirit of comparing our theory to those of SAE, let's consider the following proposal: *The beliefs that result from the reasoning strategies recommended by Strategic Reliabilism are justified.* We take this to be an inessential codicil to our view. It is no objection to our view to show that there is a scenario in which it is the considered judgment of analytic epistemologists that the belief recommended by Strategic Reliabilism is not justified. But the inessential codicil allows us to pose a question: Does Strategic Reliabilism recommend only beliefs that are justified (in whatever sense a proponent of SAE means by 'justified')? One way to put our question is as follows: Suppose God gave the analytic epistemologist the theory of justification (Theory J) that satisfied all his (the epistemologist's) desiderata. Would Theory J and Strategic Reliabilism (plus the codicil) always agree about which beliefs are justified? We will argue that no matter how the question is answered, Strategic Reliabilism is more worthy of belief than any currently available theory of SAE.

There are two ways to answer the question of whether Theory J and Strategic Reliabilism (supplemented with the codicil) would always agree about which beliefs are justified. The first answer is that all beliefs recommended by Strategic Reliabilism are justified according to Theory J. Under this scenario, we don't need the theories of Standard Analytic Epistemology. Strategic Reliabilism provides us with a straightforward theory of justification that accurately divides the justified beliefs from the unjustified beliefs. Suppose two theories of SAE (e.g., a coherentist and a reliabilist theory) disagree about a particular case. If Strategic Reliabilism yields the same judgments as Theory J, then there is an obvious way to break this deadlock: Figure out what Strategic Reliabilism would say is the best reasoning strategy for S to adopt in this particular situation, and the belief that results from that reasoning strategy is the one that is justified. If Strategic Reliabilism is a dependable deadlock breaker, then why do we need the theories of SAE? We don't.

Now let's consider the second answer to our question. Suppose that the beliefs that are the result of the best reasoning strategies (according to Strategic Reliabilism) are not always justified (according to theory J). In this scenario, Strategic Reliabilism will occasionally recommend a belief that theory J does not count as justified. So which belief should we recommend from an epistemological perspective? The belief recommended by Strategic Reliabilism is the result of excellent reasoning on the part of S. Excellent reasoning maximizes S's chances of coming to true beliefs about significant problems. This, in turn, will tend to lead in the long run to better outcomes for S than if she had adopted reasoning strategies of lesser quality. So the belief recommended by Strategic Reliabilism has a lot going for it. What about the belief recommended by SAE? Its main advantage seems to be that it is the belief that is deemed justified by a bunch of really smart philosophers who have reflected seriously on their notion of justification. Perhaps this description of the choice is unfair; perhaps this belief would be deemed justified by a much wider range of people than just really smart philosophers. Maybe it would be deemed justified by every person capable of wielding the concept. Even so, which belief is the one that deserves to be recommended from an epistemological perspective? Surely it is the belief that comes with all the practically important empirical advantages of epistemic goodness and of epistemic success.

Strategic Reliabilism plus the codicil presents the proponent of Standard Analytic Epistemology with a dilemma. Either Strategic Reliabilism recommends only justified beliefs or it does not. If it does recommend only justified beliefs, then there is no need for any other theory of justification.

Strategic Reliabilism will do. If it does not recommend only justified beliefs, then so much the worse for justification. The excellent reasoner—the person, who adopts robustly reliable strategies for problems of significance—will sometimes adopt beliefs that the proponent of SAE deems unjustified. So what would the proponent of SAE have her do? Adopt less reliable reasoning strategies or tackle less significant problems or both? If this is the sort of advice the proponent of SAE intends to offer, then perhaps we need to recognize that the orthodox concept of justification, no matter how gilded by philosophical theory, is a crude and insensitive instrument of evaluation. In the subtle causal nexus of mind and world, no good comes from wielding such a notion like a mace. Those devoted to offering a psychologically accurate picture of reasoning strategies and the useful information they provide are likely to find such "justification talk" quaint, were it not for the resources squandered by its primping.

8

Putting Epistemology into Practice: Normative Disputes in Psychology

In previous chapters, we have introduced a number of experimental findings that purport to demonstrate deep and systematic failures of human reasoning. These findings include base rate neglect, covariation illusions, the overconfidence bias, the hindsight bias, and the self-serving bias (e.g., the Lake Wobegon Effect). These findings are associated with the heuristics and biases (HB) program, championed in the ground-breaking work of Kahneman and Tversky, and influential in nearly every area of cognitive and social psychology, as well as in affiliated disciplines (Gilovich, Griffin, and Kahneman 2002). Other examples of biases found by proponents of the HB program include regression neglect, the conjunction fallacy, and the fundamental attribution error (Nisbett and Ross 1980). Unlike Ameliorative Psychology, the HB program has received a good deal of attention from philosophers (e.g., Cohen 1981, Stich 1985, 1990, Kornblith 1992, Stein 1996, Pollock and Cruz 1999).

Why do proponents of the HB program focus on people's systematic reasoning errors? Kahneman and Tversky offer three reasons:

First, they expose some of our intellectual limitations and suggest ways of improving the quality of our thinking. Second, errors and biases often reveal the psychological processes and the heuristic procedures that govern judgment and inference. Third, mistakes and fallacies help the mapping of human intuitions by indicating which principles of statistics or logic are non-intuitive or counter-intuitive. (Kahneman and Tversky 1982, 494)

While Kahneman and Tversky are reasonably cautious in their overall assessment of human reasoning, others have drawn fairly harsh pessimistic conclusions. In an oft-quoted passage, Nisbett and Borgida (1975, 935) claim that the reasoning errors uncovered by the HB program have "bleak implications" for human rationality (see also Piattelli-Palmarini 1994). These pessimistic conclusions have been repeatedly challenged (see, e.g., Cohen 1981, Lopes 1991, Gigerenzer 1991, 1996).

One line of attack against the "bleak implications" view of human rationality is to argue that it is not the subjects who are making the mistakes in solving the HB problem-tasks, it is the psychologists. Our goal in this chapter is to consider a number of these reject-the-norm arguments (Stein 1996, 239). A reject-the-norm argument purports to show that the proponents of the HB program are applying the wrong inference rules, and so the wrong norms, to the problem-tasks. As a result, people's performance on the HB problems is not evidence of any kind of irrationality or poor reasoning among lay reasoners (Stein 1996, 239–42).

Philosophers and psychologists who adopt the reject-the-norm strategy have offered a number of different arguments for their conclusion. We will not canvass all of these arguments here. Instead, we will focus only on two instances of what we will call *conceptual* reject-the-norm arguments. The premises of such arguments do not depend on any empirical facts about reasoners or their situations. Consider a subject who has neglected the base rate and so has reasoned poorly, according to proponents of the HB program. One might argue that the subject has understood the problem differently than was intended by the psychologists; and given that understanding, her answer was not an error. This is an empirical reject-the-norm argument, since it depends essentially on how subjects as a matter of fact understand the problem. Kahneman and Tversky have recognized the legitimacy of this kind of empirical reject-the-norm argument.

[N]ot every response that appears to contradict an established fact or an accepted rule is a judgmental error. The contradiction could also arise from the subject's misunderstanding of the question or from the investigator's misinterpretation of the answer. The description of a particular response as an error of judgment therefore involves assumptions about the communication between the experimenter and the subject.... The student of judgment should avoid overly strict interpretations, which treat reasonable answers as errors, as well as overly charitable interpretations, which attempt to rationalize every response. (Kahneman and Tversky 1982, 493–94)

Since we have nothing particularly new to add to the empirical findings of research on judgment and decision making, we will avoid discussion of empirical reject-the-norm arguments. Our focus will be on those reject-the-norm arguments that purport to derive normative results about reasoners tackling the HB problems without attending to the details of how they're actually reasoning.

1. Conceptual reject-the-norm arguments

Conceptual reject-the-norm arguments cast a very wide net by appealing to abstract, conceptual considerations to show that subjects are not reasoning poorly about a large set of problems. It must be clear to the reader where we come down on conceptual reject-the-norm arguments. According to Strategic Reliabilism, the relative quality of a reasoning strategy is a function of its expected costs and benefits *as well as those of its competitors.* It is an empirical question which of two reasoning strategies has a better cost-benefit ratio for a particular reasoner. So Strategic Reliabilism is committed to the view that optimism about our cognitive abilities must be held, if at all, for empirical reasons. From the perspective of Strategic Reliabilism, when the optimist assesses someone's reasoning, he must present *evidence* that these individuals have availed themselves of the best strategies.

We will focus on two conceptual reject-the-norm arguments that have received considerable attention, one from a philosopher, another from a psychologist. Perhaps the most famous (or infamous) conceptual reject-the-norm argument was put forward by the philosopher L. J. Cohen. He argued that it is impossible to empirically demonstrate human irrationality (1981). More recently, Gerd Gigerenzer has proposed an argument that is meant to show that subjects' answers to many of the HB problem-tasks are not really errors. Neither of these arguments focuses on how a reasoner interprets or approaches or even answers a particular problem; nor do they attend to the consequences of their reasoning. Gigerenzer and Cohen both attempt to commit us to a conception of rationality—or at any rate a conception of cognitive permission or approval—that precedes evidence. This strategy may satisfy a certain taste for a priori standards of rationality, but it also provides reasoning advice that can lead to relatively inferior outcomes. We would warn that when epistemologists consistently attribute positive normative status to reasoning strategies that predictably and robustly lead to inferior outcomes, the Aristotelian Principle suggests that something has gone deeply wrong.

The considerations raised by the conceptual reject-the-norm arguments tend to be highly abstract. So it will be useful to keep our discussion grounded in an example. We will focus on base rate neglect (since this is an example both Cohen and Gigerenzer discuss in their work). Base rate neglect typically occurs when people are trying to infer from symptoms to causes. John fails an exam, so he must not have studied; Julie tests positive for drugs, so she must take drugs; Kareem has a cough and a fever, so he must have the flu. How reliable are these conclusions? The standard way to approach such problems is to invoke Bayes' Rule:

$$P(C/S) = P(S/C) \times P(C) / \left[[P(S/C) \times P(C)] + [P(S/-C) \times P(-C)] \right]$$

where C is the alleged cause (not studying, taking drugs, having the flu) and S is the symptom or effect (failing the exam, failing the drug test, having a cough and a fever). (Note that Bayes' Rule may be applied even if there is no causal connection between C and S.) The probability of C given S depends essentially on the base rates—on the prior probability of C and so the prior probability of −C. And yet in a very wide array of situations, even very sophisticated subjects ignore base rates. Consider an example presented to sixty students and staff at Harvard Medical School (Casscells, Schoenberger, Grayboys 1978):

> If a test to detect a disease whose prevalence is 1/1,000 has a false positive rate of 5%, what is the chance that a person found to have a positive result actually has the disease, assuming you know nothing about the person's symptoms or signs?

Casscells et al. did not describe the diagnosis problem fully enough for someone to properly solve it without making some important assumptions. In particular, one must assume something about the test's sensitivity (i.e., the probability that a person would test positive given that she had the disease). Casscells et al. assumed that the test's sensitivity is about 100%. Given this assumption, Bayes' Rule yields the result that the probability that the subject has the disease given the positive result is about 2%. Among the faculty and staff at Harvard, almost half judged the probability to be 95%; the mean answer was 56%; and only 18% of subjects responded with the answer given by Bayes' Rule. (Despite problems with the Casscells et al. study, their finding has been replicated in studies that include all the necessary information [Gigerenzer 1996a; Gigerenzer and Hoffrage 1995].)

A reject-the-norm argument will conclude that subjects who do not give the Bayesian answer to this problem have not violated any epistemological norms. Their reasoning was neither flawed nor irrational, and their answers were not errors. Conceptual versions of the reject-the-norm argument do not depend on contingent, empirical facts about the reasoners. Let's turn first to Gigerenzer's argument.

2. Gigerenzer's conceptual reject-the-norm argument

Gerd Gigerenzer begins his conceptual reject-the-norm argument by noting that there are a number of different *interpretations* of the standard axioms of probability (1996). He then argues that on a frequentist interpretation of probability, subjects' answers to many of the HB problem-tasks are not errors. The frequency interpretation of probability states that the probability of an attribute A is the relative frequency with which A occurs in an unlimited sequence of events. So when subjects are given a problem-task that involves assigning a probability to a single event (e.g., the probability that this patient has a disease), Gigerenzer argues that from a frequentist perspective, such probability statements are meaningless. So far so good.

At this point, one might suppose that Gigerenzer's argument is going to turn empirical. After all, everyone admits that it is an interesting and important question how these subjects represent the problem to themselves. But Gigerenzer never attempts to argue that experimental subjects are in fact consistently interpreting probability statements in a frequentist way. This is ironic because when it comes to another HB problem-task, Hertwig and Gigerenzer (1999) argue that in evaluating subjects, it is essential to know how they are understanding the problem. (To be fair, Gigerenzer often argues that "the mind is a frequentist." But by this he seems to mean that our minds are set up to solve problems framed in terms of frequencies and not probabilities [e.g., Gigerenzer 1991]. Gigerenzer does not argue that subjects interpret probability statements in a frequentist way; for example, he does not offer any evidence for thinking that subjects take single-event probability statements to be meaningless.)

Putting aside worries about how subjects understand single-event probabilities, it is worth exploring the normative assumptions behind Gigerenzer's frequentist arguments. As far as we know, Gigerenzer has not spelled his epistemological presuppositions in any detail. So it might be useful to look at what he has to say about the single-event probability problems. After introducing frequentist and subjectivist views of probability, Gigerenzer argues:

> I will stop here and summarize the normative issue. A discrepancy between confidence in single events and relative frequencies in the long run is not an *error* or a *violation of probability theory* from many experts' points of view. (Gigerenzer 1991, 88–9, emphasis added)

In discussing the well-known Linda problem, where a significant percentage of subjects deem the probability of a conjunction to be higher than the probability of one of the conjuncts, Gigerenzer argues:

> For a frequentist, this problem has nothing to do with probability theory. Subjects are asked for the probability of a *single event* (that Linda is a bank teller), not for frequencies. . . .
>
> To summarize the normative issue, what is called the "conjunction fallacy" is a violation of some subjective theories of probability, including Bayesian theory. It is not, however, a violation of the major view of probability, the frequentist conception. (Gigerenzer 1991, 92)

In discussing base rate neglect, Gigerenzer's line is the same. Given certain conceptions of probability, subjects' answers are not a violation of probability theory, and so not an error.

> [S]ubjects were asked for the probability of a *single event*, that is, that "a person found to have a positive result actually has the disease." If the mind is an intuitive statistician of the frequentist school, such a question has no necessary connection to probability theory. (Gigerenzer 1991, 93)

So how does Gigerenzer handle base rate neglect? He notes that subjects are asked for a single-event probability: Does a particular patient have a disease? On a frequentist view of probability, it makes no sense to assign probabilities to single events, so this question is meaningless. For a frequentist, therefore, this problem is akin to the problem of deciding whether to wear blue socks or red socks—probability doesn't give us an answer. No matter how the subject responds, that response is not a violation of probability. As a result, subjects' answers are not errors in the sense that they are not violations of probability. But keep in mind, Gigerenzer does not try to make the case that subjects are understanding the problems in any particular way. The reason subjects' answers are not errors is that there is some interpretation of probability on which subjects' answers are not a violation of the axioms of probability. In order for Gigerenzer's frequentist argument to work, he must be assuming something like the following:

> *Gigerenzer's Normative Assumption:* If there are a number of different "legitimate" ways to solve a problem and a subject's answer is not an error on at least one of those ways of solving the problem, then regardless of how the subject understands the problem, the subject's answer is not an error.

Putting aside obvious worries about this formulation (including what counts as a "letigimate" solution to a problem), we can grant that Gigerenzer's frequentist argument shows that HB problems that ask subjects to assign probabilities to single events cannot *in some sense* make "errors." And we can perfectly well spell out the sense of "error" that is meant: Subjects' answers are not violations of probability given some particular conception (or conceptions) of probability. Rather than repeat this mouthful every time we want to talk about this particular sort of error, let's say that Gigerenzer's frequentist argument shows that for certain HB problems, those that ask subjects to assign probabilities to single events, subjects cannot make G-errors (or Gigerenzer-errors).

Granting that subjects don't make G-errors leaves the most important normative issues untouched. When someone neglects base rates and reasons on the basis of a diagnostic test to the conclusion that he very likely has cancer, there are lots of errors he hasn't made. He hasn't made a G-error or violated the laws of logic; he isn't guilty of a spelling or a grammatical mistake; he hasn't made a mistake by unwittingly engaging in activity that is criminal or immoral; he hasn't violated the rules of chess or made a stupid move by failing to protect his queen; and he has not made any errors of geometry or calculus. There is a galaxy of errors he hasn't made. But it doesn't follow that he has reasoned well; nor does it follow that he hasn't made some other sort of error. Gigerenzer's frequentist argument leaves open the possibility that Gigerenzer will win the battle but lose the war. That is, it is open to us to grant him the conclusion that subjects don't make G-errors but still argue that they reason poorly and make significant errors.

To be fair, Gigerenzer is responding to a tradition that holds that subjects are making errors because they suffer from "probability blindness" (Piattelli-Palmarini 1994, 130–32). Piattelli-Palmarini suggests the following "probabilistic law: Any probabilistic intuition by anyone not specifically tutored in probability calculus has a greater than 50 percent chance of being wrong" (1994, 132). Here is perhaps the clearest articulation from

Kahneman and Tversky of what makes a subject's answer an error: "The presence of an error of judgment is demonstrated by comparing people's responses either with an established fact . . . or with an accepted rule of arithmetic, logic, or statistics" (1982, 493). Given these views about what counts as an error, it is natural that Gigerenzer should have focused on G-errors: on whether there is some interpretation such that subjects' answers do not violate the laws of probability. But if philosophers have any useful role to play in Ameliorative Psychology, it is to critically evaluate the epistemological assumptions underlying disputes about normative matters. In this case, we suggest that these assumptions be jettisoned.

This normative debate about whether to count subjects' answers as errors culminated in a somewhat heated exchange (Kahneman and Tversky 1996; Gigerenzer 1996). From our perspective, however, this debate takes place within unnaturally narrow normative constraints. The parties to the debate take the main issue to be whether subjects have violated the laws of probability. Gigerenzer thinks that the mind is a frequentist, and given a frequentist interpretation of probability, subjects often do not violate the laws of probability (1991, 1996). Kahneman and Tversky argue that given how subjects understand the problems (i.e., they don't deem single-event probability statements meaningless), subjects do violate the laws of probability (1996). While there are any number of moves each side to this debate can make, we will proceed by breaking free of the debate's narrow normative confines. This is a strategic decision. It is not based on the assumption that this debate cannot proceed productively within its narrow normative limits. Instead, our strategy depends on realizing that the issue we're most interested in is the quality of subjects' reasoning; and that is an issue we can address with Strategic Reliabilism. In other words, Strategic Reliabilism provides us a framework for thinking about relative reasoning excellence, which is typically what we're most concerned about when assessing a subject's reasoning; and this framework will often allow us to resolve disagreements about how to evaluate a particular episode of reasoning. In some cases, when a normative disagreement has become stuck on an issue other than the relative excellence of a subject's reasoning, Strategic Reliabilism can help us to break the stalemate. We bypass the narrow issue on which we are stuck and focus on what we take to be the main issue: How well are subjects reasoning?

The fundamental problem with Gigerenzer's frequentist argument is that people can make extraordinarily serious errors of reasoning that wouldn't count as G-errors. For example, when a man tests positive for prostate cancer, he wants to know whether he has prostate cancer. In order to make decisions, he might want to ask: Given the positive result, what are the chances that I actually have prostate cancer? In such a situation, it is hard to imagine anyone seriously pointing out that frequentists would deem this a meaningless question—or worse yet, explaining to the patient that he is a frequentist, and so his own question can have no meaning for him. If a doctor tells his patient that he has a 99% chance of having cancer, the patient is surely going to have some sort of understanding of what is being said. (It is unlikely, for example, that he will react with glee.) And that understanding will play a role in what might well be life-or-death decisions. When medical practitioners make diagnoses and ignore base rates, people who are highly vulnerable will end up acting on misleading information. And those actions will too often lead to horrible results—to tragically mistaken decisions to treat or not treat a condition or to deep psychological trauma. And no amount of philosophical pussyfooting can change that. How are we to understand what sort of error the subject makes and why his reasoning is less than excellent? We will discuss the answer provided by Strategic Reliabilism in chapter 9. Our discussion will make clear the irony of our critique of Gigerenzer's conceptual reject-the-norm argument: Gigerenzer perfectly well understands and accepts our central contention—that base rate neglect involves poor reasoning and some kind of error, even if it is not a G-error.

3. Cohen's conceptual reject-the-norm argument

Perhaps the best known response from a philosopher to the HB program is L. J. Cohen's article "Can human irrationality be experimentally demonstrated?" (1981). Cohen's thesis is that it is *impossible* for empirical evidence to show that normal, adult humans are irrational. Although Cohen's article is more than two decades old, it still reflects the views of at least some analytic philosophers. For example, Pollock and Cruz briefly discuss the HB literature and state that their reading "is pretty much the same as the assessment of the irrationality literature offered by Jonathan Cohen" (1999, 130 n. 110).

Cohen begins by asking two questions: What would a normative theory that describes how we ought to reason look like? And what would a descriptive theory that describes our reasoning competence look like? Cohen's strategy is to argue that these theories would be identical: *A theory of our reasoning competence just is a theory of how we ought to reason.* Cohen puts the point bluntly. "[O]rdinary human reasoning—by which I mean the reasoning of adults who have not been systematically educated in any branch of logic or probability theory—cannot be held to be faultily programmed: it sets its own standards" (1981, 317). Cohen does not suggest that normal human adults never reason poorly. But his explanation of reasoning failures depends essentially on a performance-competence distinction. A normal adult's reasoning flaws are performance errors; her reasoning competence is flawless—and necessarily so.

Cohen's performance-competence distinction is familiar from linguistics. The idea in linguistics is that we possess a cognitive system that stores a rich body of grammatical information. A central goal of linguistics is to infer linguistic rules from intuitions that cognitive system produces. So linguists build theories of grammar. Such a theory for English would accurately capture the grammatical competence of speakers of English. In order to find out about this competence, we investigate the grammatical judgments of English speakers (e.g., judgments about whether particular sentences are grammatical). In order to make such judgments, speakers must employ not only their grammatical competence, but also various ancillary cognitive systems, such as memory, attention, and perception. As a result, some judgments of a speaker might fail to reflect her underlying grammatical competence because of the failure of one of these ancillary systems. These are performance errors. Because of performance errors, the linguist is likely to be faced with a situation in which she cannot construct a theory because her data—speakers' judgments—are messy or inconsistent. As a result, the linguist must construct an idealized grammar for the language. For Cohen, much of this story can be applied directly to the theory of reasoning competence: We possess a cognitive system that represents our reasoning competence. A descriptive theory of reasoning competence will describe the rules of reasoning that make up our reasoning competence. The data for such a theory will consist of subjects' intuitions about particular reasoning problems. For Cohen, "an intuition that p is...an immediate and untutored inclination, without evidence or inference, to judge that p" (1981, 318). Such intuitions might not reflect a subject's reasoning competence, however, because of the potential for performance errors. As a result, subjects' intuitions might well be messy or inconsistent. So the theorist must construct an idealized theory of reasoning competence.

What about a normative theory of how we ought to reason? Here again, we start with subjects' intuitions about particular reasoning problems:

> In order to discover what criteria of probability are appropriate for the evaluation of lay reasoning we have to investigate what judgments of probability are intuitively acceptable to lay adults and what rational constraints these judgments are supposed to place on one another. (1981, 319)

Because of the possibility of performance errors, some amount of idealization will be necessary in constructing a normative theory. According to Cohen, we achieve an idealized normative theory through a process of narrow reflective equilibrium: a coherent reconstruction of the subject's reasoning principles. Nelson Goodman describes this process as follows:

> [R]ules and particular inferences alike are justified by being brought into agreement with each other. A rule is amended if it yields an inference we are unwilling to accept; an inference is rejected if it violates a rule we are unwilling to amend. The process of justification is the delicate one of making mutual adjustments between rules and accepted inferences; and in the agreement achieved lies the only justification needed for either. (1965, 67)

An implication of Cohen's view is that "Nothing can count as an error of reasoning among our fellow adults unless even the author of the error would, under ideal conditions, agree that it is an error" (1981, 322). So it is not possible to empirically demonstrate that people are incompetent reasoners, and the reason is that it is impossible for people to be incompetent reasoners (i.e., it is impossible for people's reasoning competence to be defective). When we make mistakes, it is due to contingent barriers like pesky distractions or memory failures that hamper our (in principle) flawless execution.

Cohen believes that the primary data for our normative theory are subjects' intuitions—their immediate, untutored inclinations—about reasoning problems. What justifies this premise? Cohen seems to suggest that this is the only possibility unless one invokes the standards of a Higher Power.

> [I]f you claim no special revelation in matters of logic or probability, you will have to be content there too to accept the inherent rationality of your fellow adults. (1981, 321)

> One may be tempted to ask: "how do we know that any intuition of the relevant kind is veridical?" . . . The best that normative theorists can hope for in this field (and also what they need to achieve), if they do not claim any special revelation, is that the contents of all relevant intuitions—suitably sifted or qualified, if necessary—can be made to corroborate one another by

being exhibited as the consequences of a consistent and relatively simple set of rules or axioms that also sanctions other intuitively acceptable, but previously unremarked, patterns of reasoning. (1981, 322)

Keep in mind, however, that for Cohen, intuitions are immediate and untutored inclinations to judge, derived without evidence or inference. There are surely many other possibilities, even if one is inclined to construct a normative theory on the basis of the judgments of reasoners. For example, one might construct a normative theory on the basis of people's well-considered judgments (as opposed to their immediate judgments). Cohen, however, rejects such possibilities by insisting that "[t]he judgments of everyday reasoning must be evaluated in their own terms and by their own standards" (1981, 320).

What does Cohen say about base rate neglect? He argues that, at best, this is an example of subjects being ignorant of a mathematical truth. However, he rejects even this possibility by offering a number of arguments to the effect that "it is doubtful whether the subjects have made any kind of mathematical error at all" (1981, 328). Here is one of Cohen's arguments:

> You are suffering from a disease that, according to your manifest symptoms, is either A or B. For a variety of demographic reasons disease A happens to be nineteen times as common as B. The two diseases are equally fatal if untreated, but it is dangerous to combine the respectively appropriate treatments. Your physician orders a certain test which, through the operation of a fairly well understood causal process, always gives a unique diagnosis in such cases, and this diagnosis has been tried out on equal numbers of A- and B-patients and is known to be correct on 80% of those occasions. The tests report that you are suffering from disease B.

Let's pause here to consider how someone might reason who was not neglecting base rates: For every hundred patients who have either A or B in this population, on average five will have B and 95 will have A. Of those who test positive for B, four will have B (80% of 5) and 19 will have A (20% of 95). So for the 23 who test positive for B, 4 actually have B. Now back to Cohen:

> Should you nevertheless opt for the treatment appropriate to A, on the supposition... that the probability of your suffering from A is 19/23? Or should you opt for the treatment appropriate to B, on the supposition... that the probability of your suffering from B is 4/5? It is the former option that would be the irrational one for you, qua patient, not the latter.... Indeed, on the other view, which is the one espoused in the

literature, it would be a waste of time and money even to carry out the tests, since whatever their results, the base rates would still compel a more than 4/5 probability in favour of disease A. So the literature under criticism is propagating an analysis that could increase the number of deaths from a rare disease of this kind. (1981, 329)

This is a stunning line of argument. (As is Cohen's defense of the gambler's fallacy [1981, 327–28].) While Cohen is right that the literature he is criticizing defends a position that would lead to a greater number of deaths from (rare) disease B, he recognizes that his own position would lead to a greater number of total deaths—indeed, four times as many—from both diseases A and B. Out of 100 people, Cohen's strategy can be expected to lead to 20 deaths (1 person dies from B, 19 die from A), while the other strategy can be expected to lead to 5 deaths (all of those with disease B). Cohen grants that "[t]he administrator who wants to secure a high rate of diagnostic success for his hospital at minimal cost would be right to seek to maximize just that probability, and therefore to dispense altogether with the tests." Note also that Cohen admits that in order not to violate Bayes' Rule, the subject must ignore the given base rate and "suppose equal predispositions" (1981, 329).

Cohen suggests that base rate neglect is superior to a Bayesian reasoning strategy because, although base rate neglect will lead to more overall deaths, it will lead to fewer deaths from a rare disease. This is a real head-scratcher. Philosophers and their loved ones, after all, get sick too. If you have the same symptoms as 200 other people and there are two treatments, one with a survival rate of 95% and the other with a survival rate of 80%, Cohen's argument implies that the rational person will choose the treatment with the lower survival rate. If that's what rationality dictates, we don't want it. Cohen's optimism is the result of an a priori attachment that exacts a heavy price so that we may save cognitive face. But then any conceptual reject-the-norm argument is by its very nature deeply antithetical to the scientific spirit that animates not just Ameliorative Psychology but all inquiry about the natural world.

Like with Gigerenzer's conceptual reject-the-norm argument, Cohen is defending a rather eccentric normative category. Cohen's conception of what it is to be "rational" is distinctly Protagorean—"man is the measure of all things." But subjects who neglect the base rate might well be "rational" in a Protagorean sense and yet reason extraordinarily badly. In fact, in chapter 9, we will argue that most subjects who neglect base rates are reasoning badly. To see this intuitively, consider someone whose behavior makes him a very low risk for HIV, who takes a very reliable HIV test, and who tests positive. What is an AIDS counselor supposed to tell this patient? Should the counselor ignore the fact that the subject is low risk and advise him that there is a 99% chance he has HIV? Or should the counselor take that fact into account and tell the subject that the chances are more like 50-50? How to reason about this situation has literally life-and-death consequences: "Former Senator Lawton Chiles of Florida reported at an AIDS conference in 1987 that of 22 blood donors in Florida who were notified that they tested HIV-positive with the ELISA test, seven committed suicide. In the same medical text that reported this tragedy, the reader is informed that 'even if the results of both AIDS tests, the ELISA and WB (Western blot), are positive, the chances are only 50-50 that the individual is infected' (Stine, 1996, 333, 338)" (Gigerenzer, Hoffrage, and Ebert 1998). Now consider the AIDS counselor who ignores the base rate and tells his clients that they have a 99% chance of having HIV, when in fact only about 50% of his clients who test positive have HIV. Ignoring the base rate in this situation may well be "rational" in Cohen's sense. But it would be lousy reasoning—the sort of reasoning that would quite properly haunt one the rest of one's days.

Cohen is surely right to suggest that there is some sort of a distinction between our performance and the cognitive capacities that make it possible. But it is not the distinction seen in linguistics. It is the distinction familiar from any activity that requires skill and dedication. People who have the competence to sing Weber's desperate aria "Wo berg ich mich" might on occasion perform it badly, but even at our best, most of us really can't perform it at all. In this case, no one is inclined to suppose that everyone's capacities are similar or that everyone's contingent collection of capacities *just is* the measure of excellence. Some people sing better than others. Further, everyone recognizes that there are differences in people's native mathematical and logical abilities. And both of these are crucial to reasoning competence. So surely it is not too much of a stretch to suppose that some people reason better than others. But Cohen denies that different normal adults might have different reasoning competences; he insists that any apparently different intuitions about particular reasoning problems must always be resolvable.

> No doubt two different people, or the same people on two different occasions, may sometimes have apparently conflicting intuitions. But such an apparent conflict always demands resolution. The people involved might come to recognize some tacit misunderstanding about the terms of the problem, so

that there is no real conflict; or they might repudiate a previously robust intuition, perhaps as a result of becoming aware that an otherwise preferred solution has unacceptable implications; or they might conclude that different idiolects or conceptions of deducibility are at issue. (1981, 319)

This is an empirical speculation, and we will now turn to some fascinating evidence that suggests that it is false.

4. Evidence for irresolvable differences in how people reason about certain problems

In *Who is Rational* (1999), Keith Stanovich sets as his goal to investigate individual differences across the various HB tasks (as well as other cognitive tasks). He argues that many views about the HB tradition have focused too much on subjects' modal (average) response patterns to the tasks. As a result, debates about how to properly reason about the tasks are too often framed in terms of who is wrong—the subjects or the psychologists (i.e., the proponents of the HB program). That is precisely how Cohen understands the debate. (But this is not true of Gigerenzer's frequentist argument. According to that argument, for tasks asking for single-event probabilities, no answer is an error. No psychologists or subjects are making an error.) The problem with framing the debate in terms of whether the psychologists or the subjects are wrong is that some subjects give the response that the psychologists think is the right one. "Thus, the issue is not the untutored average person versus experts..., but experts plus some laypersons versus other untutored individuals" (61).

There are a number of studies that show that there is considerable correlation in subjects' scores on different reasoning tasks associated with the HB tradition. In other words, subjects who did well on one reasoning task tended to do well on other tasks. For example, Stanovich and West (1998) gave subjects four reasoning tasks: syllogistic reasoning, the selection task, statistical reasoning tasks (pallid statistics vs. vivid single examples), and argument evaluation (informal reasoning). They found that "five of the six correlations between these four tasks were significant at the .001 level" (Stanovich 1999, 36). Further, Stanovich and West found that SAT scores correlate significantly with all four rational thinking tasks. Interestingly enough, however, for most of the tasks, the subjects who agreed with the psychologists did not (on average) have more math education (Stanovich 1999, 40–2).

Another series of studies that might be relevant to properly understanding the HB literature suggests that when subjects are forced to
articulate justifications for their answers (or otherwise are made account-
able), fewer subjects offer the answer considered wrong by the proponents
of the heuristics and biases tradition (Miller and Fagley 1991, Sieck
and Yates 1997, Takemura 1992, 1993, 1994). On the HB view, this makes
sense—forced to provide a justification, more people get the right answer.
Cohen, and anyone who claims that subjects' modal answers are correct,
seems forced to claim the opposite—forced to provide a justification,
more people get the wrong answer.

Stanovich reports on a series of studies in which subjects are offered
arguments for and against a particular solution to a task (Stanovich 1999,
81–3). Consider an example of base rate neglect. Subjects were asked to
judge whether the base rate of a fictitious disease (Digirosa) is relevant to
the issue of whether a subject with a red rash has the disease. As expected,
most subjects did not deem the base rates to be relevant. Subjects were
then asked to evaluate one or both of the following arguments.

> The percentage of people with Digirosa is needed to determine the prob-
> ability because, if Digirosa is very infrequent in the population and some
> people without Digirosa also have red rashes, then the probability of
> Digirosa might still be low even if the person has a red rash.

> The percentage of people with Digirosa is irrelevant because this particular
> patient has a red rash, and thus the percentage of people who have Digirosa
> is not needed when trying to determine the probability that someone has
> Digirosa given that they have a red rash.

The question was: How many subjects would change their mind after being
given one (or both) of these arguments? After being given the argument for
attending to base rates, subjects more often changed their mind in the
"correct" (according to the HB program) direction, and this was a statistically significant difference (39% of those who originally took base rates to
be irrelevant changed their minds after reading the first argument and took
base rates to be relevant, while 15% of those who originally took base rates
to be relevant changed their minds after reading the first argument and
took base rates to be irrelevant). After being given the argument for
neglecting base rates, subjects more often changed their minds in the
"incorrect" direction, but this difference was not statistically significant
(15.7% vs 30.8%). After being given both arguments, subjects more often
changed their minds in the "correct" direction, and this was a statistically
significant difference (27.2% vs. 11.1%) (Stanovich 1999, 81–3).

There are three general facts about the studies Stanovich cites that raise problems for Cohen's reject-the-norm argument (and for any reject-the-norm argument that takes subjects' modal answers to be correct). The first is that subjects who tend to reason "correctly" on one problem also tend to reason "correctly" on other problems ("correctly" from the perspective of the proponents of the HB program). The second fact is that many subjects' responses to these tasks are quite malleable:

> Collapsed across all of the problems in this chapter that were tested with the argument evaluation procedure, when presented with an argument on each side of the question, an average of 22.1% altered their responses on a re-administration of the task. When presented with a single normative argument, 42.5% of the non-normative subjects switched to the normative response on a readministration of the task. Note that, in the procedure used, subjects were not told that the argument was correct. They were simply told to evaluate the argument, and were free to rate it as very weak.... Nevertheless, fully 25.4% of the non-normative subjects shifted after seeing one conflicting argument along with a compatible one. (Stanovich 1999, 95–6)

And the third fact is the mirror image of this one—lots of people don't change their minds on these problems. In fact, most people did not change their minds even in the face of arguments against their view (including some quite powerful arguments). What this suggests is that it is quite likely that subjects will have irreducible disagreements on some of these problems. (We mean that a significant percentage of subjects who aren't explicitly trained to solve these problems a certain way will adopt quite different solutions.)

If the irreducible disagreement hypothesis is true, what this means is that Cohen (and anyone who takes subjects' modal answers to be correct) will be pushed toward an uncomfortable dilemma. Cohen can insist on one set of norms—either his or those of the HB program. If he accepts the norms of the HB program, then he has totally abdicated his position. If he insists on his own (anti-HB) norms, then he ends up having to argue for more than he bargained for. It's not just that the psychologists are wrong; it's that the psychologists and lots of subjects are wrong. But this is not a particularly comfortable position to take. Recall that the subjects who reason according to the anti-HB norms also tend to do worse on various cognitive and aptitude tests. While it is not clear what these tests actually test *for*, they are correlated with academic success. So if given a choice between reasoning norms that tend to be followed by better students and reasoning norms that tend to be followed by worse students, it would be prima facie odd to insist upon the latter. In order to avoid abdication (by embracing the HB norms) or embarrassment (by embracing the anti-HB norms), an obvious move is to not insist on just one set of norms. The proponent of the Cohen-type reject-the-norm strategy might insist that different norms are right for different reasoners. In this way, Cohen-style reject-the-norm strategies seem drawn to some kind of "anything goes" epistemic relativism. But this won't work. Cohen *can't* be a relativist. After all, he argues that the proponents of the HB program are insisting upon the *wrong reasoning rule* in assessing the reasoning of their subjects. This is not consistent with relativism. So those, like Cohen, who advance a conceptual reject-the-norm argument to defend the view that subjects' modal answers are correct, are stuck with the abdication-or-embarrassment dilemma.

5. Conclusion

According to Strategic Reliabilism, the quality of a reasoning strategy is a function of its expected costs and benefits *as well as those of its competitors*. But which of two reasoning strategies has a better cost-benefit ratio for a particular reasoner is an empirical question. From the perspective of Strategic Reliabilism, when one assesses positively someone's reasoning, he must present *evidence* that these individuals have availed themselves of the best strategies of which they are cognitively capable. Of course, conceptual reject-the-norm arguments don't do this. They conclude that proponents of the HB program are mistaken in their negative evaluations of their subjects' reasoning (or of the reasoning that leads to the modal answer given by subjects). But these arguments do not appeal to the contingent, empirical factors that are relevant to the proper assessment of the quality of a reasoning strategy. Therefore, conceptual reject-the-norm arguments are incapable of making the case that our actual reasoning strategies are epistemically excellent.

It's useful to note that *any* argument—whether purely conceptual or not—that aims to show that our actual reasoning strategies are epistemically excellent is doomed. There are two reasons for this. First, the conclusion is known to be false. Ameliorative Psychology offers us a number of reasoning strategies that are superior to the ones most of us actually use. Second, suppose the conclusion weren't known to be false. Suppose that as far as we know, our actual reasoning strategies are the best available. It would still be extraordinarily unlikely that there aren't better strategies out there, just waiting to be discovered. So an argument can't be sound if it purports to show that when it comes to our reasoning we don't need no stinkin' badgerers.

There is a way for reject-the-norm arguments to avoid these objections. They can change the subject. They can employ or define an epistemic notion such that our actual reasoning strategies are unbeatable according to that notion. We suspect that something like this is going on with the conceptual reject-the-norm arguments of Gigerenzer and Cohen. But as long as these arguments don't touch upon the quality of subjects' reasoning—the focus of Strategic Reliabilism—there is no reason for proponents of the HB program to worry. They can grant that a reject-the-norm argument shows that there is some Pickwickian sense in which subjects are "rational" or not making an "error," and then point out that on this view, one can be "rational" and "error-free" while regularly engaging in atrocious reasoning, reasoning that (among other things) predictably leads to massively suboptimal outcomes. There is, admittedly, an esthetic drawback to taking this line against reject-the-norm arguments: It requires the use of an annoying number of scare quotes. The substantive lesson to draw, however, is that unbridled, a priori optimism about our cognitive capacities inevitably leads to normative evaluations that either are meant to be prescriptive and are in practice absurd or are empty of prescriptive force.

We have argued that two conceptual reject-the-norm arguments fail; and we have also argued that any conceptual reject-the-norm argument must fail. It doesn't follow, however, that every normative assessment made by proponents of the HB program is correct. When it comes to assessing the quality of a particular reasoning strategy, there is no substitute for attending to the costs and benefits of that strategy and its competitors. What does Strategic Reliabilism say about the reasoning strategies that proponents of the HB program claim result in biases (e.g., base rate neglect)? We turn to this issue in the next chapter.

9

Putting Epistemology into Practice: Positive Advice

E pistemology is but a hollow intellectual exercise if it does not ultimately provide a framework that yields useful reasoning advice. Strategic Reliabilism provides a framework for figuring out how one ought to reason about particular problems. The quality of a reasoning strategy is a function of the significance of the problems it addresses, of its robust reliability, and of its costs. Reasoning strategies are better to the extent they are cheaper, are more robustly reliable, and address more significant problems. Our aim in this chapter is to employ the tools of our normative theory as well as various empirical findings to offer some practical advice. While there are some conclusions to be drawn (perhaps sometimes only tentatively), we can only go as far as the empirical data take us. Such is the naturalist's lot. One virtue of our theory is that, when conjoined with empirical evidence, it can yield specific reason-guiding recommendations. But another virtue that is perhaps as important is that our theory can point us to important gaps in our knowledge. It can tell us specifically what empirical evidence is missing if we want to offer reasonable guidance about a reasoning strategy or a range of reasoning problems. In this way, our theory can help direct us to empirical investigations that can effectively lead us to better reasoning and (in the long run) better decisions.

1. Diagnostic Reasoning

In chapter 8, we explored the conceptual reject-the-norm arguments of Cohen and Gigerenzer that held that subjects who neglected base rates were not making an error. Base rate neglect occurs when subjects are trying to come to a conditional probability judgment (e.g., given that a subject tests positive on a drug test, what is the probability he has drugs in his system?). Subjects who neglect the base rate typically take the inverse conditional probability (the probability that the test will be positive given that the subject has drugs in his system) to be the conditional probability they're after. So suppose a subject is told that a test is 80% accurate (i.e., if S is positive, the test will say so 80% of the time; and if S is negative, the test will say so 80% of the time). The subject who suffers from base rate neglect will judge that if someone tests positive (negative) there is an 80% chance that they are positive (negative). But simply because the probability of P given Q is 80%, it doesn't follow that the probability of Q given P is 80%. The probability that S is pregnant given that she has had sex is not the same as the probability that S has had sex given that she is pregnant.

The standard way to solve such problems is with Bayes' Rule: $P(C/S) = P(S/C) \times P(C) / \{[P(S/C) \times P(C)] + [P(S/-C) \times P(-C)]\}$. As a mathematical identity, Bayes' Rule is, of course, true. But a mathematical formula isn't by itself a reasoning strategy. A reasoning strategy is a cognitive representation of a rule we can often characterize in terms of four elements: (a) the *cues* used to make the judgment; (b) the *formula* for combining the cues to make the judgment; (c) the *target* of the judgment (i.e., what it's about); and (d) the *range* of objects (states, properties, processes, etc.), defined by detectable cues, about which the rule makes judgments that are thought to be reliable. So we can characterize a Bayesian reasoning strategy as follows:

1. *Cues*: Conditional Probability of Q given P; Prior Probability of P; Conditional Probability of Q given not-P
2. *Formula*: $P(P/Q) = P(Q/P) \times P(P) / \{[P(Q/P) \times P(P)] + [P(Q/-P) \times P(-P)]\}$
3. *Target*: Conditional Probability of P given Q
4. *Range*: Indefinite

The first three features are self-explanatory, but we should say something about the range of the Bayesian reasoning strategy. It is indefinite, in the same sense that the range of deductive logic is indefinite: As long as the problem facing a reasoner has the right sort of formal structure, it can be about anything.

So far, we have two ways to solve diagnosis problems. We can neglect base rates (which seems to involve confusing a conditional probability with its inverse) or we can apply Bayes' Rule. As we have argued (in chapter 8), neglecting base rates leads to errors on highly significant problems. So we should avoid that reasoning strategy if possible. But there is considerable evidence that subjects don't find it easy to use the Bayesian reasoning strategy. For example, the study by Casscells, Schoenberger, and Grayboys (1978), even though flawed (see our discussion in chapter 8, section 1), suggests that the faculty and staff at Harvard Medical School had a difficult time using Bayes' Rule. This is disturbing. Consider, first, that medical doctors are, as a group, very intelligent; second, they (unlike most people) have been introduced to Bayes' Rule in their studies (at least, we hope they have); third, medical doctors are faced with diagnosis problems all the time; and fourth, these problems are highly significant for medical doctors. They have very weighty moral and prudential reasons to be as accurate as they can be in drawing conclusions about their patients' health on the basis of medical tests. And surely most doctors must know that diagnosis problems are highly significant. When it comes to implementing a reasoning strategy, one would think that these conditions are about as ideal as one can realistically hope for. So if the faculty and staff at Harvard Medical School can't get diagnosis problems right, this suggests there's trouble. Gigerenzer and Hoffrage describe three physicians who dropped out of an experiment in which they were asked to engage in diagnostic reasoning. One university professor "seemed agitated and affronted by the test and refused to give numerical estimates." The professor said, "This is not the way to treat patients. I throw all these journals [with statistical information] away immediately. One can't make a diagnosis on such a basis. Statistical information is one big lie" (Hoffrage and Gigrenzer 2004, 258). We can't help but worry about this doctor's patients. These are people who might have a serious disease and who need to make treatment decisions. Surely, they would benefit from a clear idea of the likelihoods facing them.

From our perspective, these results strongly suggest that the Bayesian reasoning strategy (as represented above) is not particularly tractable for most people. For most people, the start-up costs are high (i.e., it's hard to learn) and the benefits are low (i.e., it's hard to successfully apply to cases given the cognitive resources most of us bring to such problems). It is worthwhile to investigate whether there is some other reasoning strategy that avoids the inaccuracies of base rate neglect and that also avoids the high costs of the Bayesian strategy. Fortunately, Gigerenzer and Hoffrage (1995) have shown how to dramatically improve people's reasoning on diagnosis problems without a lot of complicated statistical training. It turns out that people do much better on these sorts of problems when they are framed in terms of frequencies rather than probabilities. The best way to see this is with an example. Here are two mathematically equivalent formulations of a diagnosis problem:

> Probability format. The probability of breast cancer is 1% for women at age forty who participate in routine screening. If a woman has breast cancer, the probability is 80% that she will get a positive mammography. If a woman does not have breast cancer, the probability is 9.6% that she will also get a positive mammography. A woman in this age group had a positive mammography in a routine screening. What is the probability that she actually has breast cancer?
> —%.

> Frequency format. 10 out of every 1,000 women at age forty who participate in routine screening have breast cancer. 8 of every 10 women with breast cancer will get a positive mammography. 95 out of every 990 women without breast cancer will also get a positive mammography. Here is a new representative sample of women at age forty who got a positive mammography in routine screening. How many of these women do you expect to actually have breast cancer?
> ___out of___.

People with no training in statistics tended to do much better on problems in the latter frequency formats. Gigerenzer and Hoffrage report that 16% of subjects faced with probability formats got the Bayesian answer, while 46% of subjects faced with frequency formats got the Bayesian answer (693).

These results suggest an obvious reasoning strategy: When faced with a diagnosis problem framed in terms of probabilities, people should learn to represent and solve the problem in a frequency format. The frequency format solution to this (or any) diagnosis problem would involve five steps (adapted from Gigerenzer and Hoffrage 1995):

1. Draw up a hypothetical population of 1,000. (Literally, draw a rectangle that represents 1,000 people.)
2. Base rate cut: How many (of 1,000) have the disease? Answer: 10 (1% of 1,000).
3. Hit rate cut: How many of those with the disease will test positive? Answer: 8 (test sensitivity is 80%). (In a corner of the rectangle, color in the space representing the 8 true positives.)

4. False alarm cut: How many of those (990) without the disease will test positive? Answer: 95 (9.6% of 990). (In another corner of the rectangle, color in the space representing the 95 false positives.)
5. Comparison step: What's the fraction of true positives (8) among the positives (8 + 95)? Answer: 8/103, or about 7.8%.

There is no mystery why subjects have an easier time with the frequency format than the probability format. First, the frequency format makes the base rate information transparent. Second, the frequency format requires performing a much easier calculation.

The calculation for the probability format: $.01 \times .08 / [(.01 \times .08) + (.99 \times .096)]$

The calculation for the frequency format: $8/(8 + 95)$

Studies like the ones cited here provide a lot of evidence for thinking that people can reason better about frequencies than they can about probabilities (Gigerenzer et al. 1999). So here is a piece of advice that drops out naturally from our naturalistic epistemological theory: When tackling diagnosis problems, repackage the problem-task so that it will (for many people) naturally trigger a cognitive mechanism that will quickly and reliably get the Bayesian answer. By framing diagnosis problems in terms of frequencies rather than probabilities, people can reason about significant problems more reliably.

The start-up costs of adopting and implementing the frequency format are not negligible. One must learn to frame a diagnosis problem in terms of idealized populations and frequencies, and one must learn to apply the format's five steps to problems. The reliability of the frequency format is considerably higher than that of neglecting the base rate; and we can confidently assert (having taught undergraduates both strategies) that the frequency format is significantly easier to learn to use than the Bayesian strategy. Should everyone learn to use the frequency format? This is very much an empirical issue, but we suspect not. Certainly any person whose profession involves drawing inferences from diagnostic tests (whether for disease or drug use) who cannot easily apply the Bayesian reasoning strategy should learn to use frequency formats (which is the recommendation of Gigerenzer and Hoffrage 1995). If there are institutions, policies, or practices in place that make it highly unlikely that people will suffer because of the mistakes of experts involved in diagnosing important conditions, it is not clear that everyone would need to go to the trouble of learning frequency formats. There might be good reasons for people to do so (e.g., to understand how highly reliable tests for rare conditions can generate many more false positives than true positives, to check on the diagnostic judgments of experts, etc.). But given the evidence we have reviewed, it seems unlikely that we are in a situation in which the risk of poor diagnosis is very low. If this is right, then it would behoove just about everyone who has the potential to get a serious disease or who has a loved one who has the potential to get a serious disease to understand how frequency formats work.

Here is a natural objection to the advice that (some) people adopt frequency formats: "Anyone who uses the frequency format is really computing Bayes' Rule. Both are computing the same function—given a set of inputs, Bayes' Rule and the frequency format will have the same answer as an output. So this advice provides no grounds for rejecting Bayes' Rule." (One might respond that they aren't the same function, since they presuppose different views about probability. While this might be a legitimate objection, we intend to focus on what we think is a more serious problem with the argument.) The problem with this objection is that it confuses two things that must be kept distinct: Bayes' Rule as a mathematical identity and Bayes' Rule as a reasoning strategy (as a psychological process). As a mathematical identity, Bayes' Rule is true. But most people can't use the Bayesian reasoning strategy very well. So even though (in some sense) these two strategies compute the same formula, for reasons of computational difficulty, the Bayesian reasoning strategy just isn't as good as the frequency format. In fact, the frequency format is quite different from the Bayesian strategy (described above). There are a number of different ways we might characterize the frequency format. But Gigerenzer and Hoffrage (1995) introduce it primarily as a means of improving *doctors' reasoning about diagnostic inferences*. Narrowing its range in this way, we can characterize it as follows:

1. *Cues*: Base rate of disease; hit rate of the test; false positive rate of the test
2. *Formula*: true positives/total positives
3. *Target*: The likelihood that someone who tests positive for a disease actually has the disease
4. *Range*: Medical diagnoses based on medical tests

There are various ways one might try to extend the range of this reasoning strategy. (For example, one might extend it to apply to drug and alcohol tests.) While extending the strategy's range would make it a more robust reasoning strategy, it is a thoroughly empirical claim whether or not this would improve it. This will depend in part on how well a reasoner can be expected to employ the more robust reasoning strategy; and it will also depend on how significant those extra reasoning problems are likely to be for the reasoner. On our view, it might well be that given the range of reasoning problems most people expect to face, the full Bayesian reasoning strategy is not worth the trouble. It is possible that the only significant reasoning problems most people are likely to face that require Bayesian reasoning are diagnosis problems (e.g., medical and drug tests). In that case, when it comes to offering normative guidance, the mathematical question of whether the frequency format calculation is identical to the Bayesian one is near enough irrelevant. The relevant issue is which of the two *clearly different* reasoning strategies people should adopt.

We suspect that many epistemologists will want to raise a version of the triviality objection: "Why does this example exhibit the superiority of your naturalistic theory over any other (remotely plausible) epistemological theory? Conjoin the empirical results discussed above with an epistemological theory. If the theory is remotely plausible, it will hold that under normal circumstances, for any diagnosis problem, the justified belief is delivered by Bayes' Rule. So any plausible view can recommend the frequency format. Given our cognitive abilities, the frequency format will lead people to reason to justified beliefs better than alternative reasoning strategies." This objection explicitly relies on the distinction between Bayes' theorem as a mathematical identity and as a reasoning strategy. But it does so by divorcing from epistemology the issue of what reasoning strategy to adopt. The objection suggests that any plausible epistemological theory—foundationalist, coherentist, reliabilist, pragmatist, contextualist—will be consistent with any reasonable normative guidance about reasoning one might offer on the basis of psychological findings. But if this is really true, then how reason guiding could these theories possibly be? If the practical normative content of all these very different theories is something like "Adopt justified beliefs, but we have no resources to tell you how to do this," then these theories are like the financial advisor who takes his commission after offering the advice "Buy low and sell high." This describes a desirable state of affairs, but it's hardly *guidance*.

2. Overcoming overconfidence

If error is the constant companion of inquiry, so is overconfidence. People are systematically prone to giving more credence to their beliefs than they deserve. The literature demonstrating overconfidence is very large. To cite one representative example mentioned earlier (chapter 2, section 3.4),

Fischhoff, Solvic, and Lichtenstein (1977) asked subjects to specify the most frequent cause of death in the U.S. and to estimate their confidence that their choice was correct. It turns out that when subjects set the odds of their answer's correctness at 100:1, they were correct 73% of the time; even when they were so sure as to set the odds between 10,000:1 and 1,000,000:1, they were correct only between 85% and 90% of the time. The overconfidence effect is systematic (it is highly replicable and survives changes in task and setting) and directional (the effect is in the direction of overconfidence rather than underconfidence—except when it comes to objectively easy problems [Lichtenstein and Fischhoff 1980].) Given these findings, one might hope that expert training reduces or eliminates overconfidence. This does not appear to be so. Physicists, economists, and demographers have all been observed to suffer from this bias, even when reasoning about the content of their special discipline (Henrion and Fischoff 1986). In fact, it might be useful for readers of this book to know that people who score better on SATs are also more prone to overconfidence (Stanovich 1999, 120). Overconfidence is not the mere result of individual differences in personality or of clinical delusions of grandeur. It is the normal consequence of routine cognitive activity.

Overconfidence in highly significant reasoning problems can lead to fatally inaccurate judgments—for example, that guilt has been proven beyond a reasonable doubt. There have been 110 people who were convicted of murder who have been found to be not guilty on the basis of DNA evidence. Most of these errors have been found to be the result of mistaken eyewitness testimony and the overconfidence of eyewitnesses and juries in the reliability of such testimony (Wells, Olson, and Charman 2002).

Are there any reliable strategies for counteracting this overconfidence? Arkes, Dawes, and Christensen (1986) found that accuracy incentives did not improve accuracy of judgments (also see Arkes 1991). Lord et al. (1984) found that simple motivational declarations do not reduce bias either. So, for example, offering subjects $1 for each correct answer or urging subjects to be unbiased do not reduce overconfidence. There are some ways to reduce bias, but they involve introducing elements that are unlike what people tend to face in daily life. For example, when subjects are made to feel accountable for their judgments (by being told that their answers will be discussed after the session), they assimilated evidence in a less biased way. Further, overconfidence can be eliminated when subjects are persistently exposed to a rigorous schedule of specially prepared feedback (Arkes, Christensen, Lai, and Blumer 1987). These sorts of findings are important for thinking about what sorts of procedures to implement when deliberations occur in stable social settings (such as a jury or a policy panel). These sorts of calibration exercises can prompt groups of people to be less overconfident than each individual, reasoning alone, might have been. Indeed, it may be that controlled environments, where debiasing decision-making procedures can be implemented, offer our best hope of overcoming overconfidence.

The most prominent of the individual, subjective debiasing methods is the *consider-the-opposite strategy.* One of the groundbreaking studies on debiasing argued that people "have a blind spot for opposite possibilities" when making social and policy judgments (Lord, Lepper, and Preston, 1984). When subjects were asked to generate pros and cons for a judgment they had made, Koriat, Lichtenstein, and Fischhoff (1980) demonstrated that overconfidence bias was reduced. Indeed, they found that it was the generation of *opposing* reasons that did all of the bias-reducing work. The most effective version of the consider-the-opposite strategy involves a simple rule: "Stop to consider why your judgment might be wrong" (Plous 1993, 228). Here are some beliefs that we might hold with undue certainty. If S believes that New York State is the largest state on the Eastern Seaboard, S might consider that he might be wrong because New York gets a lot more press than South Atlantic states. If S believes that Los Angeles is west of Reno, he might ask himself whether he might not have a clear sense of the orientation of the American landmass. If S believes that a defendant is guilty beyond a reasonable doubt, he might consider that he might be mistaken because of his confusion over the DNA evidence.

While we are somewhat hopeful about the ability of the consider-the-opposite strategy to reduce our overconfidence, there are a number of issues that need to be resolved before we can embrace it wholeheartedly. One serious worry is whether the consider-the-opposite strategy can be exported to a setting in which it can be usefully implemented. This is not a criticism of the ecological validity of the experiments; there is no question that if you could get people in natural settings to perform the same experimental debiasing task, overconfidence would be reduced. The question instead is whether, as people go through their daily lives, they will have the discipline, motivation, and concentration required to implement the consider-the-opposite strategy. This kind of worry drops out of our view quite naturally. Strategic reliabilism is a view that explicitly recognizes our psychological limitations. If it is part of our psychological functioning that we tend to ignore or undervalue corrective strategies, this is something we must take seriously.

But even if we can implement the consider-the-opposite strategy to good effect, there is another serious worry: What is its range to be? After all, it would surely be a mistake for us to adopt the strategy for every belief we entertain. Such a strategy would turn us into unhappy, neurotic nebbishes, impossible to get along with. (One of us is reminded of the student who was obviously having serious life troubles and explained that it was because he had really taken Descartes' *Meditations* to heart.) Recall our discussion in chapter 3 of the Four Ways to better reasoning. We noted that there could be occasions when one could become a better reasoner by replacing a reliable but expensive strategy with another that was less reliable but less expensive. Replacing a wide ranging consider-the-opposite strategy with a consider-the-opposite strategy with a narrower range might be an example of this. If a consider-the-opposite strategy is a good idea, it is surely one whose range is to be limited to highly significant problems in which short-term reliability is very important.

3. Causal reasoning

Many of the most significant problems we face involve reasoning about causal connections. But thinking clearly about causal claims is a very tricky business. For one thing, in colloquial speech the term 'cause' is used in a number of different ways (e.g., to signify a probabilistic causal connection or a necessary or sufficient causal condition). Further, there are various ways in which controlled experiments can go awry—and these are often quite difficult to detect. We don't intend to give an easy-to-use strategy for reasoning about any and all causal claims. In fact, we doubt such a strategy exists. But there is a fairly simple strategy for avoiding a certain kind of pitfall when it comes to causal reasoning. (This strategy is implicit in much of Robyn Dawes's work, e.g., 2001.) The neglected risk involves accepting as a causal explanation a narrative that lacks a control. To see this, consider two points: the importance of controls in causal reasoning and our tendency to accept plausible sounding narratives (Trout 1998, esp. chapter 8).

Suppose we want to know whether Snake Oil Hooch is an effective cure for the common cold. We give the Snake Oil Hooch to 100 people with a cold, and all of them get better within a week. Is that good evidence for thinking we have a cure for the common cold? Of course not. We would expect (near enough) all 100 people who get over a cold to get over it without a medical cure. To know whether the Snake Oil Hooch had an effect, we would want to run a controlled, double-blind experiment. We would want to study a control group—a group of people with colds who aren't given the Snake Oil Hooch. And we would want the experiment to be double-blind (neither the subjects nor the people who diagnose the subjects know whether subjects are in the control or experimental group). If there is no significant difference in outcomes, then it is reasonable to suppose that the Snake Oil has no effect.

Most people recognize the importance of controls in causal reasoning. And yet, we have a tendency to accept compelling narratives as evidence for causal claims. Let's consider a somewhat amusing example. Some people believe that shaving hair causes it to grow back thicker. This is supported by observation: When people start shaving, their hair does tend to start coming in thicker. And people also often support this causal claim with some sort of "intuitive" explanation. We've heard two. One likens hair to certain plants that when pruned come back thicker; another holds that the razor "stimulates" the hair follicles. But this is an old wives' tale. It is an example of correlation but not causation. Those who propose this hypothesis don't have a control group. While they know that shaving and thicker hair are correlated, they don't know what would have happened to the hair without the shaving. And in fact, merely raising the question leads to an obvious alternative hypothesis: Most people start shaving in early puberty, when their facial and body hair begin to grow in. But puberty itself explains the increased hair growth.

This problem suggests a relatively simple debiasing strategy. When faced with a causal hypothesis of the form *X causes Y* that is supported by a narrative but no control, it is often useful to ask a very simple question of the form: What would have happened to Y without X? It is important to recognize that this debiasing query, by itself, doesn't immediately lead us to the right conclusion about what's causing what. But if one has no idea what would have happened to Y without X, and if one recognizes the importance of controls in causal reasoning, then at the very least this should give one pause. Perhaps one doesn't have particularly powerful reasons to believe the causal claim. So while the consider-the-control strategy is only a first step in thinking about causal claims, it is often an effective first step in opening up fruitful lines of investigation that can perhaps help us to avoid the temptation of falling for an intuitive but mistaken story. Let's see how this might work with three high-stakes examples.

3.1. The regression fallacy

Someone is guilty of the regression fallacy when they propose an unnecessary causal explanation for what is, in fact, an instance of regression to the mean (Gilovich 1991). Kahneman and Tversky (1973) reported on the classic example of the regression fallacy. Israeli air force instructors had been urged (presumably on the basis of psychological results) to use positive (rather than negative) reinforcement in pilot training. However, these instructors claimed to know that punishment is more effective in training than praise. The reason? Punishment was typically followed by improved performance, while praise was typically followed by a worse performance. However, the instructors failed to control for a regression effect: Wherever performance tends toward a mean, a poor outcome (one that is deep in the left tail of a normal distribution) is far more likely to be followed by an outcome that is better than an outcome that is even worse. And an outstanding outcome is far more likely to be followed by a worse one. When regression was controlled for in the Israeli air force example, reward did mold behavior more effectively than punishment.

There is an important lesson to be drawn for those of us who raise children. Many parents and coaches believe that rewards inhibit performance while punishment enhances it. In fact, we can predict that those who have the most experience with children should believe this falsehood most strongly. After all, they do have observations to support their view: After rewarding a very good performance, the next performance *really is* likely to be worse; and after punishing a very bad performance, the next performance *really is* likely to be better. These falsehoods not only have the "observations" on their side, but they also have "theory." It is very easy to come up with plausible narratives to "explain" the observations. Punishment improves performance because it concentrates the mind; and reward diminishes performance because it leads to overconfidence and self-congratulation and so ultimately to a loss of effort and concentration. As we have seen, such stories come easy. But the failure of parents to call into question this hypothesis—to consider the control by asking whether they know what would have happened to the performance without the intervention—has undoubtedly led to needless unhappiness for countless children and regrettable frustration for parents.

3.2. *Policy assessment*

In thinking about how to intervene in the world, we often have need for beliefs about what sorts of policies (general strategies for dealing with certain situations) are effective and which are not effective. For example, many people have opinions about what sorts of social policies are best suited to overcoming poverty in our country. These opinions (we hope) rest on judgments about the effectiveness of various social policies; and these judgments (we hope) rest on good evidence. But what counts as good evidence for thinking that a social policy has been effective? Long and technical books have been written about policy analysis. While we can't expect ordinary reasoners to master the complexities of policy analysis, the consider-the-control strategy might help people to overcome some glaring errors associated with the assessment of policy.

Policy assessment is applicable to much more than issues of social policy. It is also relevant to the assessment of different approaches to personal and professional matters. To take an example close to home, everyone knows that it's hard to get good jobs in philosophy. Different people and schools take different approaches to job searches. At the national conference where job interviews are conducted, some job seekers are more aggressive than others about seeking out and chatting up prospective employers at receptions. Some departments are more aggressive than others when it comes to lobbying for their graduate students. On the other side of the job search, different departments take different approaches to the hiring process. For example, some don't conduct conference interviews, while others conduct many short (15-minute) interviews. Which of these strategies is most effective in finding a job (or hiring a job seeker)? Presumably, many of our colleagues have firm opinions about these matters— or at least opinions that are firm enough for them to act on. But does their evidence support their opinions? We suspect that in most cases, the answer is no. The reason is that most people involved in the job search don't know how well they would have done if they'd adopted different search policies. (Actually, the truth is a bit more disturbing than this. At least some of our colleagues know about, or have heard about, the interview effect; so they have some evidence that their job searches would have gone, on average, better if they'd not insisted upon short unstructured interviews.)

We often employ strategies in social matters as well. In trying to win friends and influence people at a party, we might try being funny or charming or "coming on strong" or drinking to the point of imbecility. Of course, often these strategies aren't consciously adopted—they're not the result of an explicit decision procedure in which alternatives are considered and rejected. But many of us sometimes reflect on our social behaviors (perhaps after a particularly humiliating episode) and wonder whether we might try to change our ways in the future in order to obtain better results. Reflecting on these issues requires that we think about what social strategies are most likely to help us achieve our social goals. For many, this is a particularly significant kind of policy assessment.

There is a serious problem associated with policy assessment that arises as soon as we consider the control. The problem is particularly acute when it comes to the assessment of large-scale policies or seldom used policies (like job search policies). The problem is that it's hard to know how the world would have been if we *hadn't* adopted those policies. Gilovich (1991) calls this the problem of hidden data (or hidden evidence). For example, we don't know what the current state of poverty would be like if we'd not adopted certain poverty programs; and we don't know how we'd have done on the job market if we'd gone about things differently. Since we can't turn back time to see how the world would have turned out if we would have adopted different policies, the best way to deal with the problem of hidden data is to compare different policies (implemented in relevantly similar circumstances) against each other. Sometimes, the problem of hidden data is so severe that we would do better just to accept fewer causal hypotheses than we do and to be a lot less confident about the ones we do accept.

3.3. *Rare events*

If we accept the need for controls, then it becomes quite difficult to provide a causal explanation for very rare or unique events. For example, after someone commits a horrible crime, there is the inevitable spate of "explanation" stories in the media. These reports focus on some sordid or unhappy aspects of the person's background—a taste for music with violent lyrics or violent video games, a broken home, distant parents, adolescent alienation, or a childhood tendency to be cruel to animals. Such themes make for a narrative that seems to culminate naturally with the crime. These are often very good stories—memorable, dramatic, and they satisfy our subjective sense of understanding. But do they accurately identify the causal factors that led to the crime? After all, those who come up with these narratives (and those of us who believe them) are seldom constrained by any knowledge of base rates or serious empirical research on violence.

How many of us have lived such fortunate lives that if a gaggle of reporters were set loose on us, not one could construct a narrative on the basis of our youth that plausibly culminated in a horrible crime (fictitious, we trust)? In our cases, the greenest cub reporter could whip out a blood-curdling narrative along the lines of "quiet alienated youth goes bad" in a day. As pillars of our communities, we intend to keep these stories to ourselves. But it's not just that lots of kids have stories uncomfortably similar to those told in the media about criminals. It's also that we don't even know if those whose pasts are free of alleged "danger signs" really are less prone to violence than the rest of us. The lesson we would draw is not that narrative modes of inquiry are irreducibly or intrinsically unsound. All of us offer narrative explanations, particularly for people's behavior. Rather, we would contend that storytelling forms of inquiry are less reliable than most of us believe; and narrative explanations deserve much less confidence than they typically get. Without knowledge of base rates and without an accurate causal model, we can only rely on sweet anecdote and the subjective plausibility of a good story. On some occasions, these stories may act as useful heuristics. But too often these stories rely on background knowledge that has not risked the painful test of disconfirming feedback. Without awareness of our own boundedness and frailty, then, we can only proceed with blithe innocence, assuming that a good story is good enough. But as the literature we have considered so far indicates, good stories come easy. True stories are harder to find.

4. Conclusion

We have presented just some of the advice there is to extract from Ameliorative Psychology about how people might reason better about matters of significance. It is easy to envision how this kind of "applied epistemology" might serve as the basis for an interesting critical thinking course—one very different from the courses taught by most philosophers. Many critical thinking texts written by philosophers seem designed to provide students with the resources to puncture the pompous absurdities of psychics, faith healers, and political pundits. An epistemological tradition that took seriously its normative, reason-guiding function would naturally suggest a different kind of critical thinking course, one that took Ameliorative Psychology seriously. Such a course would be based on empirical findings in psychology (e.g., Gilovich 1991, Nisbett 1993, Hastie and Dawes 2001), as well as in negotiation (e.g., Thompson 2001) and managerial decision making (e.g., Bazerman 2001). It would introduce students to reasoning strategies that can help them improve their retirement savings, that can help them increase joint outcomes in cooperative group behavior, that can help them draw reasonable inferences from a positive or a negative test for cancer, and that can help them safeguard their neighborhoods from human predators.

Can such courses do any good? We don't know, but there is reason for hope. In a paper that found that people improved their reasoning after formal instruction, Lehman, Lempert, and Nisbett drew the following conclusion:

> The truth is we know very little about reasoning and how to teach it. The one thing we knew—namely, that formal discipline is an illusion—seems clearly wrong. Just how wrong, and therefore just how much we can improve reasoning by instruction, is now a completely open question. (1993, 335–36)

These are sobering words from a distinguished team of researchers. If they strike philosophers as pessimistic, that is because we have assumed for too long that our courses help people reason better without bothering to test the assumption. When it comes to offering epistemic guidance, the prospects for Ameliorative Psychology are good. We have plenty of evidence of what we do wrong, and a fair bit of evidence about what we can do to correct it. Do we have the cognitive wherewithal to appreciate the need for those corrections? Do we have the resolve and the stamina to make them? These are worthwhile questions. But if the answer to these questions is no, it is not because Standard Analytic Epistemology is a better alternative. One of the general findings we have pressed in this book is that when it comes to matters of human and social judgment, our unaided reasoning abilities are no match for sound, empirically-based reasoning methods. It is high time to apply this lesson to the practice of epistemology.

Conclusion

E pistemology is a normative enterprise. This means, in part, that it aims to give direction to our cognitive lives. Certain parts of psychology also aim to give direction to our cognitive lives. Our primary goal in this book has been to marry these normative endeavors, or better yet, to remarry these endeavors. For much of the intellectual history of the West, from Plato to Kant, it is not too much of an overstatement to say that psychology was a branch of philosophy. But in the mid-nineteenth century, psychology filed for divorce, and the divorce was finalized in Wundt's lab. Since then, philosophy has behaved like many a jilted lover and erected barriers between itself and psychology. But it is psychology that has thrived. Psychology has proven that it can offer effective reason-guiding advice without input from philosophy; epistemology has shown no comparable talent. Nonetheless, we have argued that both epistemology and psychology would benefit from closer collaboration. Gin is better than vermouth, but they're still better together.

The history of science shows that humans have a tremendous capacity to learn how to better learn about the world. We can discover and adopt new and better ways of reasoning. In the past half-century or so, psychology has made dramatic advances in this area. We can learn to reason so that there are fewer violent recidivists on the streets, so that graduate and professional schools accept higher-quality students, and so that medical decisions are made on the basis of more accurate diagnoses of psychiatric conditions, of cancer prognoses, and of the location and cause of brain damage. Most Standard Analytic Epistemology proceeds as if these sorts of empirical findings can have no effect on the outcome of normative theorizing. This book stands as a repudiation of this assumption. When we take these findings as the starting point of our epistemological theorizing, we end up with a theory completely unlike the theories of Standard Analytic Epistemology.

There is still much for a reason-guiding epistemology to do. For as with so much in life, our knowledge of our defects far exceeds our ability to correct them. We know, for example, that because people took a good story to be a causally accurate story, mothers were led to feel guilty about and responsible for their children's autism (chapter 2, section 4.2). We know that the regression fallacy has led countless parents to be overconfident about the effectiveness of punishment in molding their children's behavior. We know some of the dangers of the fundamental attribution error (i.e., the tendency to explain behavior primarily in terms of dispositional factors, such as motives, capacities, and personality traits, and to underestimate the causal influence of situational factors, such as whether the subject is pressed for time or is in an uncomfortably warm room [Ross 1977]). The fundamental attribution error can lead to unfairly harsh views of the poor, explaining poverty primarily in terms of negative personal attributes and radically underestimating situational causes. We also know that we commonly exhibit the regression fallacy, overconfidence and hindsight biases, and a host of other less-than-ideal forms of reasoning. No one can tally the needless burdens these habits of mind have inflicted upon us, but they are likely to be substantial. We need a reason-guiding epistemology that has something to say about these matters.

The dramatic divide between the discipline that studies reasoning (psychology) and the discipline that is supposed to assess that reasoning (epistemology) has harmed epistemology. But it has done psychology no good either. Psychologists occasionally disagree, sometimes strongly, about the normative status of some instance of reasoning. These disputes cry out for a clear, compelling epistemological framework for thinking about such normative issues. We think that Strategic Reliabilism is such a framework. While we would not presume that it is the final word on the subject, it is a subject that merits quite a few more words from philosophers. We are not above appealing to philosophers' prodigious sense of pride: It must be galling to you that when people and institutions look for normative, reason-guiding advice, they ignore epistemology and turn to psychology. If you think you can do epistemology better than the psychologists (and you know you do), then why not prove it in the marketplace of ideas?

The views developed and defended in this book replace the subjective judgments of the traditional epistemologist with objectively tested material of documented integrity. They transform epistemology from a quest for justified belief into a demand for meaningful action. This is a deeply interdisciplinary project, and it is in its infancy. If we are to achieve a powerful, reason-guiding epistemology, there are a number of important projects we have not sufficiently emphasized. Let's briefly explore three of these. First, and most obviously, an effective epistemology needs to continue to discover handy new heuristics that help us reason reliably about significant matters. To do this, however, we need a firmer grasp on significance. This leads to a second project that is essential to a mature, reason-guiding epistemology: We need to better identify what is involved in human well-being. There is a wealth of literature on the conditions that promote human welfare, and it is pretty clear already that at least some of these conditions are so counterintuitive that they cannot be discovered by a process of introspective philosophical analysis. This literature is far outside most epistemologists' comfort zones (e.g., Wilson and Gilbert 2003). Indeed, it has thus far only received modest attention from ethicists, and social and political philosophers, the fields most likely to draw on these findings (but see Goldman 1993, Harman 1998, and Doris 2002). A third project essential to the development of a prescriptive, reason-guiding epistemology is social epistemology (see, e.g., Goldman 1999). The robust reliability of a reasoning strategy owes much to the environment, including the social institutions that are so important to our well-being. There are policies, programs, and institutions that if implemented can foster significantly improved reasoning. For example, Gary Wells has offered a number of practical recommendations about how to make eyewitness testimony more reliable. Among other suggestions, Wells recommends that any lineup contain only one suspect and that lineups be sequential, where individuals or their photographs are shown to the eyewitness one at a time, rather than simultaneous, where all are shown to the eyewitness at the same time (Wells et al. 1998; Wells 2001; Wells, Olson, and Charman 2002.). What is so powerful about this kind of example is that it shows how we can dramatically improve the reasoning of eyewitnesses about an extraordinarily significant problem without the eyewitnesses incurring any start-up costs. In other words, the eyewitness doesn't have to learn a new way to think about anything. The ameliorative work is all done with the implementation of a new law enforcement policy, a policy that costs almost nothing to implement.

The aim of philosophy might be self-knowledge. But there is reason to doubt that self-knowledge can be achieved by an introspective study of ourselves. There was a time, not so long ago, that a philosopher might soberly and honestly claim that he had learned pretty much everything that there was to know, as Descartes did in the *Meditations*. Philosophers could construct their philosophical theories confident that they were informed by the best science of the day—sometimes because they were among the best scientists of their day. No more. We have argued that an explicitly naturalistic approach can yield a useful, reason-guiding epistemology; and we believe that this approach promises to make epistemology far richer than the standard twentieth-century fare. But it also promises to make epistemology considerably more demanding. A reason-guiding epistemology must be a deeply interdisciplinary affair, and philosophers who want to play a role in the development of a usefully prescriptive epistemology will have to have a grasp of some science—of at least some economics and psychology. Further, given how philosophy is done, philosophers will not be the dominant figures in the development of a reason-guiding epistemology. We are likely to be theoreticians trying to make sense of a kind of normative engineering—we'll be sometimes useful but seldom central. Some philosophers might find that relinquishing our perch as Queen of the Sciences is much too bitter a pill to swallow. In response, we would ask for a moment's indulgence: Imagine philosophers playing a useful, and perhaps even essential, role in the development of a reason-guiding epistemology that brings significant tangible benefits to people's lives. If this role is less central than some philosophers had dreamed, so be it. No discipline, including philosophy, can have more noble a goal than to fully and honestly explore and execute the charge that nature defines.

Appendix
Objections and Replies

We address objections we expect to be leveled at our view. We identify the objections of our imagined critic with italicized type. We won't pretend to have addressed all the serious objections to our view; and we won't pretend to have given conclusive answers to all the objections we do consider. Our goal is to give the reader some sense of the resources available to Strategic Reliabilism for dealing with some important issues, many of which articulate longstanding epistemological concerns.

1. Skepticism

Any epistemological theory worthy of the name must address the skeptical challenge. The skeptic begins with a fund of presumptively justified beliefs and proceeds to argue that one can't legitimately make inferences that go beyond that evidence. For example, a skeptic about the material world argues that on the basis of our sensory beliefs, we can equally well support the brain-in-the-vat hypothesis, the ideational world hypothesis, the evil demon hypothesis, the material world hypothesis, etc. All of these hypotheses are underdetermined by the evidence. The skeptical challenge is that since the evidence does not support any one of these hypotheses over any other, we cannot justifiably believe any of them.

A central problem with naturalistic approaches to epistemology, including the one defended in this book, is that they fail to address the skeptical challenge. Naturalists begin their epistemological investigations by making substantive assumptions that skeptics are unwilling to grant: that there is a material world, that there are other minds, etc. You face a dilemma. Either you ignore the skeptical challenge, in which case your theory does not deserve to be called an epistemological theory, or you beg the question against the skeptic.

Let's begin with a "live and let live" response to the skeptical problem. Our approach to epistemology does not provide a solution to skepticism. But what do we really want from an epistemological theory? It would certainly be nice to have a theory that solved the problem of skepticism. But it would also be nice to have a theory that provided useful guidance to reasoners. An epistemological theory that provided a framework for how to reason in an excellent manner could have many practical benefits. It could provide a framework for thinking about diagnosis that led to better medical outcomes, a framework for thinking about parole board decisions that led to a less violent society, a framework for thinking about public policy that helped the electorate support policies that better serve its values, and so on. Now, one might legitimately wonder whether a useful reason-guiding theory is possible; but one might equally well wonder whether a theory that solves the problem of skepticism is possible. Our point is that if philosophers insist that a theory of reasoning excellence that has this ameliorative aim is not *epistemology*, well then, so much the worse for epistemology.

The "live and let live" response notes that many successful theories don't do everything we might like them to do. Newton's theory of motion was highly successful even though it does not explain all physical phenomena (e.g., electromagnetic phenomena). So a theory of reasoning excellence might be highly successful at providing useful guidance to reasoners even though it does not solve some other epistemological problems. In particular, it might well not solve the skeptical problem. So we admit that we don't have a solution to the skeptical challenge, but we're proposing a theory that aims to meet a different goal. Unless one rejects this as a legitimate goal of epistemology, then the skeptic's criticism fails to uncover a problem with any theory, naturalistic or not, that has this goal. And of course that includes Strategic Reliabilism.

The "live and let live" response is problematic for any naturalistic theory, like yours, that takes reasoning excellence to be partly determined by the reliability of reasoning strategies. You argue that according to Strategic Reliabilism, one ought to use Goldberg's Rule in making tentative diagnoses of psychiatric patients on the basis of the MMPI. That's because Goldberg's Rule has low costs and is reliable on problems that are significant. But the skeptic can reformulate her challenge so that it is about reasoning excellence. If a skeptical hypothesis is true, if, for example, there are no other minds or other people, then Goldberg's Rule would not be reliable after all. Given this possibility, how could we ever know how to reason in an excellent fashion? The problem with the "live and let live" response is that it fails to recognize that the skeptical problem is so pervasive that it cannot be sidestepped or avoided.

In the face of this challenge, our inclination is to restrict our theory to *normal worlds*—that is, non-skeptical worlds that are presumed to be like our own (Goldman 1986, 107–9). A reasoning strategy is reliable when it has a high truth ratio on the assumption that the world is as we presume it to be, i.e., nonskeptical.

But the move to "normal worlds" is cheating. You escape the skeptical challenge simply by ruling by fiat that the skeptical hypotheses are false. Is there some principled reason that warrants the move to "normal worlds"? Or is this move simply motivated by the understandable but unprincipled desire to avoid a difficult problem?

Technically, we are not ruling that the skeptical hypotheses are false. Our point is that judgments of reasoning excellence are insensitive to whether or not a skeptical hypothesis is true. There are two principled reasons for this move to normal, non-skeptical worlds. First, the goal of Strategic

Reliabilism is not to solve the problem of skepticism. It aims to be a useful reason-guiding theory. This is a legitimate goal of epistemology. Strategic Reliabilism should be assessed in terms of whether it meets this goal. If it does, then the fact that it does not meet a different goal (solving the skeptical problem) does not by itself give us a reason to doubt it. Rather, it suggests that the epistemological theory that guides reasoning is not the theory that will solve the problem of skepticism. Second, recall that Strategic Reliabilism is supposed to articulate the normative principles that guide the prescriptions of Ameliorative Psychology. A cursory examination of Ameliorative Psychology makes evident that it ignores the skeptical challenge; for example, it employs the processes and categories of contemporary psychology. So given that our aim is to articulate the normative presuppositions of Ameliorative Psychology, it is perfectly reasonable for our theory to ignore the possibility of skepticism if the sciences does. And the science does.

There are good, principled reasons for restricting Strategic Reliabilism to normal worlds. Still, some might be disappointed. After all, Strategic Reliabilism does not even hold out the hope of solving the problem of skepticism. Is this a reason to have doubts about our theory? Perhaps. Who wouldn't prefer a lovely theory that both guided reason and solved the problem of skepticism? For those who might be disappointed, however, it's important to recognize two points. First, there might be no unified epistemological theory that meets all our goals. We suggest that Strategic Reliabilism reflects the fact that you can't always get what you want, but if you try sometimes, you just might find you get what you need. Second, even if the failure of Strategic Reliabilism to address the skeptical challenge is a mark against it, that is not by itself a mark in favor of any other approach. In particular, it is not a reason to believe that the standard analytic approach to epistemology can yield a satisfying solution to the skeptical problem.

Strategic Reliabilism recognizes that for most people dealing with everyday issues, skepticism is not a significant problem. This is a point contextualists make in defense of their account of justification (e.g., DeRose 1995). Our point is about what problems the excellent reasoner will tackle and what problems she will ignore. At the risk of undermining our own "live and let live" response to the problem of skepticism, we should note that as children of the 60s, we are nothing if not reflexive: our theory of reasoning excellence applies to us as epistemologists as well. The philosopher who takes skepticism seriously has made judgments, perhaps implicit, about what problems are important in epistemology. If naturalists have not been sufficiently sensitive to the problems posed by the skeptical challenge and other concerns of SAE, perhaps it is because we recognize that there is a need for a genuinely prescriptive epistemological theory— one that provides a framework for improving the reasoning of individuals and institutions about significant issues. It's not that skepticism and other concerns of SAE are insignificant. But Standard Analytic Epistemology so often ignores so much of the world that we do not believe that the values implicit in its practice accurately reflect the values of its proponents.

If improving the world is so important to you, why don't you give up epistemology and devote your lives to charity?

Our account of significance does not depend on a kind of maximizing consequentialism. Significance ultimately is based on the conditions that promote human flourishing, and given our physical and psychological makeup, we take those conditions to be variable but also constrained. So we would deny that people's reasoning or action must always aim to maximize some notion of the good.

On what grounds, then, can you criticize proponents of SAE for focusing attention on skepticism? Let's grant for the sake of argument that skepticism is not the most significant problem facing epistemology. You admit that people can be excellent reasoners even if they do not always address the most significant problems. So your criticism of proponents of SAE depends on holding them to standards you admit are unnecessarily high.

This objection fails to understand the nature of our criticism. We are critical of epistemology as a field of study in the English-speaking world. We are critical of the way resources (everything from human talent to institutional support) are distributed in epistemology. We are happy to grant that a healthy intellectual discipline can and should afford room for people to pursue highly theoretical issues that don't have any obvious practical implications. So we do not object to any particular epistemologist tackling the skeptical challenge. We object to the fact that proponents of SAE insist (rightly) that epistemology has a prescriptive reason-guiding function, while precious few resources are devoted to developing an epistemological theory with useful prescriptive, reason-guiding advice.

2. Circularity worries

You begin your epistemological investigations with empirical findings, i.e., some findings of Ameliorative Psychology. Any epistemological project that begins with empirical findings raises a circularity objection. We can put it in the form of a dilemma. Why did you begin your epistemological investigations with these particular empirical findings? In particular, do you have good reasons for believing them? If so, you are presupposing epistemological principles before you begin your epistemological investigations. And this is viciously circular. If not, if you don't have good reasons for believing the empirical findings on which your epistemological theory is based, then how can you defend this book with a straight face?

Your theory, Strategic Reliabilism, raises a particularly dramatic form of this circularity objection. Chapter 1 says that a good epistemological theory doesn't just mimic the findings of Ameliorative Psychology, and chapter 8 employs your theory to resolve disputes in Ameliorative Psychology. But when you constructed your epistemological theory in the first part of the book, it could not have been "informed" by the instances of Ameliorative Psychology you argue are mistaken in chapter 8. So you must have been making decisions about which instances of Ameliorative Psychology are good and which are not-so-good in the construction of your theory. If so, you must have been presupposing epistemological principles in deciding which empirical findings to accept, and these empirical findings informed your normative theory, which in turn justified those very empirical findings. Again, isn't this viciously circular?

In doing any sort of science, including physics, biology or Ameliorative Psychology, scientists bring substantive normative assumptions to bear in deciding what theories are good or true or worthy of pursuit. But this point is not restricted to scientists. *Anyone* who provides reasons of *any* kind in support of *any* kind of doctrine is up to their ears in substantive epistemological assumptions. And that includes epistemologists. We challenge the proponent of the circularity objection to show us the epistemological theory that begins without relying on any judgment that is informed by some kind of substantive epistemological assumption. Such an epistemology would not begin by assuming, for example, that we have beliefs (for that assumes that we have good *reason* to reject eliminativism, the view that propositional attitudes don't exist). It would not begin by assuming that certain ways of reasoning about normative, epistemic matters are superior to others (for that would require epistemological assumptions about how we *ought* to reason about epistemology). The circularity objection seems to require that we begin construction of an epistemological theory without making *any* normative, epistemic assumptions whatsoever. And that's a fool's errand.

I'm certainly not insisting that epistemology proceed without any normative assumptions whatsoever. Rather, our epistemological investigations should be based on some privileged class of normative, epistemic assumptions. These are the epistemological assumptions of a priori epistemology.

The circularity objection seems to leave us with a choice. But it is not a choice between beginning our epistemological theorizing with substantive epistemological assumptions or without substantive epistemological assumptions. It is a choice between beginning our epistemological theorizing with the epistemological assumptions of a priori epistemology (whatever they may be) or the epistemological assumptions of science (whatever they may be). On what grounds do we make this choice? It is certainly *not* based on the relative success of a priori epistemology (or a priori philosophy in general) over science in coming up with theories that are fruitful and can lay some claim to being true. In fact, if we were to use any reasonable version of the major philosophical theories of justification (reliabilism, coherentism or foundationalism) to assess itself and our best scientific theories, each would surely return the verdict that our best scientific theories are far more justified than the epistemological theory. If this is right, why not embrace the normative presuppositions of the theories that all parties to this debate agree are superior?

But the epistemological assumptions of a priori epistemology are superior to those of naturalistic epistemology. The reason is that the former are a subset of the latter. Naturalists give themselves permission to reason about a priori matters and a posteriori matters when doing epistemology; a priori epistemologists permit only the former. Therefore, the epistemological assumptions of a priori epistemology are safer and more likely to be true.

Even if we grant this point, why is safer better? Epistemologists have a choice about what sorts of epistemic assumptions to adopt when doing epistemology. We suspect that many epistemologists haven't explicitly made a choice about this. They have simply absorbed a tradition still haunted by Descartes and the neurotic abhorrence of error. But error isn't the only enemy—or even the greatest enemy—in life, or in philosophy.

Our approach does risk error by taking Ameliorative Psychology seriously. But what is the risk of constructing an epistemological theory in happy ignorance of such findings—findings that have a half-century's worth of empirical support? Two possible risks stand out. First, if our a priori theories contradict such findings, we risk error. Second, if our a priori theories imply nothing very specific about such findings, we risk irrelevance. And if the proponent of a priori epistemology insists that his approach does not carry these risks, we wonder: How on earth could he possibly be so sure? *Any* choice we make about where to begin our epistemological investigations carries risk of some kind. From our perspective, there are moral, political and pragmatic grounds for doing what we can to make sure that our epistemological theory is informed by our best scientific findings about how we can reason better about significant matters (for an interesting discussion of failures to meet this standard in moral reasoning, see Sunstein 2003). After all, when people fail to heed the advice offered by Ameliorative Psychology about how best to reason about diagnosing disease or predicting violence, people die. Why build an epistemological theory that risks endorsing or not condemning such epistemic practices?

Let's end our thoughts about the circularity objection by considering why the objection is supposed to be damning. The problem, presumably, is that the epistemological assumptions the naturalist begins with will ultimately be vindicated by the naturalist's epistemological theory. In this way, the naturalist's epistemology is self-justifying and so viciously circular. There are three points to make about the viciousness contention. First, it can be made equally well against any epistemological method or theory, no matter how pristinely a priori. After all, the a priori epistemologist must begin her investigations with epistemological assumptions of some sort. Presumably, these assumptions will be vindicated by her epistemological theory. So a priori epistemologies are just as viciously circular as naturalistic epistemologies. Second, it is hard to see how the viciousness claim can be reasonably made with any confidence (including the viciousness claim we just made against a priori epistemology). After all, no one has a clear and compelling account of what epistemological assumptions are being presupposed by epistemologists, naturalists or otherwise. Without knowing this, how can anyone be sure that the prescriptions coming out of such theories will be the same as those that went in? And how can anyone be sure that the prescriptions coming out of such theories will *vindicate* those that went in? Third, suppose that Strategic Reliabilism really does end up vindicating the epistemological assumptions of science. Would that mean that the naturalistic method was vicious? Not unless there was something *necessary* or *inevitable* about this outcome. But let's stop to consider what it would be for Strategic Reliabilism to vindicate every epistemological assumption of all of our best scientific theories. This would mean that the methods and substance of every scientific theory and discipline presuppose epistemological principles that yield prescriptive judgments that are identical to those of Strategic Reliabilism. As we've already admitted, we have no idea whether this sort of vindication is in the offing (although we have serious reservations). But we are most eager to see this case made by the proponent of the circularity objection. We are confident that after articulating the epistemological assumptions of (say) nuclear physics, cognitive psychology and evolutionary biology, and then determining if these assumptions are vindicated by Strategic Reliabilism, our overwhelmed philosopher will grant that there is nothing inevitable about the outcome. And let's suppose that after decades of work, the proponent of the circularity objection finds—to everyone's surprise—that Strategic Reliabilism does vindicate all the epistemological assumptions of our best science. Given that this result was not inevitable, we would have no need to take this as an objection. We could simply conclude that science makes even more terrific epistemological presuppositions than we thought.

3. Is Ameliorative Psychology really normative?

Ameliorative Psychology is no more normative than any other science. Like Ameliorative Psychology, physics, chemistry and biology give us new reasoning strategies that are better than old ones all the time. We ought to adopt these reasoning strategies for solving certain problems, and people often do. So the mere fact that Ameliorative Psychology is in the business of giving us new and better ways to reason doesn't make it any more normative than physics, chemistry, biology, etc. This calls into question your philosophy of science approach to epistemology. There is no reason for us to begin our epistemological speculations with Ameliorative Psychology rather than with any other successful branch of empirical science.

When there is a theoretical improvement in (say) chemistry, it improves our thinking *only* by improving our knowledge of the world—our knowledge of the subject matter of chemistry. Theoretical advancements in chemistry do not improve our knowledge of ourselves as human cognizers. They get us closer to the truth about the chemical world. Ameliorative Psychology is like chemistry in that it improves our thinking about certain aspects of the world. For example, Goldberg's Rule improves our thinking about diagnosing psychiatric patients, credit scoring models improve our reasoning about credit risks, etc. So, like any science, Ameliorative Psychology helps us get closer to the truth about the world. But Ameliorative Psychology also improves our knowledge of ourselves as reasoners. At its best, Ameliorative Psychology identifies how people reason about a problem and offers ways to better reason about the problem. And from these findings, we can pretty immediately draw generalizations about how we ought to reason. From our perspective, what makes Ameliorative Psychology special from a normative perspective—what differentiates it from other sciences—is that the generalizations drawn about how we ought to reason can (in principle at least) put pressure on our deepest epistemological judgments about how we ought to reason.

You claim that Ameliorative Psychology yields generalizations about how we ought to reason while other sciences do not. But this is not obvious. It is clearly possible that we might be able to draw generalizations about how we ought to reason from attending to the character of theoretical advances in the natural sciences. Further, given that the natural sciences offer us the most powerful ways of reasoning about the world that we have, it seems, in fact, plausible to suppose that we might be able to extract lessons about how we ought to reason. For example, suppose one believed that unification is an important virtue in successful scientific theories (Friedman 1974, Kitcher 1981). One might reasonably draw a generalization about how we ought to reason—we ought to seek unification in our belief systems. If this is right, then there really is no distinction in the 'normative' status of Ameliorative Psychology and other sciences.

This is a tricky objection. We expect to be criticized for our extreme naturalism. But this objection suggests our approach is not extreme enough. It says that it's not just that we can extract epistemological lessons from Ameliorative Psychology, we can extract epistemological lessons from *all* the sciences (or at least all the successful sciences). So epistemology isn't just the philosophy of psychology (or the philosophy of Ameliorative Psychology), it's the philosophy of all the (successful) sciences! We have no principled objections to this attempt to push us toward a more radical naturalism. Perhaps we can extract epistemological lessons from (say) physics that can put pressure on our deepest epistemological judgments about how individuals ought to reason. Whatever else might be said about this project, it is certainly going to be *difficult*. It is going to be hard to extract surprising lessons from physics about how people ought to reason in their day-to-day lives. As we argue in chapters 2 and 9, the lessons of Ameliorative Psychology for how people ought to reason are fairly clear. So this objection does nothing to undermine our approach. There are fairly clear—and quite surprising—epistemological lessons to extract from Ameliorative Psychology. That's what we have tried to do. If it should turn out that there are surprising lessons to extract from other areas of science, that's great! We await those results.

4. The grounds of normativity, or Plato's Problem

In the Euthyphro, Plato famously asks whether something is pious because it is loved by the gods or if it is loved by the gods because it is pious. Your approach to epistemology raises an analogous issue. You often appeal to Ameliorative Psychology in the assessment of epistemological excellence. So: Is a reasoning strategy excellent because Ameliorative Psychology says it's excellent, or does Ameliorative Psychology say it's excellent because it really is excellent?

We have argued that on occasion, proponents of Ameliorative Psychology are mistaken about epistemic excellence. So even though we think that attending to the results of Ameliorative Psychology is a reliable way to discover excellent reasoning strategies, it is not perfectly reliable. So on our view, epistemic excellence is a feature of the world discovered by Ameliorative Psychology. Our access to it is akin to our access to any theoretical posit of natural science.

Our empirical investigation into the epistemic excellence begins with the Aristotelian Principle, which says that in the long run, poor reasoning tends to lead to worse outcomes than good reasoning. This principle allows us to take empirical results and infer with confidence that one way of reasoning is better than another. For example, when it comes to medical diagnosis, using frequency formats brings substantially better outcomes than using probability formats (see chapter 9, section 1). The Aristotelian Principle licenses the inference that frequency formats are epistemically superior to probability formats. The construction of an empirical theory of epistemic excellence can begin with many such examples. But a catalog of such examples will not be enough. A theory of epistemic excellence will also lean on what is known about the causal dependence between reasoning and well-being. There is a substantial body of evidence concerning the conditions of human well-being and the conditions for the exercise of human capabilities. For example, people are notoriously unreliable at forecasting their affective reactions to events in their lives (Wilson and Gilbert 2003). A piece of friendly advice: Don't underestimate the impact of a long commute to work on your psychological well-being, when, for example, buying a house (Stutzer and Frey 2003). One would expect a theory of epistemic excellence to evolve with discoveries about human well-being, just as the theory of natural selection evolved with the discovery of the gene.

Our access to epistemic excellence derives from what we can infer about the regularities in the world that are responsible for the success of certain reasoning strategies. Like any domain of empirical inquiry, the access is sometimes indirect. In science, measurement often documents a subtle causal chain, not open to casual inspection. But measurement strategies constitute a powerful class of methods in contemporary science. Ameliorative Psychology has made use of these strategies in generating a substantial body of evidence. We expect that the very scientific methods that vindicate Ameliorative Psychology will confirm the posits of a normative theory of epistemic excellence.

5. The relative paucity of SPRs

Let's grant that Ameliorative Psychology offers some wonderful SPRs. But there just aren't that many, compared to the number of significant reasoning problems we face every day. If John had at his disposal all successful, tractable SPRs, they would not help him deal with the overwhelming majority of the significant reasoning problems in his life. Throughout this book, you attack SAE for offering theories that do not provide useful guidance to reasoners. But your theory fares just about as badly on this score. A handful of successful SPRs for making judgments about a hodgepodge of issues hardly counts as useful reasoning advice.

There are three points to make in response to this objection. First, Ameliorative Psychology provides considerably more guidance than is here suggested. There is more to Ameliorative Psychology than SPRs. For example, the consider-the-opposite strategy and the various strategies for thinking about causation (chapter 9) are potentially applicable to a very wide range of reasoning problems. Second, this objection seems to assume that the epistemological theory we defend, Strategic Reliabilism, is exhausted by the practical advice offered by Ameliorative Psychology. This is a misunderstanding. Strategic Reliabilism offers a general framework that accounts for the epistemic quality of particular reasoning strategies. While Strategic Reliabilism grounds the prescriptions of Ameliorative Psychology, it is not exhausted by those prescriptions. And third, while Ameliorative Psychology might not provide as much reason-guidance as we might hope, it does provide more than the theories of Standard Analytic Epistemology. The theories of SAE are almost entirely indifferent to issues of significance and to issues of the costs and benefits of reasoning. Such theories can perhaps advise that we should only adopt justified beliefs, and they can explain in exquisite detail what they mean by 'justified'. But this hardly counts as useful advice for three reasons. (a) We doubt that SAE embodies a reasonable method of identifying the proper goal of reasoning (see chapter 7). (b) For most of us at most times, there are infinitely many justified beliefs we could adopt. Without an account of significance or an account of the costs and benefits of reasoning, the theories of SAE have no way to advise someone to adopt one justified belief rather than any other (see chapters 5 and 6). And (c) at best, the theories of SAE define a goal of reasoning, they don't provide any useful guidance about how to achieve that goal (see chapter 9). This is reminiscent of the advice offered by one of our Little League baseball coaches who told his players, "When I tip my cap, that means you should hit a home run." Unlike proponents of SAE, the coach was joking.

6. Counterexamples, counterexamples

A number of counterexamples against reliabilist theories of justification depend on a disconnect between the reliability of a particular belief-forming mechanism and the subject's evidence for trusting that mechanism. To take a classic case, a reasoner might have a perfectly reliable clairvoyant belief-forming mechanism but no evidence for trusting it—in fact she might have positive reasons for not trusting it (BonJour 1980, Putnam 1983). The reliable clairvoyant case raises hard problems for Strategic Reliabilism (as do other examples of this sort). According to Strategic Reliabilism, what would it be for the reliable clairvoyant to reason in an excellent fashion when she has reasons not to trust her clairvoyant powers? And more generally, how does Strategic

Reliabilism handle cases in which a reasoning strategy is reliable (or unreliable) and the subject has strong reason to believe the opposite?

There are many examples that are going to be hard cases for Strategic Reliabilism, and this includes cases in which there is a disconnect between the reliability of a reasoning strategy and the subject's evidence for trusting it. The strength of Strategic Reliabilism does not reside in the ease with which it can be applied to cases in order to make straightforward, univocal epistemic judgments. The strength of Strategic Reliabilism is its reason-guiding capacity. Strategic Reliabilism provides a framework for identifying and developing excellent reasoning strategies—robustly reliable reasoning strategies for tackling significant problems. This is reversed for theories of SAE. A theory of SAE is supposed to be able to be applied to cases in order to determine whether particular beliefs are justified or not. But theories of SAE don't provide much in the way of useful reason-guiding resources (a point we have endlessly harped on in this book). And so we are content to admit that there will be plenty of hard cases in which a reasoner uses a number of different reasoning strategies and Strategic Reliabilism takes some of them to be excellent and others to be less so. The fact that Strategic Reliabilism does not always yield a simple, univocal normative judgment is a problem only if epistemic judgments of reasoning excellence must always be simple and univocal. But people reason in wonderfully complex and varied ways. Why should we expect our assessments of every instance of human reasoning to be simple?

Although we have admitted that the strength of Strategic Reliabilism is not its ability to be applied to particular cases, we should not overstate this point. There is no principled reason why we can't apply Strategic Reliabilism to very complicated cases. There are, however, two thoroughly practical reasons why the application of Strategic Reliabilism can be difficult. First, in order to apply Strategic Reliabilism to (say) the clairvoyant case, we need to know a lot about what reasoning strategies the clairvoyant is using. The SAE literature tends to ignore this, except to say that by hypothesis the subject's clairvoyance is reliable. But we are not told much about how the clairvoyance works or about the nature of the clairvoyant's second-order reasoning strategies about whether to trust her clairvoyant powers. The SAE literature does not give details about such reasoning strategies because the theories of SAE, including process reliabilism, are theories of justification; and justification is a property of belief tokens. Details about the workings of the clairvoyant's reasoning strategies are irrelevant to theories of SAE. But even if we are given lots of details about how the clairvoyant is reasoning, there is a second reason Strategic Reliabilism can be practically difficult to apply. The assessment of a particular reasoning strategy employed by the clairvoyant depends on many factors we might not know. For example, we would need to know the reliability scores of the clairvoyant's reasoning strategy; and if we wanted to make relative judgments, we'd need to know the reliability scores of its competitor strategies. (We would need to know more about these strategies as well—their robustness, their costs and the significance of the problems in their ranges.) There is no principled reason we couldn't find out about these matters. But in absence of detailed information about them, it will be very difficult to apply Strategic Reliabilism to particular cases. Strategic Reliabilism is hard to apply, but not because Strategic Reliabilism is so abstract it cannot be applied to real cases. The reason Strategic Reliabilism is hard to apply is that we need to know *a lot* in order to apply it.

7. Reliability scores

You define the reliability score of a reasoning strategy as the ratio of true to total judgments in the strategy's expected range. But what about cases (like the frequency formats) in which the strategy makes probabilistic inferences. If a reasoning strategy says that the probability of E is 1/3 (where E is a single event), and E happens (or doesn't happen), we can't say that on that basis that that's a true judgment. So reliability scores seem undefined for these sorts of reasoning strategies. And that's a serious lacuna in your theory.

This worry is analogous to the hoary problem facing the frequentist account of probability of single event probabilities. Because the frequency interpretation defines "probability" in terms of observed frequency, no probability of coming up heads (or tails) can be assigned to an unflipped coin. And, notoriously, the future posture of unflipped coins has no observed value. Our problem is similar in that we define a reasoning strategy's reliability score in terms of the relative frequency of true judgments in its expected range. If a reasoning strategy leads one to predict that there is a 1/3 chance of single event E, how do we determine what the probability of E really is? If we can't assign a probability to E, then we have no way of determining how reliable the probabilistic reasoning strategy is.

Our solution to the problem is analogous to how a frequentist might handle the problem of single event probabilities. A frequentist will not explain the probability of a single event in terms of an unobserved, independently specifiable disposition or propensity. Instead, a frequentist might say that the probability of a single event is an idealization concerning the observed values yielded under an indefinite (or infinite) number of samplings or potentially infinite sequence of trials. Turning to the problem of assigning reliability scores to probabilistic reasoning strategies, we should note that we define probability scores in terms of a reasoning strategy's *expected range* for a subject in an environment. The expected range is an idealization based on the nature of the environment in which a subject finds herself. The reliability score of a reasoning strategy applied to a single case (whether that strategy yields probability judgments or not) is, similarly, based on an idealization: It is the ratio of true to total judgments in the strategy's expected range, where this range is defined by an indefinite (or infinite) number of samplings or potentially infinite sequence of trials.

The introduction of an idealized expected range provides a way (or more likely, a number of ways) to assess the accuracy of a probabilistic reasoning strategy. Take a probabilistic reasoning strategy, R. Next take all the propositions R judges to have (say) probability 1/3. In R's expected range, we should expect 1/3 of those propositions to be true. So if we have a perfectly accurate probabilistic reasoning strategy, R, then for all propositions that R takes to have probability n/m, the frequency of those propositions that are true in R's expected range will be n/m. We can measure R's accuracy in terms of a correlation coefficient that represents how closely R's probability judgments reflect the actual frequencies of truths in R's expected range. (Notice, this is just how overconfidence in subjects was assessed. When we examine those cases in which subjects assign very high probabilities to events, those events turn out to be true at much lower frequencies. See chapter 2, section 3.4.)

8. Explanatory promises

In chapter 1 and elsewhere, you claim that a successful epistemological theory will help explain the Aristotelian Principle and the success of Ameliorative Psychology. It's not at all clear that you have kept these explanatory promises.

Let's begin with the Aristotelian Principle, which says that in the long run, good reasoning tends to lead to good outcomes. According to Strategic Reliabilism, good reasoning involves the efficient allocation of robustly reliable reasoning strategies to problems of significance. So the excellent reasoner will tend to have true beliefs about significant matters. We take it to be a true empirical hypothesis that true beliefs about significant matters tend to be instrumentally valuable in achieving good outcomes. People and institutions can more easily achieve their goals insofar as they have a true picture of relevant parts of the world. The explanation for the instrumental value of significant truth is likely to be complex (Kornblith 2002). But as long as significant truth is instrumentally valuable, the account of good reasoning provided by Strategic Reliabilism helps us to understand (i.e., plays a role in the explanation of) the Aristotelian Principle.

Strategic Reliabilism also helps us to understand the success of Ameliorative Psychology in at least three ways. First, Strategic Reliabilism is a general account of reasoning excellence, and so it applies to science. The fact that science displays excellent reasoning—that it involves robustly reliable reasoning strategies for solving significant problems—is part of the explanation for the characteristic pragmatic and epistemic success of science. In this way, Strategic Reliabilism helps us to understand the epistemic and pragmatic success of Ameliorative Psychology. Second, Strategic Reliabilism can be used to explain the success of the recommendations of Ameliorative Psychology. For example, the recommendation that Goldberg's Rule be used to make tentative diagnoses of psychiatric patients on the basis of a MMPI profile is successful because it is cheap, its reliability is unsurpassed and it tackles a problem that is significant for certain people. (On the other hand, it is not particularly robust, since its conditions of application are fairly restricted. But highly reliable reasoning strategies whose ranges are restricted to mostly very significant problems can nonetheless be excellent.) There is a third way in which Strategic Reliabilism can explain the success of Ameliorative Psychology: it can do so by helping it to be more successful. Ameliorative Psychology is not a monolith. There are occasionally disagreements about how to evaluate certain reasoning strategies. As we showed in chapter 8, Strategic Reliabilism provides a framework for understanding reasoning excellence, and so it can be used to assess the prescriptive recommendations made by Ameliorative Psychologists. So Strategic Reliabilism can be used to improve Ameliorative Psychology by identifying some of its less successful recommendations.

9. Abuse worries

You advocate the increased use of SPRs. But some SPRs depend for their success on not being widely known. For example, the details of the credit scoring models used by financial institutions are kept secret so that people cannot "play" them by engaging in activities solely for the purpose of improving their scores. Expanding the use of SPRs, particularly covert SPRs, leaves open the possibility of significant abuse. It is not hard to envision scenarios in which governments use SPRs to identify and persecute people whose political or religious views are out-of-favor, or in which (say) insurance companies use SPRs to identify people with health risks in order to restrict their access to life or health insurance.

Before we get too head-up about the potential abuses of SPRs, we must remember that honest policy assessment is comparative. We must compare the threat of the increased use of SPRs to the threat posed by expert judgment. Perhaps those suspicious of SPRs suppose that, while expert judgment is inferior in accuracy, it is also less prone to abuse. But this is by no means obvious. As Robyn Dawes has pointed out many times, expert judgment is more mysterious, more covert and less available to public inspection than SPRs (e.g., Dawes, 1994). SPRs are in principle publicly available and they come with reliability scores—they do not suffer from overconfidence. When a bank loan officer or a parole board member makes a decision, third parties typically do not know what evidence they took to be most important or how they weighed it. Indeed, most of us are considerably worse at identifying the main factors involved in our reasoning than we believe (Nisbett and Wilson, 1977). The loan officer who makes relatively more and better loans to white males than to minorities or women in the same financial situation might insist that he doesn't take race or gender into account. And unless we had pretty good evidence, provided, for instance, by an explicit model, who could doubt him? Dawes gives a terrific example of the sorts of abuses that can be avoided with more objective SPRs.

A colleague of mine in medical decision making tells of an investigation he was asked to make by the dean of a large and prestigious medical school to try to determine why it was unsuccessful in recruiting female students. My colleague studied the problem statistically "from the outside" and identified a major source of the problem. One of the older professors had cut back on his practice to devote time to interviewing applicants to the school. He assessed such characteristics as "emotional maturity," "seriousness of interest in medicine," and "neuroticism." Whenever he interviewed an unmarried female applicant, he concluded she was "immature." When he interviewed a married one, he concluded she was "not sufficiently interested in medicine," and when he interviewed a divorced one, he concluded she was "neurotic." Not many women were positively evaluated on these dimensions. . . . (Dawes 1988, 219)

This example makes clear that "expert" judgment is no defense against bias and discrimination.

We are badly in need of some cost-benefit judgment here. We know that well designed SPRs are more accurate than expert judgment. (For a treatment explicitly sensitive to the threat of SPR abuse, see Monahan, submitted.) Using SPRs will lead to fewer errors in parole decisions, clinical psychiatric diagnosis, medical diagnosis, college admission, personnel selection, and many more domains of life. While SPRs can be abused, expert judgment may leave even greater potential for abuse. In absence of some reasonable evidence for thinking that SPRs bring more serious costs than expert judgment, the case for SPRs is straightforward. For those who insist on holding out, it might be useful to imagine the situation reversed. Suppose we had found that experts are typically more reliable than the best SPRs. Would it be reasonable to insist on using SPRs because of an ill-defined concern about the potential abuse of expert judgment?

Strategic Reliabilism does not recommend SPRs because they are secret (when they are secret). It recommends SPRs because they are the tools most likely to (say) discriminate a person who will default on a loan from one who won't. Any procedure for making high stakes decisions comes with the potential of harmful errors. In the case of SPRs, we can reasonably expect certain kinds of errors. An undertrained or overworked credit-scoring employee might make a keystroke error, or a troubled employee might willfully enter incorrect information. A sensitive application of our view to a social institution would recognize the potential for such errors and would recommend the implementation of corrective procedures. Nothing in Strategic Reliabilism supports using SPRs irresponsibly—just the opposite. Still, what about the possibility of abuse that comes with SPRs being used for dastardly ends? Here we come to the limits of what epistemology can do. A monster like Hitler might employ SPRs to reason in an excellent manner. And that possibility is of course frightening. But it is no objection to our epistemological theory that it doesn't have the resources to condemn the wicked. Physics and chemistry don't either. And neither do the traditional theories of SAE. That is a job for moral and political theory.

There is another issue that may be an appropriate concern. If a SPR appeals to factors an individual cannot control, there is potential for serious abuse. For example, we can imagine a SPR that uses variables that appeal to race in making (say) credit decisions. Now, as a matter of fact, it turns out that the best models we have appeal to past behavior: "In a majority of situations, an individual's past behavior is the best predictor of future behavior. That doesn't mean that people are incapable of changing. Certainly many of us do, often profoundly. What it does mean is that no one has yet devised a method for determining who will change, or how or when . . . But if we are responsible for anything, it is our own behavior. Thus, the statistical approach often weights most that for which we have the greatest responsibility" (Dawes 1994, 105). But if someday a successful SPR does discriminate along questionable dimensions, it is always an open moral question whether we should use it.

10. The generality problem

Your view, Strategic Reliabilism, seems to fall victim to the generality problem. The generality problem arises because there is more than one way to characterize the belief-forming mechanism that produces a particular belief. Some of these characterizations will denote a reliable process, whereas other characterizations will not. Without some way of deciding which of these processes to count as the *one that produced the belief, the reliabilist runs the risk of having to say that such a belief is both justified (because it was produced by a reliable mechanism) and unjustified (because it was produced by an* un*reliable mechanism). And that's absurd (Goldman 1979, Feldman 1985). Here is Richard Feldman's characterization of the problem:*

The fact that every belief results from a process token that is an instance of many types, some reliable and some not, may partly account for the initial attraction of the reliability theory. In thinking about particular beliefs one can first decide intuitively whether the belief is justified and then go on to describe the process responsible for the belief in a way that appears to make the theory have the right result. Similarly, of course, critics of the theory can describe processes in ways that seem to make the theory have false consequences. For example, Laurence BonJour has proposed as counter-examples to the reliability theory cases in which a person believes things as a result of clairvoyance. In his examples, clairvoyance is a reliable process but the person has no reason to think that it is reliable. BonJour claims that the reliability theory has the incorrect consequence that the person's beliefs are justified. He assumes, however, that the relevant process type is clairvoyance. If one instead assumes that the relevant type is "believing something as a result of a process one has no reason to trust" the reliability theory seems to have different implications for these cases (1985, 160).

So how can Strategic Reliabilism overcome the generality problem?

In thinking about how Strategic Reliabilism handles the generality problem, it will be useful to consider a particular example. Suppose that whenever S is faced with the task of making predictions about human performance, she always uses what we might call the *human performance predictor* (HPP): She considers only the two lines of evidence she believes are most predictive, weighs them equally, and predicts that higher scores will be more highly correlated with better performance. In some sense, this is a meta-strategy, since it is a strategy for formulating strategies for making predictions about human performance. Now S is faced with some admissions problems, so she uses HPP: She considers only the two lines of evidence she deems most predictive (say, high school rank and test score rank), weighs them equally, and predicts that the best students will be those with the highest scores. We have already seen this reasoning strategy—it is ASPR (chapter 4, section 1). HPP and ASPR are nested reasoning strategies: ASPR's range (i.e., admissions problems) is a proper subset of HPP's range.

Now suppose that after having used these nested strategies to make a prediction about an admissions problem, S comes to believe that Jones will be a more successful student than Smith. Suppose further that ASPR is very reliable (i.e., it makes a high percentage of true predictions on admissions problems), but the more general HPP is not (i.e., while it leads to reliable predictions on admissions problems, it leads to very unreliable predictions on other sorts of human prediction problems). The classical reliabilist about justification is faced with a problem. S's belief was the product of a reliable belief-forming process (ASPR), and so on reliabilist grounds is justified. But S's belief was also the product of an *un*reliable belief-forming process (HPP), and so on reliabilist grounds is unjustified. The reliabilist seems committed to claiming that S's belief that Jones will be a more successful student than Smith is both justified and unjustified. Contradiction.

Goldman (1986) tries to solve the generality problem by arguing that the correct way to characterize the mechanism that produces a belief token is in terms of the narrowest causally operative process involved in its production. Thus, Goldman would argue that S's belief is justified, since the narrowest causally operative process involved in its production (i.e., ASPR) is reliable. On the other hand, if ASPR had been unreliable and the more general HPP had been reliable, Goldman would deem the belief unjustified. For our purposes, what's right about Goldman's suggestion is that any form of reliabilism need only countenance psychologically real, causally operative processes. But if we take reliabilism to be a theory about epistemic excellence rather than a theory about epistemic justification (i.e., if we accept Strategic Reliabilism instead of classical reliabilism), we can simply avoid the generality problem altogether.

How is that?

Strategic Reliabilism aims to assess reasoning processes rather than belief tokens. Suppose it is possible for a belief token to be produced by a reliable process (on one characterization) and by an unreliable process (on a different characterization). We can pass a positive judgment on the first process and a negative judgment about the second process. There is no need for the reliabilist about excellence to demand a unique character-ization of the process that produces a belief token. To take the example spelled out above, the strategic reliabilist might judge S's use of ASPR to have been epistemically excellent, though this will depend on the reliability and ease of use of competitor strategies. On the other hand, the strategic reliabilist might judge S's use of the HPP to have been not epistemically excellent (though this again will depend on the quality of the competi-tion). It is trivial that different reasoning strategies can have different, incompatible epistemic properties. So there is no need for the Strategic Reliabilist to demand a unique characterization of the process that pro-duces a belief token. And so there is no generality problem.

We should note that Earl Conee and Richard Feldman take the generality problem to be devastating to classical process reliabilism.

> In the absence of a brand new idea about relevant types, the problem looks insoluble. Consequently, process reliability theories of justification and knowledge look hopeless. (1998, p.24)

So if our view is able to overcome the generality problem, apparently this is news.

But it still seems that the generality problem raises a worry about Strategic Reliabilism. After all, a theory of epistemic excellence should tell us whether S's reasoning to the belief that Jones will be a more successful student than Smith was excellent or was not excellent. To do that, the theory needs to decide whether S's reasoning was excellent because the belief was the result of a reliable process (ASPR) or not excellent because the belief was the result of an unreliable process (HPP). So it would appear that the generality problem arises in a slightly new guise for Strategic Reliabilism.

This is not right. We take epistemic excellence to be a property of a temporal process that's dedicated to the achievement of certain specific goals. If we want to know whether a state (i.e., a belief) was the result of an epistemically excellent reasoning process, then it's important to specify what reasoning process we mean to assess. If we specify the reasoning narrowly, so that the belief is the result of ASPR, then the reasoning is excellent. If we specify the reasoning broadly, so that the belief is the result of HPP, then the reasoning is not excellent. If we want to know whether the entire voluntary reasoning process, involving both predictors, was excellent, then there is no single, univocal, uncomplicated assessment. In some ways it was excellent, and in some ways it was not. We can describe in quite a bit of detail the precise ways in which the reasoning was excellent and the precise ways in which it was not. But our theory yields no single, univocal, uncomplicated assessment of this episode of reasoning. And surely, that is a virtue of our theory.

But isn't it odd for you to simply say that there are episodes of reasoning that are in some ways excellent, and in other ways not? You don't seem inclined to say much about the epistemic quality of the reasoning in general. Resting content with this conclusion might reasonably strike one as stubbornly unambitious and perversely indolent.

There are two points to make against this worry. First, accurate theories about complicated subjects will sometimes yield complicated judgments. While the desire for simplicity is understandable, the advice often attributed to Einstein seems apt: theories should be as simple as possible, but no simpler. Second, from our perspective, epistemology is a forward-looking enterprise. So while epistemology inevitably involves passing judgments about the epistemic quality of people's reasoning and beliefs, evaluating the past is not the main point of epistemology. The main point of epistemology is to offer clear, usable criteria for epistemic excellence that will yield judgments about the relative quality of competing reasoning strategies. So going back to the example, the fundamental issue for us is not whether there is some way to characterize S's reasoning so that we may pass simple epistemic judgments. The real issue for epistemology to address is: What are the epistemically better ways S might reason about significant issues (and, of course, what makes those reasoning strategies better)?

But this still seems problematic. Besides insisting that an account of a process be "psychologically real," you do not favor any particular way of individuating belief-forming mechanisms when it comes to passing judgments of epistemic excellence. But a reasoning episode might involve dozens, or even hundreds, of such processes. Do you really want to say that for some reasoning episodes, every psychologically real belief-forming mechanism has its own epistemic worth?

Well, yes. There is no theoretical problem with this result. Some might worry that this result will make epistemology impossibly complex. It's true that it might take a superhuman effort to actually try to evaluate all the processes that went into the production of a single belief. But it's also true that as a practical matter, there is seldom a need to evaluate all the processes that went into producing a belief. Our efforts have typically been directed at voluntary reasoning strategies—strategies reasoners can choose to use or not to use. That's not to say that involuntary reasoning processes should be completely ignored. In fact, in our view, epistemology must pay closer attention to such processes. For example, a practical epistemology will offer voluntary reasoning strategies that correct involuntary reasoning processes (e.g., don't trust your visual color experiences in artificial light).

11. Strategic Reliabilism and the cannon

I understand that you haven't tried to set your view in context of (what you have been calling) Standard Analytic Epistemology. But isn't your theory, Strategic Reliabilism, really just a trivial variant of standard reliabilism (e.g., Armstrong 1973, Dretske 1981, Goldman 1986)?

Actually, our theory is unlike any traditional theory of justification defended by proponents of SAE. But we do gladly admit that there are many theories and views in contemporary epistemology that we believe point in the right direction. We will begin by briefly pointing out the ways in which our theory differs from the standard theories of SAE (see chapter 1 for a fuller discussion). We will then turn to some of the views that we think point in the right direction.

There are four ways in which Strategic Reliabilism differs from the standard theories of justification found in the SAE literature.

1. It is not a theory of justification.
2. It does not take as a major starting point philosophers' considered judgments about the epistemic status of beliefs, theories, or reasoning strategies.

3. Strategic Reliabilism is an explicitly cost-benefit approach to epistemology.

4. Strategic Reliabilism takes significance to be an ineliminable feature of epistemic evaluation.

As far as we know, no contemporary theory of justification has features 1–3. And only contextualism embraces something like 4 (DeRose 1995). Still, some of these ideas can be found in contemporary epistemology.

11.1 Not justification

At least two well-known philosophers have called for epistemological theories that do not focus on justification. In 1979, Alvin Goldman argued for an approach to epistemology he called *epistemics* that would focus on assessing and guiding our mental processes. While we clearly do not share Goldman's appreciation for our "epistemic folkways", his call for a "scientific epistemology" has not received the response it deserves (1992). In 1990, Stephen Stich defended a pragmatic account of "cognitive evaluation" and it was clearly not a theory for the assessment of belief tokens, but something very much like what we offer here: it was a theory for the assessment of a person's reasoning strategies. We could cite other philosophers' work who do not focus primarily on justification (e.g., Harman 1986), but the theory we have presented in this book is very much in the spirit of the proposals of Goldman and Stich.

What about virtue epistemology? These theories tend to focus on providing an account of epistemic virtue rather than epistemic justification (although many virtue theorists offer an account of epistemic justification in terms of epistemic virtue). There are, of course, quite different theories of virtue epistemology (e.g., Sosa 1991, Zagzebski 1996). We admire much of Sosa's epistemology. For example, we agree that "it is philosopher's arrogance to suppose mere reflection the source of all intellectual virtue" (Sosa 1991a, 266). Still, we do not take virtue theories of epistemology, as they currently stand, to be fellow travelers. Our primary worry is that current virtue theories are not sufficiently informed by empirical psychology. If we take an epistemic virtue to be (roughly) a habit of mind that tends to lead to truths, it is a thoroughly empirical question which habits of mind will do this. While virtue theorists would agree (e.g., Sosa 1991b), we suspect that they have underestimated how counterintuitive the "virtues" are likely to be. One worry is that insofar as virtues are dispositions that are reasonably stable across contexts, there is some reason to wonder whether people exhibit virtues of this sort (see Doris 2002 for a discussion of the moral virtues along these lines). Another problem is that the psychological evidence is likely to show that we just aren't as wise about epistemic matters as we think we are. Given the evidence presented in this book, it must be the case that we have a lot of mistaken beliefs about what habits of mind are virtuous. In a nutshell, the framework of virtue epistemology—roughly, that we should seek to instill in ourselves habits of mind that tend to be reliable—is fine as far as it goes. But to think we have a good intuitive sense of what those habits of mind might be strikes us as optimistic.

11.2. No theory of *"our"* considered epistemic judgments

We do not begin our epistemological investigations by focusing on our deeply considered epistemic intuitions about knowledge or justification. In contemporary epistemology, this view was championed by Stich in *The Fragmentation of Reason* (1990) and has found its most forceful defense in the recent empirical work of Weinberg, Nichols and Stich (2001). In terms of the number of our fellow travelers, this is perhaps the most radical aspect of our approach. The diversity findings of Weinberg, Nichols and Stich suggest that the attempt to provide a traditional account of knowledge is just anthropology. Once one grants the essentially anthropological nature of the standard project, one is forced to rethink whether it can lead to a genuine reason-guiding epistemology. And yet even Goldman, who for a quarter century has called for a "scientific epistemology" that does not focus on justification, insists on the traditional project (1992, 2001). It is time for naturalistically inclined philosophers to reject the traditional project—epistemology as armchair anthropology—as anathema not only to science but also to the essentially normative character of epistemology.

11.3. Costs and benefits

Many naturalistically inclined philosophers have argued against epistemological theories that require that people have brains "the size of a blimp" (in Stich's memorable phrase [1990, 27]). But as far as we know, no philosopher has explicitly proposed a cost-benefit approach to epistemology. So where does the idea come from? The idea is deeply embedded in psychology. Indeed, this book project received a withering review from a psychologist who was incensed that we would bother wasting ink on the utterly trivial proposition that good reasoning involves the efficient allocation of limited cognitive resources. Regardless of whether it is trivial, it is certainly not an implicit tenet of the philosophical discipline charged with the normative evaluation of cognition. It's not that most analytic epistemologists would deny the proposition, it's just that they appear to have no use for it in their theorizing. This is one more example—as if one more were needed—of the yawning chasm that separates the discipline that studies reasoning from the discipline that seeks to evaluate it.

11.4. Significance

Finally, what about significance? The idea that good reasoning is reasoning about significant matters is, of course, a central idea of the pragmatic tradition in epistemology. And plenty of non-pragmatists have pointed out that not all truths are created equal. But in recent years, this point has been made best by a philosopher of science, Philip Kitcher (1993, 2001). Not only has Kitcher written forcefully about significance, but the final chapter of *The Advancement of Science* (1993; see also his 1990) is a fascinating attempt to view social epistemology from a cost-benefit perspective. There are three features of this emerging trend that give reason for optimism. First, it honors what psychologists have already shown: Good reasoning is an intricate achievement of busy brains in complex environments. Second, treating cost-benefit measures as an essential component in epistemology allows economics and psychology—the current and future tools of public policy—to recruit and assimilate the normative, theory-building efforts of properly trained epistemologists. The third reason for optimism is more self-serving: This approach places epistemology not just where it belongs, but where this book began—in the philosophy of science, and in so doing, in science itself.

References

Alexander, S. A. 1971. Sex, Arguments, and Social Engagements in Marital and Premarital Relations. Master's thesis, University of Missouri, Kansas City.

Anderson, E. 1993. *Value and Ethics in Economics.* Cambridge: Harvard University Press.

Aristotle. *Nicomachean Ethics,* ed. and trans. Roger Crisp (Cambridge: Cambridge University Press, 2000).

Arkes, H. 1991. Costs and Benefits of Judgment Errors: Implications for Debiasing. *Psychological Bulletin* 110: 486–98.

Arkes, H. 2003. The Nonuse of Psychological Research at Two Federal Agencies. *Psychological Science* 14: 1–6.

Arkes, H., R. Dawes, and C. Christensen. 1986. Factors Influencing the Use of a Decision Rule in a Probabilistic Task. *Organizational Behavior and Human Decision Processes* 37: 93–110.

Arkes, H., C. Christensen, C. Lai, and C. Blumer. 1987. Two Methods of Reducing Overconfidence. *Organizational Behavior and Human Decision Processes* 39: 133–44.

Armstrong, D. M. 1973. *Belief, Truth and Knowledge.* Cambridge: Cambridge University Press.

Ashenfelter, O., D. Ashmore, and R. Lalonde. 1995. Bordeaux Wine Vintage Quality and the Weather. *Chance* 8: 7–14.

Bazerman, M. 2001. *Judgment in Managerial Decision-Making.* 5th ed. New York: Wiley.

Bettman, J. R., E. J. Johnson, M. F. Luce, and J. W. Payne. 1990. A Componential Analysis of Cognitive Effort in Choice. *Organizational Behavior and Human Decision Processes* 45: 111–39.

Bishop, M. 2000. In Praise of Epistemic Irresponsibility: How Lazy and Ignorant Can You Be? *Synthese* 122: 179–208.

Bishop, M., and J. D. Trout. 2002. 50 Years of Successful Predictive Modeling Should Be Enough: Lessons for Philosophy of Science. *Philosophy of Science: PSA 2000 Symposium Papers* 69 (supplement): S197–S208.

Bloom, R. F., and E. G. Brundage. 1947. Predictions of Success in Elementary School for Enlisted Personnel. In *Personnel Research and Test Development in the Naval Bureau of Personnel*, ed. D. B. Stuit, 233–61. Princeton: Princeton University Press.

BonJour, L. 1980. Externalist Theories of Empirical Knowledge. In *Midwest Studies in Philosophy*. Vol. 5, *Studies in Epistemology*, ed. Peter French, Theodore Uehling Jr., and Howard Wettstein. Minneapolis: University of Minnesota Press.

BonJour, L. 1985. *The Structure of Empirical Knowledge*. Cambridge: Harvard University Press.

BonJour, L. 2002. *Epistemology: Classic Problems and Contemporary Responses*. Lanham, Md.: Rowman and Littlefield.

Borges, B., D. G. Goldstein, A. Ortmann, and G. Gigerenzer. 1999. Can Ignorance Beat the Stock Market? In *Simple Heuristics That Make Us Smart*, ed. G. Gigerenzer, P. Todd, and the ABC Research Group. New York: Oxford University Press.

Bowman, E. H. 1963. Consistency and Optimality in Managerial Decision-Making. *Management Science* 9: 310–21.

Boyd, R. 1980. Scientific Realism and Naturalistic Epistemology. In *PSA 1980*, vol. 2, ed. P. D. Asquith and R. N. Giere, 613–62. East Lansing, Mich.: Philosophy of Science Association.

Boyd, R. 1988. "How to be a Moral Realist." In *Essays on Moral Realism*, ed. G. Sayre-McCord. Ithaca, NY: Cornell University Press, 181–228.

Carey, S. 1985. *Conceptual Change in Childhood*. Cambridge: MIT Press.

Carpenter, R., A. Gardner, P. McWeeny, and J. Emery. 1977. Multistage Score System for Identifying Infants at Risk of Unexpected Death. *Archives of Diseases in Childhood* 53: 606–12.

Carroll, J., R. Winer, D. Coates, J. Galegher, and J. Alibrio. 1988. Evaluation, Diagnosis, and Prediction in Parole Decision-Making. *Law and Society Review* 17: 199–228.

Casscells, W., A. Schoenberger, and T. Grayboys. 1978. Interpretation by Physicians of Clinical Laboratory Results. *New England Journal of Medicine* 299: 999–1001.

Chapman, L., and J. Chapman. 1967. Genesis of Popular but Erroneous Psychodiagnostic Observations. *Journal of Abnormal Psychology* 73: 151–155.

Chapman, L., and J. Chapman. 1969. Illusory Correlation as an Obstacle to the Use of Valid Psychodiagnostic Signs. *Journal of Abnormal Psychology* 74: 271–80.

Cherniak, C. 1986. *Minimal Rationality.* Cambridge: MIT Press.

Chi, M., R. Glaser, and E. Rees. 1982. Expertise in Problem Solving. In *Advances in the Psychology of Human Intelligence*, vol. 1, ed. R. Sternberg. Hillsdale, N.J.: Erlbaum.

Chisholm, R. 1981. A Version of Foundationalism. In *Midwest Studies in Philosophy.* Vol. 5, *Studies in Epistemology*, ed. Peter French, Theodore Uehling Jr., and Howard Wettstein. Minneapolis: University of Minnesota Press.

Clement, J. 1982. Students' Preconceptions in Introductory Mechanics. *American Journal of Physics* 50.1: 66–71.

Cohen, L. J. 1981. Can Human Irrationality Be Experimentally Demonstrated? *Behavioral and Brain Sciences* 4: 317–31.

Conee, E., and R. Feldman. 1998. The Generality Problem for Reliabilism. *Philosophical Studies* 89: 1–29.

Csikszentmihalyi, M. 1999. If We Are So Rich, Why Aren't We Happy? *American Psychologist* 54: 821–27.

Daniels, N. 1979. Wide Reflective Equilibrium and Theory Acceptance in Ethics. *Journal of Philosophy* 76: 256–82.

Dasgupta, P. 1993. *An Inquiry into Well-Being and Destitution.* New York: Oxford University Press.

Dawes, R. 1971. A Case Study of Graduate Admissions: Application of Three Principles of Human Decision-Making. *American Psychologist* 26: 180–88.

Dawes, R. 1982. The Robust Beauty of Improper Linear Models in Decision-Making. In *Judgment under Uncertainty: Heuristics and Biases*, ed. D. Kahneman, P. Slovic, and A. Tversky, 391–407. Cambridge: Cambridge University Press. First appeared in *American Psychologist* 34 (1979): 571–82.

Dawes, R. 1988. *Rational Choice in an Uncertain World.* New York: Harcourt.

Dawes, R. 1994. *House of Cards.* New York: Free Press.

Dawes, R. 2001. *Everyday Irrationality: How Pseudo-Scientists, Lunatics, and the Rest of Us Systematically Fail to Think Rationally.* Boulder, Colo.: Westview.

Dawes, R. 2002. The Ethics of Using or Not Using Statistical Prediction Rules in Psychological Practice and Related Consulting Activities. *Philosophy of Science: PSA 2000 Symposium Papers* 69 (supplement): S178–S184.

Dawes, R., and B. Corrigan. 1974. Linear Models in Decision Making. *Psychological Bulletin* 81: 95–106.

Dawes, R., D. Faust, and P. Meehl. 1989. Clinical versus Actuarial Judgment. *Science* 243: 1668–74.

DeRose, K. 1995. Solving the Skeptical Problem. *Philosophical Review* 104.1: 1–52.

DeVaul, R. A., F. Jervey, J. A. Chappell, P. Carver, B. Short, and S. O'Keefe. 1957. Medical School Performance of Initially Rejected Students. *Journal of the American Medical Association* 257: 47–51.

Diener, E. 2000. Subjective Well-Being: The Science of Happiness and a Proposal for a National Index. *American Psychologist* 55: 34–43.

Diener, E., and S. Oishi. 2000. Money and Happiness: Income and Subjective Well-Being across Nations. In *Culture and Subjective Well-Being*, ed. E. Diener and E. Suh, 185–218. Cambridge: MIT Press.

Diener, E., and M. Seligman. 2002. Very Happy People. *Psychological Science* 13.1: 81–84.

Doris, J. 2002. *Lack of Character: Personality and Moral Behavior*. Cambridge: Cambridge University Press.

Dretske, F. 1971. Conclusive Reasons. *Australasian Journal of Philosophy* 49: 1–22.

Dretske, F. 1981. *Knowledge and the Flow of Information*. Cambridge: MIT Press.

Dublin, L., and A. Lotka. 1930. *The Money Value of a Man*. New York: Ronald.

Dunham, H. W., and B. N. Meltzer. 1946. Predicting Length of Hospitalization of Mental Patients. *American Journal of Sociology* 52: 123–31.

Edwards, D., and J. Edwards. 1977. Marriage: Direct and Continuous Measurement. *Bulletin of the Psychonomic Society* 10: 187–88.

Einhorn, H. 1986. Accepting Error to Make Less Error. *Journal of Personality Assessment* 50.3: 387–95.

Einhorn, H. J., and R. M. Hogarth. 1975. Unit Weighting Schemas for Decision Making. *Organizational Behavior and Human Performance* 13: 172–92.

Faust, D., and P. E. Meehl. 2002. Using Meta-Scientific Studies to Clarify or Resolve Questions in the Philosophy and History of Science. *Philosophy of Science: PSA 2000 Symposium Papers* 69 (supplement): S185–S196.

Faust, D., and J. Ziskin. 1988. The Expert Witness in Psychology and Psychiatry. *Science* 241: 1143–144.

Feldman, R. 1985. Reliability and Justification. *The Monist* 68: 159–174.

Feldman, R. 1999. Methodological Naturalism in Epistemology. In *The Blackwell Guide to Epistemology*, ed. John Greco and Ernest Sosa. Malden, Mass., and Oxford: Blackwell.

Feldman, R. 2003. *Epistemology*. Upper Saddle River, N.J.: Prentice-Hall.

Firth, R. 1998. Epistemic Merit, Intrinsic and Instrumental. In *Defense of Radical Empiricism*, ed. John Troyer. Lanham, Md., and Oxford: Rowman and Littlefield.

Fischhoff, B., P. Slovic, and S. Lichtenstein. 1977. Knowing with Certainty: The Appropriateness of Extreme Confidence. *Journal of Experimental Psychology: Human Perception and Performance* 3: 552–64.

Foley, R. 1985. What's Wrong with Reliabilism? *The Monist* 68: 188–202.

Frey, B., and A. Stutzer. 2002. *Happiness and Economics: How the Economy and Institutions Affect Human Well-Being*. Princeton: Princeton University Press.

Friedman, M. 1974. Explanation and Scientific Understanding. *Journal of Philosophy* 71: 5–19.

Gettier, E. L. 1963. Is Knowledge Justified True Belief? *Analysis* 23: 121–23.

Gigerenzer, G. 1991. How to Make Cognitive Illusions Disappear: Beyond Heuristics and Biases. In *European Review of Social Psychology*, vol. 2, ed. W. Stroebe and M. Hewstone. Chichester, U.K.: Wiley.

Gigerenzer, G. 1996. On Narrow Norms and Vague Heuristics: A Reply to Kahneman and Tversky. *Psychological Review* 103: 592–96.

Gigerenzer, G. 1996a. The Psychology of Good Judgment: Frequency Formats and Simple Algorithms. *Medical Decision Making* 16.3: 273–80.

Gigerenzer, G., and D. Goldstein. 1999. Betting on One Good Reason: The Take The Best Heuristic. In *Simple Heuristics That Make Us Smart,* ed. G. Gigerenzer, P. Todd, and the ABC Research Group. New York: Oxford University Press.

Gigerenzer, G., and U. Hoffrage. 1995. How to Improve Bayesian Reasoning without Instruction: Frequency Formats. *Psychological Review* 102, 4: 684–704.

Gigerenzer, G., U. Hoffrage, and A. Ebert. 1998. AIDS Counselling for Low-Risk Clients. *AIDS CARE* 10.2: 197–211.

Gigerenzer, G., P. Todd, and the ABC Research Group, eds. 1999. *Simple Heuristics That Make Us Smart.* New York: Oxford University Press.

Gilovich, T. 1983. Biased Evaluation and Persistence in Gambling. *Journal of Personality and Social Psychology* 44: 1110–126.

Gilovich, T. 1991. *How We Know What Isn't So.* New York: Free Press.

Gilovich, T., D. Griffin, and D. Kahneman, eds. 2002. *Heuristics and Biases: The Psychology of Human Judgment.* New York: Cambridge University Press.

Goldberg, L. R. 1965. Diagnosticians vs. Diagnostic Signs: The Diagnosis of Psychosis vs. Neurosis from the MMPI. *Psychological Monographs* 79.9: Whole no. 602.

Goldberg, L. R. 1968. Simple Models of Simple Processes? Some Research on Clinical Judgments. *American Psychologist* 23: 483–96.

Goldberg, L. R. 1970. Man vs. Model of Man: A Rationale, Plus Some Evidence, for a Method of Improving on Clinical Inferences. *Psychological Bulletin* 73: 422–32.

Golding, J., S. Limerick, and A. Macfarlane. 1985. *Sudden Infant Death.* Seattle: University of Washington Press.

Goldman, A. 1978. Epistemics: The Regulative Theory of Cognition. *Journal of Philosophy* 75: 509–23.

Goldman, A. 1979. What is Justified Belief? In *Justification and Knowledge,* ed. George Pappas. Dordrecht: Reidel, 1–23.

Goldman, A. 1986. *Epistemology and Cognition.* Cambridge: MIT Press.

Goldman, A. 1992. Epistemic Folkways and Scientific Epistemology. *Liaisons: Philosophy Meets the Cognitive and Social Sciences.* Cambridge: MIT Press.

Goldman, A. 1993. Ethics and Cognitive Science. *Ethics* 103: 337–360.

Goldman, A. 1999. *Knowledge in a Social World.* New York: Oxford University Press.

Goldman, A. 1999a. A Priori Warrant and Naturalistic Epistemology. In *Philosophical Perspectives.* Vol. 13, *Epistemology,* ed. James Tomberlin. Boston: Blackwell.

Goldman, A. 2001. Replies to the Contributors. *Philosophical Topics* 29: 461–511.

Goldstein, D. G., and G. Gigerenzer. 1999. The Recognition Heuristic: How Ignorance Makes Us Smart. In *Simple Heuristics That Make Us Smart*, ed. G. Gigerenzer, P. Todd, and the ABC Research Group. New York: Oxford University Press.

Goodman, N. 1965. *Fact, Fiction, and Forecast.* Indianapolis: Bobbs-Merrill.

Grove, W. M., and P. E. Meehl. 1996. Comparative Efficiency of Informal (Subjective, Impressionistic) and Formal (Mechanical, Algorithmic) Prediction Procedures: The Clinical-Statistical Controversy. *Psychology, Public Policy, and Law* 2: 293–323.

Hacking, I. 1999. *The Social Construction of What?* Cambridge: Harvard University Press.

Harman, G. 1986. *Change in View.* Cambridge: MIT Press.

Harman, G. 1998. Moral philosophy meets social psychology: virtue ethics and the fundamental attribution error. *Proceedings of the Aristotelian Society* 1998–99, 99: 315–331. Revised version in *Explaining Value and Other Essays in Moral Philosophy*, ed. G. Harman. Oxford: Clarendon Press, 2000, 165–78.

Hastie, R., and R. Dawes. 2001. *Rational Choice in an Uncertain World.* London: Sage.

Henrion, M., and B. Fischoff. 1986. Assessing Uncertainty in Physical Constants. *American Journal of Physics* 54: 791–98.

Hertwig, R., and G. Gigerenzer. 1998. The "Conjunction Fallacy" Revisited: How Intelligent Inferences Look Like Reasoning Errors. *Journal of Behavioral Decision Making* 12: 275–305.

Hoffrage, U., and G. Gigerenzer, 2004. How to Improve the Diagnostic Inferences of Medical Experts. In *Experts in Science and Society*, ed. E. Kurz-Milcke and G. Gigerenzer, New York: Kluwer Academic/Plenum Publishers, 249–68.

Howard, J. W., and R. Dawes. 1976. Linear Prediction of Marital Happiness. *Personality and Social Psychology Bulletin* 2.4 (fall): 478–80.

Kahneman, D. 2000. New Challenges to the Rationality Assumption. In *Choices, Values, and Frames*, ed. D. Kahneman and A. Tversky, 758–74. New York: Cambridge University Press.

Kahneman, D., and A. Tversky. 1973. On the Psychology of Prediction. *Psychological Review* 80: 237–51. Reprinted in *Judgment under Uncertainty: Heuristics and Biases*, ed. D. Kahneman, P. Slovic, and A. Tversky, 48–68. Cambridge: Cambridge University Press, 1982.

Kahneman, D., and A. Tversky. 1982. On the Study of Statistical Intuitions. *Cognition* 11: 123–41. Reprinted in *Judgment under Uncertainty: Heuristics and Biases*, ed. D. Kahneman, P. Slovic, and A. Tversky, 493–508. Cambridge: Cambridge University Press, 1982.

Kahneman, D., and A. Tversky. 1996. On the Reality of Cognitive Illusions. *Psychological Review* 103: 582–91.

Kahneman, D., P. Slovic, and A. Tversky, eds. 1982. *Judgment under Uncertainty: Heuristics and Biases*. Cambridge: Cambridge University Press.

Keil, F. 1989. *Concepts, Kinds, and Cognitive Development*. Cambridge: MIT Press.

Kim, J. 1988. What Is "Naturalized Epistemology"? *Philosophical Perspectives* 2: 381–405.

Kitcher, P. 1981. Explanatory Unification. *Philosophy of Science* 48: 507–31.

Kitcher, P. 1990. The Division of Cognitive Labor. *Journal of Philosophy* 87: 5–21.

Kitcher, P. 1993. *The Advancement of Science*. New York: Oxford University Press.

Kitcher, P. 2001. *Science, Truth, and Democracy*. New York: Oxford University Press.

Koriat, A., S. Lichtenstein, and B. Fischhoff. 1980. Reasons for Confidence. *Journal of Experimental Psychology: Human Learning and Memory* 6: 107–18.

Kornblith, H. 1992. The Laws of Thought. *Philosophy and Phenomenological Research*, 52: 895–911.

Kornblith, H. 1993. *Inductive Inference and Its Natural Ground*. Cambridge: MIT Press.

Kornblith, H. 2002. *Knowledge and Its Place in Nature*. Cambridge: MIT Press.

Lane, R. 2000. *The Loss of Happiness in Market Democracies*. New Haven: Yale University Press.

Lehman, D. R., R. O. Lempert, and R. E. Nisbett. 1993. The Effects of Graduate Training on Reasoning: Formal Discipline and Thinking about Everyday Life Events. In *Rules for Reasoning*, ed. R. Nisbett, 361–401. Hillsdale, N.J.: Erlbaum.

Lehrer, K. 1974. *Knowledge*. New York: Oxford University Press.

Lehrer, K., and T. D. Paxson Jr. 1969. Knowledge: Undefeated Justified True Belief. *Journal of Philosophy* 66: 225–37.

Leli, D. A., and S. B. Filskov. 1984. Clinical Detection of Intellectual Deterioration Associated with Brain Damage. *Journal of Clinical Psychology* 40: 1435–41.

Lewis, D. 1996. Elusive Knowledge. *Australasian Journal of Philosophy* 74: 549–57.

Lichtenstein, S., and B. Fischhoff. 1977. Do Those Who Know More Also Know More about How Much They Know? The Calibration of Probability Judgements. *Organizational Behavior and Human Performance* 3: 552–64.

Lopes, L. 1991. The Rhetoric of Irrationality. *Theory and Psychology* 1: 65–82.

Lord, C., M. Lepper, and E. Preston. 1984. Considering the Opposite: A Corrective Strategy for Social Judgment. *Journal of Personality and Social Psychology* 47: 1231–43.

Lovie, A. D., and P. Lovie. 1986. The Flat Maximum Effect and Linear Scoring Models for Prediction. *Journal of Forecasting* 5: 159–68.

Maynard Smith, J. 1978. Optimization Theory in Evolution. *Annual Review of Ecology and Systematics* 9: 31–56.

Meehl, P. 1954. *Clinical versus Statistical Prediction: A Theoretical Analysis and a Review of the Evidence.* Minneapolis: University of Minnesota Press.

Meehl, P. 1957. When Shall We Use Our Heads Instead of the Formula? *Journal of Counseling Psychology* 4: 268–73.

Meehl, P. 1986. Causes and Effects of My Disturbing Little Book. *Journal of Personality Assessment* 50: 370–75.

Meehl, P. 1990. Why Summaries of Research on Psychological Theories Are Often Uninterpretable. *Psychological Reports* 66: 195–244.

Miller, P. M., and N. S. Fagley. 1991. The Effects of Framing, Problem Variations, and Providing Rationale on Choice. *Personality and Social Psychology Bulletin* 17: 517–22.

Milstein, R. M., L. Wildkinson, G. N. Burrow, and W. Kessen. 1981. Admission Decisions and Performance during Medical School. *Journal of Medical Education* 56: 77–82.

Monahan, J. (submitted for publication). "Determining danger: Admissible risk factors in criminal sentencing and civil commitment."

Myers, D. 2000. The Funds, Friends, and Faith of Happy People. *American Psychologist* 55: 56–67.

Newell, A., and H. Simon. 1972. *Human Problem Solving.* Englewood Cliffs, N.J.: Prentice-Hall.

Nisbett, R., ed. 1993. *Rules for Reasoning.* Hillsdale, N.J.: Erlbaum.

Nisbett, R., and E. Borgida. 1975. Attribution and the Psychology of Prediction. *Journal of Personality and Social Psychology* 32: 932–43.

Nisbett, R., and L. Ross. 1980. *Human Inference: Strategies and Shortcomings of Social Judgment.* Englewood Cliffs, N.J.: Prentice-Hall.

Nisbett, R., and T. Wilson. 1977. Telling More Than We Can Know: Verbal Reports on Mental Processes. *Psychological Review* 84.3: 231–59.

Oskamp, S. 1965. Overconfidence in Case Study Judgments. *Journal of Consulting Psychology* 63: 81–97.

Pappas, G., and M. Swain. 1973. Some Conclusive Reasons against "Conclusive Reasons." In *Essays on Knowledge and Justification,* ed. G. Pappas and M. Swain (1978), 62–66. Ithaca: Cornell University Press.

Parker, G. A. 1974. The Reproductive Behaviour and the Nature of Sexual Selection in *Scatophaga stercoraria. Evolution* 28: 93–108.

Passell, P. 1990. Wine Equation Puts Some Noses Out of Joint. *New York Times,* March 4: 1.

Payne, J. W., J. R. Bettman, and E. J. Johnson. 1993. *The Adaptive Decision Maker.* New York: Cambridge University Press.

Piattelli-Palmarini, M. 1994. *Inevitable Illusions: How Mistakes of Reason Rule Our Minds.* New York: John Wiley.

Plantinga, A. 1993. *Warrant and Proper Function.* New York: Oxford University Press.

Plous, S. 1993. *The Psychology of Judgment and Decision-Making.* New York: McGraw-Hill.

Pollock, J. 1974. *Knowledge and Justification.* Princeton: Princeton University Press.

Pollock, J., and J. Cruz. 1999. *Contemporary Theories of Knowledge.* 2nd ed. Lanham, Md.: Rowman and Littlefield.

Porter, T. 1994. Objectivity as Standardization: The Rhetoric of Impersonality in Measurement, Statistics, and Cost-Benefit Analysis. In *Rethinking Objectivity,* ed. Allan Megill. Durham, N.C.: Duke University Press.

Putnam, H. 1983. Why Reason Can't Be Naturalized. In *Realism and Reason, Philosophical Papers,* vol. 3, 229–47. Cambridge: Cambridge University Press.

Quine, W. V. O. 1969. Natural Kinds. In *Ontological Relativity and Other Essays,* 114–38. New York: Columbia University Press.

Quinsey, V. L., G. T. Harris, M. E. Rice, and C. A. Cormier. 1998. *Violent Offenders: Appraising and Managing Risk.* Washington: American Psychological Association.

Railton, P. 1986. Moral Realism. *Philosophical Review* 95: 163–207.

Rawls, J. 1971. *A Theory of Justice.* Cambridge: Harvard University Press.

Ross, L. 1977. The Intuitive Psychologist and His Shortcomings: Distortions in the Attribution Process. *10 Advances in Experimental Social Psychology 173,* ed. L. Berkowitz.

Sawyer, J. 1966. Measurement and Prediction, Clinical and Statistical. *Psychological Bulletin* 66: 178–200.

Sen, A. 2000. The Discipline of Cost-Benefit Analysis. *Journal of Legal Studies* 29.2, part 2: 931–52.

Sieck, W., and J. F. Yates. 1997. Exposition Effects on Decision Making: Choice and Confidence in Choice. *Organizational Behavior and Human Decision Processes* 70: 207–19.

Sieck, W. R., and H. R. Arkes. Overconfidence Contributes to Decision Aid Neglect. Unpublished ms.

Simon, H. A. 1982. *Models of Bounded Rationality.* Cambridge: MIT Press.

Sklar, L. 1975. Methodological Conservatism. *Philosophical Review* 84: 374–400. Reprinted in *Philosophy and Spacetime Physics* (1985), ed. Lawrence Sklar. Berkeley: University of California Press.

Smith, E., and D. Medin. 1981. *Categories and Concepts.* Cambridge: Harvard University Press.

Sober, E. 1997. Is the Mind an Adaptation for Coping with Environmental Complexity? *Biology and Philosophy* 12: 539–50.

Sosa, E. 1991. *Knowledge in Perspective.* Cambridge: Cambridge University Press.

Sosa, E. 1991a. Equilibrium in Coherence. In *Knowledge in Perspective,* 257–269. New York: Cambridge University Press.

Sosa, E. 1991b. Knowledge and Intellectual Virtue. In *Knowledge in Perspective,* 225–244. New York: Cambridge University Press. Originally published in *The Monist* 68: 224–45.

Spelke, E. S. 1994. Initial Knowledge: Six Suggestions. *Cognition* 50: 431–55.

Stanovich, K., and R. West. 1998. Individual differences in rational thought. *Journal of Experimental Psychology: General* 127: 161–188.

Stanovich, K. 1999. *Who Is Rational?: Studies of Individual Differences in Reasoning.* Hillsdale, N.J.: Erlbaum.

Stein, E. 1996. *Without Good Reason: The Rationality Debate in Philosophy and Cognitive Science.* New York: Oxford University Press.

Stich, S. 1985. Could Man Be an Irrational Animal? *Synthese* 64.1: 115–34.

Stich, S. 1990. *The Fragmentation of Reason.* Cambridge: MIT Press.

Stillwell, W., F. Barron, and W. Edwards. 1983. Evaluating Credit Applications: A Validation of Multiattribute Utility Weight Elicitation Techniques. *Organizational Behavior and Human Performance* 32: 87–108.

Stine, G. J. 1996. *Acquired Immune Deficiency Syndrome: Biological, Medical, Social, and Legal Issues.* 2nd ed. Englewood Cliffs, N.J.: Prentice-Hall.

Strayer, D. L., and W. Johnston. 2001. Driven to Distraction: Dual-Task Studies of Simulated Driving and Conversing on a Cellular Telephone. *Psychological Science* 12.6: 462–66.

Stutzer, A. and Frey, B. Under review. Stress that Doesn't Pay: The Commuting Paradox. Institute for Empirical Research in Economics, Working Paper No. 151, University of Zurich.

Sunstein, C. 2000. Cognition and Cost-Benefit Analysis. *Journal of Legal Studies* 29.2, part 2: 1059–1104.

Sunstein, C. 2003. Moral Heuristics. University of Chicago Law and Economics, Olin Working Paper No. 180 (March).

Swets, J., R. Dawes, and J. Monahan. 2000. Psychological Science Can Improve Diagnostic Decisions. *Psychological Science in the Public Interest* 1: 1–26.

Takemura, K. 1992. Effect of Decision Time on Framing of Decision: A Case of Risky Choice Behavior. *Psychologia* 35: 180–85.

Takemura, K. 1993. The Effect of Decision Frame and Decision Justification on Risky Choice. *Japanese Psychological Research* 35: 36–40.

Takemura, K. 1994. Influence of Elaboration on the Framing of Decision. *Journal of Psychology* 128: 33–39.

Thompson, L. 2001. *The Mind and Heart of the Negotiator.* 2nd ed. Upper Saddle River, N.J.: Prentice-Hall.

Thornton, B. 1977. Linear Prediction of Marital Happiness: A Replication. *Personality and Social Psychology Bulletin* 3: 674–76.

Todd, P. M., and G. Gigerenzer. 2000. Simple Heuristics That Make Us Smart (with commentaries). *Behavioral and Brain Sciences* 23: 727–66.

Todd, P. M., G. Gigerenzer, and the ABC Research Group. 2000. How Can We Open Up the Adaptive Toolbox? (Reply to Commentaries.) *Behavioral and Brain Sciences* 23.5: 767–80.

Trout, J. D. 1998. *Measuring the Intentional World: Realism, Naturalism, and Quantitative Methods in the Behavioral Sciences*. New York: Oxford University Press.

Trout, J. D. 2002. Scientific Explanation and the Sense of Understanding. *Philosophy of Science* 69.2: 212–33.

Unger, P. 1984. *Philosophical Relativity*. Minneapolis: University of Minnesota Press.

van der Heijden, A. H. C. 1998. Attention. In *A Companion to Cognitive Science*, ed. W. Bechtel and G. Graham, 121–28. Malden, Mass.: Blackwell.

Wedding, D. 1983. Clinical and Statistical Prediction in Neuropsychology. *Clinical Neuropsychology* 5: 49–55.

Weinberg, J., S. Nichols, and S. Stich. 2001. Normativity and Epistemic Intuitions. *Philosophical Topics* 29.1 and 29.2: 429–60.

Weiss, M. 1994. *Latitudes and Attitudes: An Atlas of American Tastes, Trends, Politics, and Passions*. Boston: Little, Brown.

Wells, G. L. 2001. Eyewitness Lineups: Data, Theory, and Policy. *Psychology, Public Policy, and Law* 7: 791–801.

Wells, G. L., E. Olson, and S. Charman. 2002. The Confidence of Eyewitnesses in Their Identification from Lineups. *Current Directions in Psychological Science* 11.5: 151–54.

Wells, G. L., M. Small, S. J. Penrod, R. S. Malpass, S. M. Fulero, and C. A. E. Brimacombe. 1998. Eyewitness Identification Procedures: Recommendations for Lineups and Photospreads. *Law and Human Behavior* 22: 603–47.

Wiggins, N., and E. S. Kohen. 1971. Man vs. Model of Man Revisited: The Forecasting of Graduate School Success. *Journal of Personality and Social Psychology* 19: 100–106.

Williams, M. 2001. *Problems of Knowledge: A Critical Introduction to Epistemology*. New York: Oxford University Press.

Wilson, T., and D. Gilbert. 2003. Affective Forecasting. *Advances in Experimental Social Psychology* 35: 345–411.

Wittman, M. 1941. A Scale for Measuring Prognosis in Schizophrenic Patients. *Elgin Papers* 4: 20–33.

Zagzebski, L. 1996. *Virtues of the Mind*. Cambridge: Cambridge University Press.

Index